# Lost Heirs
of the
## Medieval Crown

For my son and heir
*May he have better luck*

# Lost Heirs

### of the

# Medieval Crown

## The Kings and Queens Who Never Were

J F ANDREWS

PEN & SWORD
**HISTORY**

AN IMPRINT OF PEN & SWORD BOOKS LTD.
YORKSHIRE – PHILADELPHIA

*Every game of thrones has its losers …*

First published in Great Britain in 2019 by
**PEN AND SWORD HISTORY**
An imprint of
Pen & Sword Books Ltd
Yorkshire – Philadelphia

ISBN 978 1 52673 651 2

Typeset in Times New Roman 11.5/14 by
Aura Technology and Software Services, India
Printed and bound in the UK by TJ International Ltd.

Pen & Sword Books Ltd incorporates the Imprints of Pen & Sword Books
Archaeology, Atlas, Aviation, Battleground, Discovery, Family History, History,
Maritime, Military, Naval, Politics, Railways, Select, Transport, True Crime,
Fiction, Frontline Books, Leo Cooper, Praetorian Press, Seaforth Publishing,
Wharncliffe and White Owl.

For a complete list of Pen & Sword titles please contact

PEN & SWORD BOOKS LIMITED
47 Church Street, Barnsley, South Yorkshire, S70 2AS, England
E-mail: enquiries@pen-and-sword.co.uk
Website: www.pen-and-sword.co.uk

or

PEN AND SWORD BOOKS
1950 Lawrence Rd, Havertown, PA 19083, USA
E-mail: Uspen-and-sword@casematepublishers.com
Website: www.penandswordbooks.com

# Contents

# List of Illustrations

# List of Abbreviations

AB  Anonymous of Béthune, *Histoire des ducs de Normandie et des rois d'Angleterre*, ed. F. Michel (Paris: 1840)

Arrivall  *Historie of the Arrivall of Edward IV in England and the Final Recoverye of his Kingdoms from Henry VI, A.D. M.CCC.LXXI*, ed. John Bruce (London: Camden Society, 1838)

AU  *The Chronicle of Adam of Usk, AD 1377–1421*, trans. Edward Maunde Thompson (London: Henry Frowde, 1904; facsimile repr. Felinfach: Llanerch, 1990)

CC  *The Crowland Chronicle Continuations*, ed. Nicholas Pronay and John Cox (London: Richard III Society and Yorkist History Trust, 1986)

CH  'Chandos Herald: The Life of the Black Prince', in *Life and Campaigns of the Black Prince*, ed. and trans. Richard Barber (Woodbridge: Boydell and Brewer, 1986), pp. 84–139

CWR  *The Chronicles of the Wars of the Roses*, ed. Elizabeth Hallam, trans. Richard Mortimer et al. (Godalming: Bramley Books, 1996)

Froissart  Jean Froissart, *Chronicles*, trans. Geoffrey Brereton (London: Penguin Classics, 1978)

GB  'Geoffrey le Baker: Chronicle', in *Life and Campaigns of the Black Prince*, ed. and trans. Richard Barber (Woodbridge: Boydell and Brewer, 1986), pp. 41–48 and 60–82

GC          Gervase of Canterbury, *The Historical Works of Gervase of Canterbury*, ed. W. Stubbs, 2 vols (London: Rolls Series, 1879–80)

GH          *Gest Regis Henrici Secundi Benedicti Abbatis: The Chronicle of the Reigns of Henry II and Richard I, AD 1169–1192*, ed. W. Stubbs, 2 vols (London: Rolls Series, 1867)

GHQ         *Gesta Henrici Quinti: The Deeds of Henry the Fifth*, ed. and trans. Frank Taylor and John S. Roskell (Oxford: Clarendon, 1975)

Grafton, *Cont.*   Grafton, Richard, 'A Continuacion of the Chronicle of England Begynnyng where John Hardyng Left', in *The Chronicle of John Hardyng*, ed. H. Ellis (London, 1812), pp. 431–607

Grafton, *Hist.*   Grafton, Richard, *Grafton's Chronicle of History of England*, 2 vols (London, 1809)

Gregory     'William Gregory's Chronicle of London', in *The Historical Collections of a Citizen of London*, ed. James Gairdner (London: Camden Society, 1876), pp. 55–239

GS          *Gesta Stephani*, ed. and trans. K.R. Potter, with notes and introduction by R.H.C. Davis, Oxford Medieval Texts (Oxford: Clarendon, 1976)

GW          Gerald of Wales, *On the Instruction of Princes*, trans. Joseph Stevenson (London: Seeleys, 1858; facsimile repr. Felinfach: Llanerch, 1991)

Hardyng     *The Chronicle of John Hardyng*, ed. H. Ellis (London, 1812)

HH          Henry of Huntingdon, *The History of the English People 1000–1154*, trans. Diana Greenway, Oxford World's Classics (Oxford: Oxford University Press, 2002)

HWM         *History of William Marshal*, ed. and trans. A.J. Holden, S. Gregory and D. Crouch, 3 vols (London: Anglo-Norman Text Society, 2002–06)

JB       *The True Chronicles of Jean le Bel, 1290–1360*, trans. Nigel Bryant (Woodbridge: Boydell, 2015)

JF       *Jordan Fantosme's Chronicle*, ed. and trans. R.C. Johnston (Oxford: Clarendon Press, 1981)

JS       *The* Historia Pontificalis *of John of Salisbury*, ed. and trans. Marjorie Chibnall (London: Nelson and Sons, 1956)

JW       John of Worcester, *The Chronicle of Florence of Worcester with Two Continuations*, trans. Thomas Forester (London: Henry G. Bohn, 1854)

Mancini       Dominic Mancini, *The Usurpation of Richard III*, ed. and trans. C.A.J. Armstrong (Gloucester: Alan Sutton, 1984)

Margam       The Annals of Margam, in *Annales Monastici*, ed. H.R. Luard, 5 vols (London: Rolls Series, 1864–9), vol. I

MP       Matthew Paris, *Matthaei Parisiensis monachi Sancti Albani, Historia Anglorum*, ed. F. Madden, 3 vols (London: Rolls Series, 1865–69)

ODNB       *Oxford Dictionary of National Biography*, online edition, www.oxforddnb.com

OV       Orderic Vitalis, *The Ecclesiastical History of Orderic Vitalis*, ed. and trans. Marjorie Chibnall, 6 vols, Oxford Medieval Texts (Oxford: Clarendon, 1968–80)

Paston       *The Paston Letters 1422–1509 AD*, ed. James Gairdner, 3 vols (Edinburgh: John Grant, 1910)

RCaen       *The* Gesta Tancredi *of Ralph of Caen: A History of the Normans on the First Crusade*, trans. Bernard S. Bachrach and David S. Bachrach (Aldershot: Ashgate, 2005)

RCog       Ralph of Coggeshall, *Radulphi de Coggeshall Chronicon Anglicanum*, ed. J. Stevenson (London: Rolls Series, 1875)

RH          Roger of Howden, *The Annals of Roger of Hoveden*, trans. Henry T. Riley, 2 vols (London: Henry Bohn, 1853; facsimile repr. Felinfach: Llanerch, 1997)

RT          Robert de Torigni, *The Chronicles of Robert de Monte*, trans. Joseph Stevenson (London: Seeleys, 1856; facsimile repr. Felinfach: Llanerch, 1991)

RW         Roger of Wendover, *Roger of Wendover's Flowers of History*, trans. J.A. Giles, 2 vols (London: Henry G. Bohn, 1849; facsimile repr. Felinfach: Llanerch, 1995–96)

TW         Thomas Walsingham, *The St Alban's Chronicle: The Chronica Maiora of Thomas Walsingham*, ed. J. Taylor, W. Childs and L. Watkiss, 2 vols (Oxford: Oxford University Press, 2003–11)

Wace       *The History of the Norman People: Wace's* Roman de Rou, trans. Glyn S. Burgess (Woodbridge: Boydell, 2004)

WB         William the Breton, *Philippide*, in vol. 2 of *Oeuvres de Rigord et de Guillaume le Breton*, ed. H.F. Delaborde (Paris: Renouard, 1882)

WM, *Chron.*  William of Malmesbury, *Chronicle of the Kings of England*, trans. J.A. Giles (London: Henry G. Bohn, 1847)

WM, *Hist.*    William of Malmesbury, *Historia Novella*, ed. and trans. K.R. Potter, Nelson Medieval Texts (London: Nelson and Sons, 1955)

Quotations from texts originally written in Latin, Old French or Anglo-Norman have been taken from published English translations where possible; where works are only available in their original language, translations into English are my own. I have modernized the spelling of quotations from texts written in Middle English.

# Introduction

William the Conqueror died on 9 September 1087. He had held England in his iron grip for almost twenty-one years, wiping out the old aristocracy and causing untold misery and suffering across large parts of the realm as he went. He had seized the throne by violence in 1066, but he did not want his own death to result in another Hastings, or in a revival of any Anglo-Saxon claims; no, he would create his own Anglo-Norman dynasty, which would rule England by blood right. With this in mind, he made it clear that the English crown should pass to his son … his second son.

Naturally, his eldest son had a few thoughts of his own on the subject, and thus began four centuries of bloody disputes as the English monarchy's line of hereditary succession was bent, twisted out of shape and finally broken when the last Plantagenet king fell in battle in 1485. History is written by the winners, but every game of thrones has its losers too, and their fascinating stories bring richness and depth to what is a colourful period of history. King John would not have gained the crown had he not murdered his young nephew, who was in line to become England's first King Arthur; Henry V would never have been at Agincourt at all had his father not seized the throne by usurping and killing his cousin; and as the rival houses of York and Lancaster fought bloodily over the crown during the Wars of the Roses, life suddenly became very dangerous indeed for a young boy named Edmund.

This book will tell the stories of all of these people and more; the many medieval kings – and the occasional queen – who could have been but never were. It features a very distinct group of people: it does not include illegitimate children who had no expectation of ruling; nor those who sought to invade and claim the throne by conquest, as Prince Louis of France did in 1216; nor unrelated impostors such as Lambert Simnel, who unconvincingly pretended to be Edward, earl of Warwick, whose untimely death closes our story. Instead it focuses on those who were genuinely considered to be next in line to the throne and who expected to be crowned but who – for a number of different reasons – never made it to the top. Very few of them reached old age; those who did went to their graves disappointed or imprisoned, and those who did not were in many cases the victims of violence or murder.

Each chapter will open with a simplified family tree, making it clear how each of our 'lost heirs' was related to the previous monarch, and why they expected to sit on the throne themselves. We will then explore how and why each of them failed to reach their ultimate goal. Readers should be aware that there are very few happy endings in store ...

# Chapter 1

# Robert Curthose and William Clito

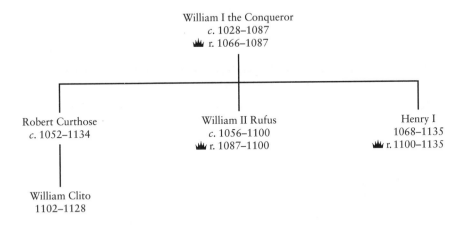

In September 1100, Robert, duke of Normandy, the eldest son of William the Conqueror, returned in triumph from the Holy Land. He was a hero of the First Crusade, his name renowned throughout Christendom. He was newly married to a rich and beautiful wife and he was the recognized heir to the throne of England. He was, at long last, a success. But his joy was to be short-lived; as Robert neared his native Norman soil, the shocking news reached him that the king of England was dead and that, for the second time in his life, he had been beaten to the crown by a younger brother. What, his followers wanted to know, was he going to do about it?

\*\*\*

Robert had been born sometime around 1052 at a time when his father was duke of Normandy and not expected to be crowned king of anywhere.[1] He was approximately 14 years old when William embarked for England with the intention of conquering it; he remained in Normandy where, as its recognized heir, he governed under the guidance of his mother,

Matilda. When she too sailed for England in 1068, to be crowned and later to give birth to her youngest son Henry, Robert was deemed to be of an age to assume the reins of Norman rule in his own name.

Robert was a very different man from his father. They had one physical similarity, in that Robert had William's burly physique and barrel chest – useful attributes for a man who was expected to take part in armed combat – but he inherited his mother's relative lack of height.[2] This resulted in his being given the nickname 'Curthose' ('Short-breeches' or 'Short-legs') in his youth, an epithet that stuck for the rest of his life and by which he is generally known today. They were also different in character; Robert was affable and easy-going, not adjectives generally applied to the king, and he was also described as 'talkative and extravagant'.[3]

There was no specific conflict between father and son for around ten years, as William concentrated on subduing resistance in England and Robert took his first steps into governance in Normandy. But as he grew out of his teens and into his twenties he gained in confidence and in expectation, and not unnaturally wanted more responsibility. He was supported in this by a group of companions of his own age who were the sons of his father's Norman magnates and who encouraged him to be extravagant. They urged him to ask William for more money and more power: 'It is a great dishonour to you and injury to us and many others that you should be deprived of royal wealth [...] why do you tolerate it?'[4]

Although Robert was in nominal charge of Normandy, the duchy that had once been the height of his expectation and the heart of the family's power base, he was actually by now on the periphery of his father's lands, as England took up more and more of his time and energy. Robert was not helped by the fact that his brothers Richard and William Rufus were in England at their father's side and therefore had more of his attention and more of a chance to impress him at first hand. Richard was killed in an accident sometime in the early 1070s, when he was in his mid-teens, but William Rufus continued to prosper.[5] He took after his father in temperament as well as physique, and Robert – his status as the eldest aside – may have justifiably felt that Rufus was supplanting him as the favoured son. He needed to bolster his position; in 1077 he asked William to relinquish Normandy to him permanently.

William's answer was in the negative. He might be king of England, but he was also duke of Normandy; he had spent his youth fighting for it – had narrowly escaped being murdered for it several times – and he was not inclined to let the reins of power slip from his own grasp. Robert, having worked himself up to make the demand, now suffered a disastrous loss of face at being denied and felt obliged to leave the duchy entirely. He was, however, fortunate in having relatives and friends in high places who were ready to help him out and to cause some mischief for King William, whom they felt to be too powerful. Robert was welcomed both in Flanders, where the count was his maternal uncle, and at the court of Philip I of France.

Within a short time, Robert found himself fighting in Philip's campaign in the Vexin (an area lying on the border between Normandy and France, which was to be the scene of much conflict between the rulers of the two territories over the years). He held a castle at Gerberoy and was able to cause trouble from there by launching raids into his father's territory; William, who had crossed the Channel to deal with matters in Normandy in person, moved to assault it at the end of 1078. During one of the skirmishes that took place at the beginning of 1079, he was wounded. In another, Robert apparently nearly killed William when they met in the heat of battle, before recognizing the man behind the helmet, at which point he let him escape.[6] But their relationship was damaged, and an attempt by his magnates to broker a peace was met with angry words from William: 'He [Robert] has stirred up civil dissent against me, lured away my young knights [...] Which of my ancestors from the time of Rollo ever had to endure such hostility from any child as I do?'[7] Robert got on well with everyone else – to the point that he was regularly exploited because he was so generous – but he and his father seemed to have a blind spot when it came to each other.

Outright and catastrophic war between them was more or less averted thanks to the strenuous efforts of Queen Matilda, who mediated between her husband and her son. Such was the reconciliation she effected that Robert accompanied William when he returned to England in 1080; now he could start to stake his claim as the heir to the kingdom. On his father's behalf, Robert led a campaign north against Malcolm Canmore, king of Scots, but in his characteristic genial style he managed to end it both on friendly terms with Malcolm and as godfather to Malcolm's infant daughter Edith.

Robert stayed in England until the spring of 1081 before returning to Normandy, but he remained dissatisfied with his position. He was nearly 30 but was still only his father's regent in Normandy, not duke in his own right, and he had not been publicly declared heir to the throne of England either. Queen Matilda managed to keep the peace for a while longer, but her death in November 1083 broke the hearts of her husband and her son and led to a more serious breakdown in the relationship. Robert went into exile once more, and he was still away from Normandy in September 1087 when news reached him of King William's death.

Now was Robert's chance. He first made sure of Normandy: his accession as duke there was not contested, as he was the eldest son of the previous incumbent and had been recognized as heir since at least 1063.[8] With that title firmly under his belt, Robert could turn his attention to England, but he had already been outmanoeuvred and he was hit by two unwelcome pieces of information: that William Rufus had already been crowned king, and that this had been done with his father's prior blessing.

The fact that this could happen perhaps requires some explanation. The practice of the dukes of Normandy for several generations had been that all sons should have at least some share in the inheritance, with the tendency being to leave the patrimony – the inherited family lands – to the eldest son, and any additional gains made through conquest or marriage to the second. Third or subsequent sons could be left money or minor lordships, or be given to the Church.[9] Under this system the idea of leaving Normandy to the eldest son, Robert, England to the second surviving brother, William Rufus, and a bundle of cash to young Henry was logical. However, the system did not often have to cope with the fact that the supplementary gain comprised a greater title and more extensive lands than the patrimony – never mind a crown – so Robert could feel himself hard done by.

The situation with regard to the transfer of the English crown was also unclear. Although there had been a tendency in the past for kings to favour their own sons, and for one selected individual to be name *Aetheling* (literally meaning 'man of royal blood', but understood more precisely to mean the designated heir to the throne) the Anglo-Saxons had in practice used an elective system whereby all men of royal blood might be considered candidates. This had the dual advantages of keeping it all in the family while also ensuring that the vagaries of fertility and birth order did not result in a child, a woman or an unsuitable man ascending the throne.

Taking into account the customs in both kingdom and duchy, William would have felt entirely justified in overlooking his eldest son for the crown. Moreover, it kept the two entities distinct. England was one kingdom, under one crown: it was therefore not to be divided and the rule of it could not be shared between two of his sons. But equally, England and Normandy were not one entity: they were separate titles that both happened to be held by the same man, so it was entirely legal and acceptable for him to leave them to different sons. The union that had chanced to occur for twenty-one years while William was both king and duke would now be dissolved, on the assumption that Rufus and Robert would each have sons of their own who would inherit England and Normandy separately.

However, this fine plan failed to take into account several factors. The first was that although the union of kingdom and duchy had been in place for only a generation, many of the magnates by now welcomed it; they held lands on both sides of the Channel and it made their lives easier to have only one overlord in both places. The second was that Robert felt aggrieved that, as the eldest, he had not been left the greater title. And the third was that Rufus, having inherited his father's kingdom and his bellicose temperament, did not see why he should not have Normandy as well as England. Conflict, therefore, seemed inevitable.

However, in one of the strange lapses of initiative that would come to characterize his career, Robert does not seem to have been champing at the bit to take immediate action to claim the crown. Perhaps he wanted to consolidate his hold on Normandy first; perhaps he wanted to consider his options. After all, Rufus now had control of England's royal treasury, which far outweighed Robert's resources. But he was not to be allowed to let matters lie, and was pushed into action by others. Chief among these were three close relatives: his youngest brother Henry (now in his late teens and with no expectation of inheriting any lands or titles, and therefore ripe for causing trouble between his older siblings); and his uncles, Bishop Odo of Bayeux and Count Robert of Mortain, the maternal half-brothers of William the Conqueror. Henry kick-started his own territorial ambitions by exchanging the £3,000 he had been left by his father for Robert's lands in the Cotentin – an area now more commonly known as the Cherbourg Peninsula, comprising at the time around a third of Normandy – while Odo and his brother travelled to England to prepare the way for an invasion and to garner support for it among the magnates there. They succeeded in causing some agitation but, in the event, Robert never got round to raising an army or sailing himself, so they were forced to return in some humiliation.

This was to become a pattern in Robert's life. He was skilled in combat and keen to take part in war – nobody doubted his personal courage or prowess – but he simply had no head for strategy; he preferred direct and simple action while others took care of the long-term planning and the logistics. He often started things that he did not have the inclination or the will to carry through.

Meanwhile, William Rufus had his own designs on Normandy, and, in contrast to his brother's apparent lethargy, he actually put his plans into action and arrived there in February 1091. All-out war did not ensue; as noted above, many of the magnates held lands in both territories, or they were members of families that held such lands between them, so there was no great enthusiasm to fight against their brothers and kin. Instead, Robert and Rufus negotiated; neither was married, and neither had a legitimate child, so the outcome of the talks was that each would name the other as his heir. Robert was not the king of England, but he was secure in his possession of Normandy and he now had official recognition of his status with regard to the English throne – and all without having to organize a campaign to claim it.

Rufus sailed back to England and Robert turned his attention to the business of ruling his duchy. Unfortunately for him, and indeed for all concerned, he turned out to be ill-equipped for the task. The geniality that had won him friends in his youth and helped him to make peace with the rather saintly royal family in Scotland was no use in ruling Normandy. The magnates there were in general an unruly lot, who had only been kept in tolerable order by the iron fist of the Conqueror and the harsh punishments he was liable to deal out if crossed. 'All men knew that Duke Robert was weak and indolent; therefore troublemakers despised him and stirred up loathsome factions when and where they chose,' said one chronicler,[10] and Robert certainly experienced many more problems than his father had in keeping peace in the duchy. Throughout the period 1092–4 he was busy putting down small-scale revolts in Normandy, some incited by William Rufus and others by lords out for their own self-interest. He had no time to think of England, where his best prospect was simply to hope for the natural death of his brother.

Then, in 1095, an event occurred that was to change Robert's life and his reputation forever. Pope Urban II preached his great call to crusade, and Robert – for once motivated and impassioned enough to get himself organized – was one of the first and highest-ranking among those who responded. This was his great opportunity, but he needed money to equip a force, and he needed it quickly. Without, perhaps, thinking of the long-term consequences, he pawned the whole of Normandy to William Rufus for the sum of 10,000 marks in cash,[11] mustered his troops and set off in the autumn of 1096.

The crusade was a situation that played to Robert's strengths. He was free from the boring and difficult aspects of administering a duchy and therefore able to concentrate more fully on his military exploits, and moreover he could claim to be fighting in the just cause of the holy Church. He lived up to expectations, demonstrating personal courage and dedication to the ideal, as noted by a number of contemporary or near-contemporary chroniclers: he was 'the invincible duke of the Normans'[12] who 'performed many fine deeds there [...] he won great renown as a result of his exploits'.[13] When surrounded by the Turks in battle and in dire peril, Robert rallied his comrades:

> There, at last, one who was of the royal blood of William recalled to himself his lineage and the fact that he was a fighter. He uncovered his head and shouted 'Normandy! [...] We should make our stand here for we will have either the glorious punishment of the defeated or the victor's crown. I say that both of these chances are glorious, but the first is even more blessed.'[14]

Robert was greatly esteemed by his fellow crusaders; his prowess was admired, and as many of the other lords who had taken up the call were of Norman descent, they saw him as their natural leader. He was apparently offered the crown of Jerusalem after the capture of the holy city in 1099, but declined it, 'not through awe of its dignity, but through the fear of endless labour'.[15] This sounds like the Robert who is depicted similarly by other contemporaries, but it should also be noted that – unlike many other crusaders – he also declined to make a personal profit by plundering. He was crusading out of idealism, not to gain riches or a crown.

With Jerusalem now in Christian hands, Robert's mission was accomplished and he began his journey home, travelling via Constantinople and southern Italy, where he married Sybil, daughter of the count of Conversano, who was of Norman stock. With William Rufus still unmarried and childless, Robert could now hope to return to Normandy with a renewed and enhanced reputation and the possibility of fathering a son who would inherit both Normandy and England in due course. The dowry he received along with his bride was in cash and would enable him to redeem his duchy when he got home.

However, by the time Robert reached Normandy in September 1100, circumstances had conspired against him. William Rufus had died unexpectedly in a hunting accident the previous month, exactly the situation that would have been favourable to Robert, had he been in England or even in Normandy. But he was not, and so another man had taken the initiative: Robert's youngest brother Henry, who had conveniently been on the spot in the New Forest, had hurriedly secured the royal treasury at Winchester, rushed to London and had himself crowned as king of England, all within a week of Rufus's death.

What is important to note here is that, at this time, it was the act of coronation that turned an ordinary mortal into a king, God's chosen. The death of a king did not mean that the throne passed automatically to his nearest heir or designated successor; rather it signalled an interregnum until a new king was crowned – and once he was crowned, he was the king. It would not be until 1272 that an English king was proclaimed on the death of his predecessor rather than on the occasion of his own coronation (following the death of Henry III, at which time his eldest son Edward I was on crusade abroad),[16] and the phrase 'the king is dead, long live the king' was not used until the fifteenth century. That was all in the future; in 1100, following his coronation and anointing, Henry's kingship was considered divinely approved, and it could not be undone. Whether Robert liked it or not, his youngest brother was now King Henry I of England, and he had been passed over once more.

The situation was very different from that of 1087. Robert had been the elder brother of the new king in both cases, but now he had the additional status of being the designated heir (since his agreement with Rufus in 1091), so he could consider himself even more hard done by; moreover, he had spent the last four years fighting for Christendom and winning renown while Henry had stayed safely at home. This time he needed to take more decisive action. Leaving his new wife in Normandy to act as his regent, Robert mustered troops and sailed; he landed in England in July 1101.

However, once again armed conflict inexplicably failed to ensue. A tale circulated that Robert had withdrawn from his approach to Winchester because he had heard that Henry's queen was within the city and in the final stages of pregnancy; chivalrous hero that he was, he did not wish to frighten or disturb a woman in her condition. However, the date does not fit with the dates of birth of either of the queen's known children, so unless she had another that nobody thought to mention, the story is apocryphal. Still, the fact that it was taken at face value shows that contemporaries believed such behaviour from Robert to be plausible. Of perhaps greater import is that the queen in question was Matilda, formerly known as Edith, the daughter of King Malcolm Canmore of Scots, so she was not just Robert's sister-in-law but his goddaughter as well. This was not a conflict of enemies but of close family, so bloodshed should be avoided if possible.

Whatever the precise reasons, Robert ended up negotiating again, in which endeavour he was no match for the cunning Henry. The one bonus that Robert would get out of the deal was that he would redeem the Cotentin from his brother using the money he now had at his disposal. But the rest was negative. Robert was persuaded once more to give up his immediate claim to the throne in favour of being named his brother's heir if he should remain childless, and vice versa. This might sound like a similar deal to the one he had struck with Rufus ten years previously, but it was much less favourable this time round. For a start, Henry was some fifteen or sixteen years younger than Robert and in robust health, and thus likely to outlive him; and secondly, Henry was newly married to a young wife and had already fathered a brood of illegitimate children, so the chances were that his queen would provide him with an heir of his body soon. In fact, if we look closely at the dates, we can deduce that she was indeed in the early stages of pregnancy at the time, though it is possible that Henry was not yet aware of this. The Treaty of Winchester formalized the agreement and was sealed in August 1101.

Robert returned to Normandy, where he celebrated the birth of a son, William, in October 1102, although tragically at the cost of his wife's life; Duchess Sybil died from childbirth complications several months later. Henry's first child had been born earlier that same year, but as she was a girl, there was still some hope for Robert and his English claims. They were dashed in the summer of 1103 when Queen Edith/Matilda gave birth to a son, also called William. Both these boys would carry competing claims to the English throne, and they were each given a nickname that reflected this: Henry's son was known as William Adelin (a Norman-French version of *Aetheling*), and Robert's son was William Clito, which derived from the similar Latin term *Inclitus*.

Robert now had more to fight for, but he had little leisure at this point to push either his own or his son's rights in England, for he was once again embroiled in trying to keep peace among squabbling parties in Normandy. He was unable to do so effectively, and some of the Norman magnates began to make overtures to Henry. By 1106 there were two distinct factions in Normandy, one supporting each brother, and open warfare had broken out.

The climax of the conflict came in September of that year when Henry was besieging the castle of Tinchebrai, held for Robert.[17] Robert brought his army up behind the encircling forces in an attempt to relieve the castle, and there was a pretence of mediation, but Robert found Henry's offer unacceptable. He called his older brother 'a duke in name only, openly mocked by your own servants', and suggested that he should hand over control of the duchy to Henry so he could live 'without toil or responsibility' in a kind of semi-retirement: 'You can then enjoy feasts and games and all kinds of amusements in comfort. I for my part will undertake all the labours necessary to preserve peace, and will faithfully keep my promises while you rest.'[18] Robert not unnaturally found this patronizing, and finally found the will to face one of his brothers on the field of battle.

Both sides dismounted to fight, a conventional tactic at the time as it encouraged the common soldiers to hold their ground as they knew that the knights could not flee on horseback, leaving them to face the enemy alone. Robert's knights charged Henry's line, Robert foremost among them – he was, as his crusading experiences had demonstrated, no coward. They pushed the line back but did not break through it, and soon became mired, the press growing so thick that there was hardly room to swing a sword. But Henry had kept a cavalry wing in hiding; they swept into Robert's troops as they were trapped in the press and routed them. The commander of Robert's rearguard fled, leaving him exposed; many of his men were killed and others captured, including Robert himself.[19]

Closely guarded, Robert was taken first to Rouen, and then, sometime before the end of the year, across the Channel to either Wareham or Corfe in Dorset. This was to be his final voyage to England, but it was not in triumph, not to be crowned king; rather it was to lifelong incarceration as his brother's prisoner.

Henry, meanwhile, moved to the ducal castle at Falaise, where he was brought face to face with William Clito. William was said to be 'trembling with fear',[20] as well he might be, given that he was not quite 4 years old and now found himself entirely at the king's mercy. In a rare act of clemency, Henry released the boy, confiding him to the care of one Helias de St Saëns, who was married to a much older half-sister of William's, an illegitimate daughter of Robert Curthose's youth.[21] The reasons for Henry's generosity are unclear, but we can guess at a combination of trying to keep his own reputation intact (even by the standards of twelfth-century Normandy, the murder of an infant would be considered shameful) and thinking that little William Clito posed no threat.

Henry brought peace and stability to Normandy – but at a price. A contemporary dismissed Robert by saying that 'none could be more pleasant […] yet, through the easiness of his disposition, was he ever esteemed unfit to have the management of the state', but the same writer noted that Henry 'suffered nothing to go unpunished which delinquents had committed repugnant to his dignity' and 'restrained the rebellious by the terror of his name'.[22]

Robert was never to see Normandy again. After landing on the south coast of England he was taken to the strongly fortified castle at Devizes and placed in the custody of Roger, Bishop of Salisbury, Henry's justiciar (the chief administrative officer of the kingdom, who was left as regent when the king was overseas). He remained there for twenty years. In 1126 Robert was handed over to Earl Robert of Gloucester, the eldest of Henry's many illegitimate sons; he was moved to one of the earl's castles at Bristol and then later to another at Cardiff, getting further away from Normandy, and his son, every time.

Henry could not simply murder his brother; he was, after all, the rightful duke of Normandy and a crusading hero. So he initially broadcast the fiction that Robert was still duke but that Henry was ruling for him (Henry did not immediately add the style 'duke of Normandy' to his titles, though it slipped in quietly later on). Robert was apparently well treated: one contemporary quotes Henry telling the pope that 'I have not kept my brother in fetters like a captured enemy, but have placed him as a noble pilgrim, worn out with many hardships, in a royal castle, and have kept him well supplied with abundance of food and other comforts and furnishings of all kinds',[23] while another says that 'he was captured and remains in open confinement until the present time, having to thank his brother's praiseworthy sense of duty that he has nothing worse to suffer than solitude'.[24] Entries in the one surviving Pipe Roll of Henry's reign, from 1129–30, show expenditure of £23 10s for clothes and £12 for furnishings for his brother; not inconsiderable sums and evidence that Robert was indeed kept in some comfort.[25]

During all this time, Robert apparently never made an attempt to escape. In the following decades chroniclers could not quite believe this, so they cast about for reasons why; eventually, in the thirteenth century, a rumour started that Henry had ordered Robert to be blinded, but there is no contemporary evidence for this at all and it is almost certainly untrue. It appears, rather, that he had simply given up. He was no longer young (in his mid-fifties at the time of his capture) and had never wanted the administrative responsibilities of duchy or kingdom anyway; how could he possibly organize a rebellion now, and who would support him in the endeavour? No, he would remain where he was, and all hope for his own line must rest in his son.

***

At the time of Robert's capture in 1106, the Norman magnates had made no protest; those who had supported Henry basked in their victory, and those who had supported Robert quickly came to terms in their own interest. But after years of Henry's authoritarian and sometimes harsh rule they became restless again. Robert, far away in the west of England, was almost forgotten, but they had a ready-made figurehead in the form of William Clito.

By 1119 William Clito was a young man of 16, the age his father had been when he had assumed the regency of Normandy, but of a very different personality. Clito had been forged in adversity, hardly knowing a safe moment in his entire life. After Robert's capture and subsequent imprisonment in 1106 he had been effectively orphaned; he temporarily found a peaceful home in the household of his half-sister and her husband

Helias de St Saëns, but in 1109 Henry attempted to have him captured, perhaps realizing the danger his earlier leniency might cause. Helias managed to get the boy out of Normandy, and after a stay in France he ended up in Flanders in 1113, where he was sheltered by the count, who was at that time Baldwin VII, William's second cousin.

William stayed in Flanders for some years, being knighted by Baldwin in 1116, and Baldwin began to launch raids into Normandy on his behalf. By 1117 there was full-scale warfare between Henry I and a coalition that included William, Baldwin, Louis VI of France and some of the Norman magnates. William Clito's supporters were not, at this stage, trying to place him on the throne of England, but they did see him as the natural heir to Normandy following his father's imprisonment – and who knew what he might achieve once he had the duchy under his control?

The pivotal moment in this war came in the summer of 1119. Flanders had withdrawn from the conflict following the childless death of Baldwin VII and the accession of his cousin Charles I, so Clito and Louis were short of a major ally when they met Henry's forces at Brémule (in the Norman Vexin) on 20 August. William's aims in the engagement were twofold: he 'armed himself there so that he might free his father from his long imprisonment and recover his ancestral inheritance'.[26] But he was to be disappointed, undone partly as a result of Henry's superior experience and tactics, and partly by a lack of resource.

Once Henry received the intelligence that a small army including both his opponents was nearby, he split his own, larger, host in two: a small division of mounted knights and a larger contingent of dismounted men. The latter group stood to receive a charge by Louis's knights, who were all on horseback, but it was ill-disciplined and easily beaten back by the well-organized formation of infantry. A large number of the knights were unhorsed, causing confusion, and many of them were captured. Louis and William Clito were not among these but were forced to flee the field without their horses; and although Louis lived, the result was decisive enough for him to agree to negotiate on the question of Normandy.[27]

A peace treaty was brokered by Pope Callixtus II in October 1119, but it was not entirely successful. William Clito, revealing a human side sometimes obscured in the contemporary documents, pleaded for the release of his father, whom he could hardly have remembered after a separation of thirteen years, and promised tearfully that they would both go to Jerusalem and never return if they could only have each other. Henry was not about to set Robert free, but he did offer Clito a place at his court and a position as earl of three counties in England if he would give up his other claims. This was declined, and Clito then had no choice but to resume his exile from Normandy, leaving Henry very much in the ascendant.

With Robert growing old in captivity and his son a landless exile, the claims of the senior branch of William the Conqueror's line looked extinguished. But they were re-ignited by a tragedy that was to have far-reaching implications; in an episode that will be explored more fully in the next chapter, Henry lost his only legitimate son, William Adelin, when he was drowned in the disaster of the *White Ship* in November 1120. This threw all his carefully laid succession plans into disarray.

William Clito was now the obvious candidate to succeed Henry in both England and Normandy. As the only son of the Conqueror's eldest son, his claims would surely override those of anyone else; he was 18, healthy, popular and a veteran of a number of military campaigns. But Henry was adamantly opposed to this move – he had not spent much of his life fighting against his brother only to cede all his gains to his brother's son. And besides, questions might also be asked as to why, if Clito was by birth Henry's heir, he was not in fact king already.

If William Clito thought his path to the throne was going to be smooth, he was mistaken; indeed, Henry turned against him with even more vigour than before. In 1123 William made a strategic alliance by marrying Sybil, the daughter of Count Fulk of Anjou, whose lands bordered Normandy to the south, thus bolstering his position. Within a year Henry managed to have the union annulled by the pope on the grounds of consanguinity (that is, by claiming that the two parties were too closely related to each other) – despite the fact that his son William Adelin had been married to Sybil's sister Matilda, and that he would later arrange a match for his daughter Matilda with Sybil's brother Geoffrey, and that both of these couples were related to precisely the same degree as Clito and Sybil.

Deprived of resources, Clito was forced once more to resume his wandering life of exile, but worse was to come. At the end of 1126 Henry formally named a new heir; it was not Clito but Henry's only remaining legitimate child, his daughter Matilda. She had been sent overseas in childhood to marry the Holy Roman Emperor but had returned, widowed and childless, in 1125, giving Henry a final option to leave the crown to his own blood.

Henry had all his magnates swear an oath in January 1127 that they would crown Matilda after his death. Intimidated by him, they all did so, but there were murmurs of dissent. Some would have favoured William Clito as heir, partly due to their fear of the unprecedented prospect of a woman ruler, partly due to his birth and hereditary claim, and partly due to his burgeoning reputation. This was a chink of light that Clito could exploit, and his position was boosted by more or less the only two strokes of luck he ever had in his life. First, his backer Louis VI, anxious to do anything that would counter Henry I's growing influence, arranged a marriage between his own wife's sister and Clito, and agreed to give him the French Vexin as dowry. This gave Clito lands and castles right on the border with Normandy, a useful foothold since he had lost his alliance with Anjou. Second, Charles, count of Flanders, was murdered. In the uproar that followed and the scramble to succeed him (he had no children and no brothers), Louis persuaded the lords of Flanders to accept Clito, who, as great-grandson of Count Baldwin V, had a blood claim.

William Clito now had titles, lands and riches with which to challenge his uncle. He rode to Gisors to make a formal claim to Normandy, and in a charter he granted on 14 April 1127 to the town of St-Omer in Flanders, he promised to confer privileges on the townsmen if ever 'he should rule over England'.[28]

Almost the antithesis of his father, William Clito was energetic, organized and resourceful. His star seemed to be on the rise: he was descended from kings and dukes, he was a fit and healthy 24 years of age, he had a reputation for gallantry and daring, and he was already a hugely experienced military leader. He had so far managed to achieve a great deal with very little resource, as evidenced by the fact that he was still touted as a possible heir to England and Normandy some twenty years after his father's capture and imprisonment. He was popular with his followers, who were in the main equally young and spirited, and was portrayed in a positive light by contemporaries:

> William made up for the small size of his forces by his inextinguishable prowess. All his armour stained with enemy blood, he hacked into the enemy's squadrons with

his lightning sword. The enemy could not withstand
the awesome weight of his youthful arm, and took flight
in terror.[29]

However, Henry I had not finished with his nephew. Wicked uncles
will feature frequently in this book, as we shall see, and Henry would
not be satisfied until he had trampled young William into the dust. He
had already had Clito's favourable Angevin marriage annulled; now he
supported a rival claimant to the county of Flanders, one Thierry of
Alsace (who was also a great-grandson of Baldwin V), and threw both
his influence and his money into the fray. Henry used his alliances in the
surrounding lands of Lorraine and Boulogne – held by his father-in-law
and his nephew Stephen of Blois respectively – to put pressure on Clito's
borders, sending Stephen over in person to challenge the new count. In
the meantime, he used a combination of bribes and economic sanctions
against the towns of Flanders in order to turn them against Clito; most
of their wealth was founded on trade with England, so this could have a
severe impact on the prosperity of the whole region.

    William, in marked contrast to his father, did not take this lying down.
He was not nearly as rich or as powerful as Henry, but he had a loyal
band of knights, and youth and energy were on his side. He waged a
campaign throughout the summer of 1127, easily beating back Stephen,
who sued for a three-year truce. But it was not enough and Clito just could
not compete with the influence wielded by his uncle. By now Henry's
economic sanctions against the towns of Flanders had begun to cut more
deeply, and the result was a general rebellion against Clito as the citizens
were forced to act in their own interest. Once more he refused to give
up; with the depleted means at his disposal, he marshalled his forces
and began a series of sieges of opposing strongholds, hoping to drive
Thierry's supporters out.

    Sadly for William Clito, his efforts were just starting to turn the
tide in his favour when he suffered a sudden and fatal reverse. In July
1128 he was besieging Thierry's castle of Aalst in eastern Flanders
when he was wounded in the hand, necessitating what he thought was a
temporary withdrawal from the field in order to have it treated. But due
to inflammation of the wound 'he was compelled to retire to his bed [...]
his whole arm up to the shoulder turned as black as coal',[30] and he died
in agony from blood poisoning five days later. This was the end of the

line. William Clito had spent his entire life fighting to gain what he saw as his and Robert's by right, but despite two marriages he had fathered no children, so there was nobody to take up his cause.

Clito was generally looked on by contemporaries with favour and sympathy, and the epitaphs left to us by chroniclers reflect this: he was 'noble' and 'greatly loved by his knights', and his death caused 'great sorrow'.[31] In 'his short life this most noble of youths earned eternal fame [...] Mars has died on earth, the gods lament an equal god'.[32] His ill luck was recognized:

> This young prince was born to misfortune, from which he was never altogether free as long as he lived. He was brave, handsome and high-spirited; desperately fond of warlike adventures [...] he was the cause of more misery than profit to the multitude who adhered to him.[33]

William Clito had never forgotten his father, or what was due to his lineage, but he was buried at St-Omer without a single member of his family in attendance. The legend of the doomed youth grew over the years, increasing his fame long after his death; sometime in the 1180s a spectacular effigy was added to his tomb as a memorial to him.

News of William's demise eventually made its way to Cardiff, where Robert Curthose, now in his late seventies, was said to have had a premonition of it in a dream. He had long given up any hope of his own restoration, and any aspiration to which he still clung on behalf of the son he had not seen since the latter was 4 years old died in a field outside Aalst. Robert somehow managed to survive another five and a half years, spending his time learning Welsh and writing poetry, before finally dying at the age of around 80 in February 1134, in the twenty-eighth year of his captivity. He had long outlived his own relevance – and also, it would seem, his own desire. A poem attributed to him contains three lines that give us an insight into his state of mind towards the end of his long life:

> Woe to him that is in the power of his enemies;
> [...]
> Woe to him that is not old enough to die;
> [...]
> Woe to him that beholds what is not Death.[34]

Between them, Robert Curthose and William Clito had been claimants to the English throne for over forty years from 1087 to 1128, but despite being thorns in the side of the Anglo-Norman kings neither of them could quite succeed against the combination of the determination of the Conqueror's other sons and the might of the English royal treasury. What Robert may have lacked in political acumen, he made up for in personal courage; his son inherited the courage and added grit and determination in spadefuls. Had they ever been fated to join forces they might have enjoyed more success, but it was not to be.

In contrast to the lamentations on the untimely death of the gallant young William Clito, epitaphs of Robert Curthose were more subdued:

> For although the duke was bold and daring, praiseworthy for his knightly prowess and eloquent in speech, he exercised no discipline over either himself or his men. He was prodigal in distributing his bounty and lavish in his promises, but so thoughtless and inconstant that they were utterly unreliable. Being merciful to suppliants he was too weak and pliable to pass judgement on wrongdoers; unable to pursue any plan consistently, he was far too affable and obliging in all his relationships, and so earned the contempt of corrupt and foolish men [...] Through his wish to please all men he either gave or promised or granted whatever anyone asked.[35]

Robert was buried in Gloucester Abbey, where, like his son, he later had an effigy added to his tomb; his was of oak and dated to many years after his death, around the middle of the thirteenth century. It depicts a tall, slim figure in armour of its own day and is therefore unlike him in either appearance or apparel, but it shows that he was not forgotten, a hundred years after his unsuccessful attempts to claim the English throne.

Both the kingdom of England and the duchy of Normandy remained in the hands of Henry I, and contemporary wisdom had it that they were both better off under his strict and somewhat ruthless rule; affable fellows did not make good kings. But Henry, as we are about to see, was to have succession problems of his own.

# Chapter 2

# William Adelin and Empress Matilda

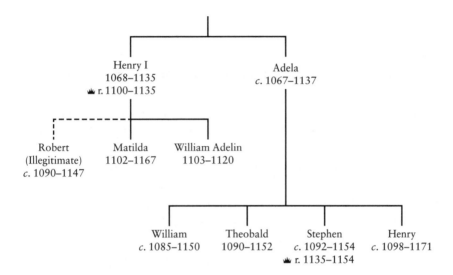

Although he fathered at least twenty illegitimate children, Henry I had only two by his wife: Matilda, born in 1102, and William, in 1103.[1] Matilda was shipped overseas at the age of just 8 to marry Henry V, the Holy Roman Emperor, and it appeared that her future would lie there; William, meanwhile, was kept with his father and brought up as befitted the heir to both England and Normandy.

As we saw in the previous chapter, Henry I had himself assumed the throne by riding roughshod over the claims of his elder brother and had then taken Normandy from him too; but he was in no doubt that both territories would pass to his son and heir by hereditary right. There could be no question that William Adelin would be the next king. His very name denoted it, and he was Henry's only legitimate son; moreover, he had been born 'in the purple' – that is, born when his father was already a king, something that Henry had made much of himself, given that he was the only one of the Conqueror's sons to be born after 1066.

Indeed, young William was of royal stock on both sides: through his father he was descended from the Anglo-Norman kings and the dukes of Normandy, and through his mother not only from the Celtic kings of Scotland but also from the ancient Anglo-Saxon line. He had it all.

William Adelin was given the best twelfth-century education that money and influence could buy. As the designated heir from birth he was educated and trained 'with the fondest hope and surpassing care'[2] for the throne from his earliest years, not only in letters but also in governance, politics and the knightly arts – this was a time when kings were expected to lead their armies from the front. William was brought into the public gaze and associated with Henry's rule at an early age; he was only 10 when he began attesting royal documents, but it all served to familiarize him with the world of kingship and equally to acquaint the magnates with the fact that William would one day rule over them.

An advantageous marriage was soon arranged for the young prince with Matilda, daughter of Count Fulk of Anjou, whose lands bordered Normandy to the south and who, therefore, would be an important ally. Fulk also controlled the neighbouring county of Maine in right of his wife, and he agreed to bestow it on the young couple (then aged 10 and 2) as a dowry whenever the wedding should take place. William's introduction to the world of politics then proceeded apace; he received the homage of the barons of Normandy in 1115 and those of England in March 1116. Following the death of his mother Queen Edith/Matilda in May 1118 he was officially Henry's regent in England during the king's absences in Normandy, though it is difficult to judge from the surviving evidence whether he exercised personal control or whether he acted under the guidance of one of Henry's officials.

In 1119, the year he turned 16, William was considered an adult. It was to be a momentous year for him: his marriage took place, and he was present at the Battle of Brémule, at which his father's forces defeated an army led by Louis VI of France and William Clito.[3] The extent of his participation in the actual combat is not clear, but we do know that after the battle he came into possession of the horse belonging to his cousin Clito; he returned the animal to its owner, although whether this was a gesture of chivalry or a cruel taunt is open to interpretation.[4] William Adelin was also, in the same year, listed in a charter as *rex designatus*, 'king-designate', so there can be no doubt that he was publicly recognized as heir to the English throne. He seems to have enjoyed his position, surrounding himself with youths of his own age who encouraged him in drinking and indulgence – much as the companions of his uncle Robert Curthose had once done, to his detriment.

On 25 November 1120 William Adelin was at Barfleur with his father, various other members of his family and friends, and the rest of the royal court. In his dual role as king of England and duke of Normandy, Henry needed to cross the Channel relatively frequently and today seemed nothing out of the ordinary; it was late in the year, yes, but the weather was fair and crossings had been successfully made as late as December in the past.

A ship's captain came to Henry. His name was Thomas fitzStephen; he noted that his father had conveyed William the Conqueror across the sea in 1066, and wondered if the king would do him the honour of sailing in his new, sleek, fast vessel, the *White Ship*? Henry had already made other arrangements, but William was keen to travel in such an upmarket fashion, hoping to race his father across the Channel while enjoying the company of his friends. Henry obligingly agreed, and William collected together his young and riotous companions so they could board and sail with the evening tide. Among them were his illegitimate half-siblings Richard fitzRoy and Matilda, countess of Perche; his cousins Stephen of Blois, count of Mortain, and Stephen's sister Matilda of Blois; and Matilda's husband, Richard, earl of Chester. Neither William's wife Matilda nor his eldest half-brother Robert, earl of Gloucester, travelled on the *White Ship*; they were too young and too old, respectively, to form part of his close entourage. Stephen of Blois disembarked just before they were due to sail, thus unwittingly changing the course of English royal history; his excuse was that he was suffering from a stomach upset, but it is also possible that he left because 'there was too great a crowd of wild and headstrong young men on board'[5] and he felt disinclined to travel in such company.

It all started well. King Henry's ship sailed first, and while the *White Ship* waited its turn William ordered casks of wine broached and distributed to the passengers ... and the crew. The result was that all on board were rowdily drunk by the time they weighed anchor, at which point William urged Thomas fitzStephen to race out of the harbour to try to catch the rest in order to overtake them and arrive in England first. Thomas obliged – no doubt hoping that it would be to his future advantage if he were to make a good impression on the heir to the throne – and ordered his men to row, due to a lack of wind.

Unfortunately, eased by the wine, neither the oarsmen nor the helmsman were paying proper attention to what they were doing, and on its way out of the harbour the port side of the *White Ship* smashed into a rock that lay just under the surface of the water. Known as the *Quilleboeuf*, it is still identifiable today.

The horror of that dark and freezing night can only be imagined, as nobody of sufficient literacy survived the wreck in order to record it. The sole survivor was a butcher from Rouen who managed to grab hold of a spar and cling to it all night; all others perished. The butcher was later in great demand to tell his tale and he put about some stories that might or might not be true: that William had initially survived and was being taken to safety in a small boat when he turned it back on hearing the cries of his half-sister, only to have it overwhelmed and capsized, throwing him into the water; and that Thomas fitzStephen also survived the initial impact only to hear of William Adelin's death and then let himself drown rather than face the wrath of the king.[6] William Adelin's surviving friends may have encouraged the circulation of such tales on the basis that it was better to have him remembered as a hero who had died attempting to rescue a lady than as a reckless and drunken youth whose actions resulted in 300 deaths, including his own.

Henry disembarked safely at Southampton and then made his way to Clarendon, in Wiltshire, to await the rest of the household. When the awful news arrived, those who heard it were too terrified to tell him, whether at the thought of causing him such severe grief or in fear of being the target of his anger. In the end, a weeping young boy, an innocent whom Henry could not possibly blame, was pushed in front of him to break the news. Henry immediately fell to the ground, overcome by his anguish, and needed to be helped to his chamber. 'He suffered grief; he could have had none greater. He fell back on his bed so that no one dared speak to him, and he spoke to no one.'[7]

Many of the other magnates had lost relatives and friends, so the grief at court was extreme. 'O God, what a catastrophe and what sorrow there was!', laments one chronicler, and 'no ship', says another, 'was ever productive of so much misery to England'.[8] A very few bodies were recovered from the Norman shore, but most were lost forever, including William's; he has no known grave.

Contemporary verdicts on William Adelin were mixed. His virtues were extolled by some:

[William] gave and spent generously and dwelt with his father, who loved him very much. He did what his father asked and avoided what his father forbade. The flower of chivalry from England and Normandy set about serving him and had great hopes of him […] but He who is in control of the destiny of all things had arranged matters differently.

However, others were less sympathetic, attributing the deaths of those on the *White Ship* to 'the glittering vengeance of God' for their sins and extravagant lifestyles: 'They perished and almost all of them had no burial. And so death suddenly devoured those who had deserved it, although the sea was very calm and there was no wind.'[9]

These differing opinions, coupled with his lack of years – he was just 17 when he died – make it difficult for us to guess what sort of king William Adelin might have made. On the one hand, he was rumoured to be rash and riotous with his friends, but this was far from unusual in a youth of his age at the time (or indeed at any other time), so perhaps he was simply unfortunate in that an irresponsible action of his led to tragedy and multiple deaths while others might have acted similarly and got away with it. A few more years might have made all the difference; William had, after all, been brought up in the expectation of the crown and his father would have instilled in him the responsibilities as well as the privileges, so perhaps he might have calmed down as he grew older, as princes had done before and would continue to do afterwards.

The one undoubted consequence of the *White Ship* disaster was that King Henry was left with no legitimate son, and he would therefore have to make alternative plans for the succession. As noted in Chapter 1, the candidate who seemed to be the obvious choice was William Clito, he and his father Robert being Henry's only remaining relatives in the Conqueror's male line. But this, as we have seen, was unacceptable to Henry. This left him with a number of options, none of them ideal.

Henry's thoughts may have turned to his nephews. His other brothers had produced no children, but he also had five or six sisters, one of whom, Adela, countess of Blois, had four sons: William, Theobald, Stephen and Henry. William had been put aside by his mother in his youth[10] and Henry was a clergyman, but the two middle brothers, Theobald and Stephen, had been sent to King Henry when they were young and were familiar figures around the royal household. They were plausible candidates but Henry, after all his planning over the years, had a preference to be succeeded by a child of his own.

This left him two options. First was his eldest son Robert, earl of Gloucester, a powerful magnate who had proved himself both loyal and able. He was at this point around 30, a man in his prime – but he was illegitimate, and this therefore barred him from consideration; even Henry could not overturn the might of the Church. Robert's grandfather, William the Conqueror, had of course been illegitimate, but the Church's stance on the sanctity of marriage had hardened in the intervening years and Robert's bastardy now disqualified him completely from any pretensions to the throne (this would continue to be the case: no English or British monarch since 1087 has been illegitimate).

And finally, Henry had one other legitimate child: his daughter, Matilda.

***

At this point, in December 1120, Matilda was married to the Holy Roman Emperor (hence her being known throughout her life as the empress).[11] She was 18 and had been abroad for more than half her life. Still, Henry had received good reports of her – he and his son-in-law were allies and they kept up a frequent correspondence – and although she was at present childless, if she should have more than one son there was a possibility that one might succeed to England and Normandy while his brother ruled the Empire. In the absence of a son of his own, Henry would rather leave his crown to a grandson than a nephew. Matilda herself could not at this point be considered as an heir, for her marriage meant that she belonged to her husband rather than her father, and thus she must remain with him in the Empire.

However, Henry could not place all his hopes in theoretical grandchildren who were not yet conceived, so he took a more direct course of action. He had been a widower since Edith/Matilda had died in 1118, so he now hastily arranged a new match and was married to Adeliza of Louvain within three months of the *White Ship* disaster. She was a teenager less than half his age; he had a long history of fecundity; he took her everywhere with him. His plan was evidently to produce another legitimate son and then live long enough to see him grow up to be acknowledged as heir. In the event, neither of these things was to happen: after five years of marriage Adeliza had not conceived, and Henry, by now approaching 60, was forced to think again. Then, in the spring of 1125, another option became available to him when Emperor Henry died. Matilda, widowed and with no children who might need her to remain in the Empire as regent, could be recalled.

Matilda, as noted above, had been ripped from her family as a small child and sent abroad to live among strangers. Emperor Henry was one of the most powerful men in Europe, so the situation was no doubt intimidating to a little girl of 8. However, far from collapsing in a heap, she had made the best of her situation and profited from the opportunities it afforded. Her husband, who was many years older than her, arranged for her education and she studied hard; within a few years she was fluent in several languages and had a strong grasp of the history, politics and governance of the Empire. By the time she was 16 Henry trusted her enough, and had sufficient faith in her abilities, to leave her as his regent in Italy; that is to say, she ruled that part of the Empire on his behalf while he was in Germany. This is not something he would have done had he not felt her equal to the task, however lofty her rank, so it speaks well of her capabilities.

After a couple of years, however, Emperor Henry's need for an heir overrode other considerations and Matilda was recalled to Germany. She remained at his side both in court and on his travels, but they were still childless when he died of an illness, possibly cancer, in 1125. Matilda was 23 and many of the options available to her – a long widowhood, for example, or retirement to a nunnery – did not appeal.

Matilda had, of course, heard of the *White Ship* disaster four and half years previously, but although she presumably grieved on a personal level, she must have felt at the time that it could have little impact on the course of her career, established as she was in the Empire. But now, things were different, and the prospect of rule in her own right must have been enticing. She had coped well during her taste of power in Italy, and the English crown would give her scope for her ambitions and autonomy of the sort afforded to few women.

Resigning the lands she still held in the Empire and cutting her ties there, Matilda returned to Normandy, where she remained with her father through 1126. She needed to re-learn her native language and re-acquaint herself with the major players at court, while he needed to see what she was made of. The king decided that he liked what he saw (influenced, of course, by the fact that she was his own child), and he decided to name her as his heir. And it was she alone who was designated – not any future husband or son, but her. England seemed destined to have its first female king,[12] and Henry organized a large-scale ceremony in January 1127 at which all the magnates and bishops swore that they would uphold Matilda's claim to the throne once he was dead.

Matilda no doubt looked forward to the prospect of the crown, but there was a catch: she would have to marry again. Although she had been named personally as heir, there would be little point in her ascending the throne if she then had no children of her own, or the situation would merely be repeated and Henry's dynasty would die out anyway. He therefore cast about for a suitable match, and his eye turned once again to Anjou. As well as the two daughters who had been briefly married to William Adelin and William Clito, Count Fulk had two sons. The elder, Geoffrey, was his heir; Fulk and Henry arranged the match to their mutual satisfaction and Matilda was dispatched to Anjou for the wedding in the spring of 1128.

From Henry's point of view the arrangement was extremely satisfactory, but Matilda did not share his opinion. She had been an empress; now she was to marry the mere son of a count. It was humiliating, and the situation was made even worse by the fact that she was 26 and he just 14. The marriage was a disaster from the start, and within a year Matilda and Geoffrey had separated. But this was not part of Henry's plan, so in 1131 he forced her to return to her husband; he did, however, reiterate her position as his heir by having the magnates swear once more, in September of that year, that they would uphold her right to the throne once he was gone. Matilda's cousin and major rival, William Clito, had died in 1128, so her path to the throne seemed clear, all the more so when her reunion with Geoffrey produced two sons, Henry and Geoffrey, in 1133 and 1134 respectively.

But Matilda's husband had ambitions of his own, and his position was ambiguous. Was he simply a consort, or would he in due course be king of England in right of his wife, as a man might become earl or count by marrying an heiress? And more to the point, was he to control Normandy, a territory he and his family had long coveted? Any hopes on this point were dashed when Henry not only pointedly omitted Geoffrey's name at the oath-taking of 1131, but also refused to hand over three castles in Normandy that were supposed to form Matilda's dowry.

Geoffrey, annoyed at his lack of recognition, needled and challenged Henry; the king, 'provoked by these irritations to anger and bitter ill-feeling',[13] went to war against his son-in-law. This left Matilda in an almost impossible position, but she ended up siding with her husband against her father, with the result that she was nowhere near either England or Normandy when Henry died, fairly suddenly, in December 1135. By the time news of his death even reached her, her cousin Stephen of Blois had raced across the Channel, seized the royal treasury (with the help of his brother Henry, who was bishop of Winchester), claimed the throne, ridden to London and had himself crowned.

Matilda was furious, as well she might be, but she was not in a position to do anything about it immediately. She was stuck in Anjou, she was pregnant (which made travelling difficult), and she could not hope to compete with the immense wealth that Stephen now had at his disposal. Stephen, meanwhile, had surprised his contemporaries with the speed and success with which he had seized the throne: he was neither the designated heir nor even the eldest son in his own family, and moreover he had sworn – twice – to uphold Matilda's rights. But, as was the accepted tradition, his coronation was irrevocable.[14] The rapidity with which the magnates accepted the situation and came to terms with Stephen might also seem surprising, or at least it would have been had Matilda been male. It is difficult to see that an only legitimate adult *son* of the previous monarch would have been overlooked so completely in favour of a cousin – and a cousin who was, moreover, both a royal descendant only in the female line and a younger son himself. But Matilda was not male, and therein lay her downfall: 'All the bishops, earls and barons, who had sworn fealty to the king's daughter and her heirs, gave their adherence to King Stephen, saying that it would be a shame for so many nobles to submit themselves to a woman.'[15]

It was four long years before Matilda could muster enough support to mount an invasion of England. She left Geoffrey and her three sons behind and sailed in the autumn of 1139, landing at Arundel where she was welcomed and initially sheltered by the dowager Queen Adeliza, who held the castle there. Matilda had two principal allies: her illegitimate half-brother Robert, earl of Gloucester, and her uncle King David of Scotland, who was the younger brother of Matilda's late mother Edith/ Matilda. David had already pre-empted Matilda's actions by launching an invasion of his own in 1138, ostensibly on her behalf, but he had been defeated at the Battle of the Standard in August of that year and forced to come to terms with Stephen. However, having Matilda now on English soil gave him the incentive to act on her behalf once again.

Robert, who had sailed with Matilda, rode swiftly westwards to his own castle of Bristol to raise an army, leaving her behind the high walls of Arundel castle. Stephen immediately moved to surround her position but Matilda outwitted him and, without a sword being drawn, ended up with a safe-conduct that allowed her to travel unmolested to Bristol to join Robert, escorted by none other than Stephen's brother Henry, the bishop of Winchester.[16]

And thus began a war that was to rage for another fourteen years, each party having its gains and its losses, its triumphs and its tragedies, but neither able to make the final and decisive breakthrough. It started quietly enough, with a number of the realm's magnates deserting Stephen and swearing allegiance to Matilda, either because they thought they should (rather belatedly) uphold their oaths to her, or because they thought it was in their own interests. This did not immediately cause an all-out war, but rather many smaller-scale local rebellions, and Stephen was forced to rush about to all corners of his kingdom to extinguish them. Meanwhile, Matilda positioned herself not as a noble in rebellion against the king, but rather as the lawful monarch in her own right – thus claiming the moral high ground and implying that those who adhered to Stephen were the ones in the wrong. She did this in a number of ways, including moving from being Robert's guest in Bristol to take up residence in the royal castle of Gloucester, having coins minted bearing her likeness and making grants of lands and titles. This last, incidentally, caused much confusion in many parts of England, as some counties nominally had two earls, one named by Matilda and one by Stephen.

One thing Matilda did not do was to call herself queen of England, for this title was already held by another Matilda, Stephen's wife. In any case, 'queen' meant merely the wife of a king, and this is certainly not how Matilda saw herself.[17] Her husband Geoffrey was almost forgotten: she did not call herself countess of Anjou, either, preferring to stick to 'empress', 'queen of the Romans'[18] and 'daughter of King Henry', all titles that enhanced her prestige without making her subordinate to the men involved, given that they were both long dead.

After a year or so of guerrilla warfare, of castles being captured and recaptured, Matilda enjoyed a major breakthrough early in 1141. In January of that year Ranulf, earl of Chester, had seized the castle of

Lincoln – more for his own gain than Matilda's, but the loss to Stephen was the same. Stephen, unable to ignore such an act of insubordination, moved to retake it; however, he ended up in a precarious position sandwiched inside the city walls but outside the castle. This was Matilda's chance, and despite the winter weather she sent an army under Robert of Gloucester to Lincoln. Robert was keen to get there as soon as possible, partly due to his loyalty to Matilda, and partly because his daughter was Ranulf's wife; in his plea for assistance, Ranulf had been careful to note that she was trapped inside the castle while the king was assaulting it.

The army reached Lincoln much more quickly than Stephen might have expected. He did not retreat, 'refus[ing] to sully his name by the disgrace of flight';[19] but, rather than risk fighting in the close confines between the two sets of walls, he elected to come out of the city to give battle on a plain to the west. The two armies met on 2 February 1141, but Stephen's unenthusiastic forces were no match for Matilda's; his earls all fled the field, leaving him to be captured.[20]

Stephen was taken to Gloucester and brought before Matilda, an interview at which it might have been interesting to be a fly on the wall. She had to decide what to do with him: although she considered him a usurper, the fact remained that he was a crowned king, and to murder him in cold blood was out of the question. Had he been 'accidentally' killed in the heat of battle then that would be different, but here he was, alive and uninjured, and with the status of God's anointed. Matilda had no choice but to place him in custody, and, as he was taken to Bristol, Stephen may have tried to blot out thoughts of the sad fate of his uncle Robert Curthose.

Once Stephen was confined, the war seemed to be over. Matilda held talks with England's highest-ranking clergyman, who happened to be Henry, bishop of Winchester, her cousin and Stephen's brother. Normally the archbishop of Canterbury would be the senior churchman in England, but Henry, although only a bishop, held the additional status of papal legate, meaning that he was a direct representative of the pope and thus he leapfrogged the archbishop in the Church hierarchy. Matilda met with Bishop Henry in March; he abruptly abandoned Stephen's cause and declared his support for her, proclaiming her 'Lady of the English'. Preparations for her coronation were begun, and in June she travelled to Westminster for the ceremony.

However, Matilda had greatly underestimated one crucial factor: the absolute resistance of men to the idea of a female ruler. Although she had a few supporters who were resolutely loyal to her personally, many of the other magnates had supported her (or rebelled against Stephen without actually swearing allegiance to Matilda) because they were unhappy with Stephen and his erratic rule. Now that they were faced with the idea that a woman might actually rule over them, they panicked.

A smear campaign developed among contemporary chroniclers, who, we should note, were all male; indeed, as clergymen they would have had even less contact than normal with capable women – or indeed any women at all – so they tended to treat the entire sex with suspicion. Once Matilda reached London, one of them tells us, 'she was lifted up to an insufferable arrogance [...] and she alienated the hearts of almost everyone'.[21] Had she been discovered in some hitherto unknown character flaw? It seems not. It does not require a particularly close analysis to see that the comments made about her preparations for kingship were all pointedly gendered. She:

> At once put on an extremely arrogant demeanour instead of the modest gait and bearing proper to the gentle sex, began to walk and speak and do all things more stiffly and haughtily than she had been wont [...] she actually made herself queen of all England and gloried in being so called.[22]

Well, yes: she was about to be crowned queen, so she started to act like one.

The criticism continues: 'Then she [Matilda], on being raised with such splendour and distinction to this pre-eminent position, began to be arbitrary, or rather headstrong, in all that she did'; she no longer relied on the advice of her closest advisors but instead 'arranged everything as she herself thought fit and according to her own arbitrary will'; she spoke 'not with unassuming gentleness, but with a voice of authority'.[23] A monarch making their own decisions and speaking with authority? How singular. Sarcasm aside, it is clear that these accusations, if levelled at a man, would have sounded ridiculous – Matilda was only considered to be 'arrogant' because she was a woman seeking power.

In the twelfth century women had their allotted place in life and they were expected to stick to it. As it happened, noblewomen were often called upon to undertake what might be considered traditionally 'masculine' activities, such as running estates or defending lands, and the men around them expected them to be able to cope with such responsibilities. But this was only safe for society as long as the women were acting on behalf of a male relative – a husband, a brother, a son – so that female authority could be kept within acceptable male-defined parameters. The double standards of the chroniclers became even more apparent when a new player entered the game: Queen Matilda, the wife of Stephen. She could be active, she could raise and command troops, she could assume control, because she was acting in the name of her imprisoned husband. And so it is that the same chronicler who criticized the empress by saying that 'she, with a grim look, her forehead wrinkled into a frown, every trace of a woman's gentleness removed from her face, blazed into unbearable fury' could with a completely straight face a few lines later praise the queen for being 'a woman [...] of a man's resolution'.[24]

And it was Queen Matilda who took the initiative now, having the interests of both a husband and a son to look out for. She incited a mob of Londoners, who stormed Westminster the very night before Matilda's planned coronation, forcing her and her companions to flee so suddenly that the attackers found the food still warm on the table. Empress Matilda, together with Earl Robert and King David, rode to Oxford to regroup – but without Bishop Henry, who headed to Winchester and promptly changed sides again, declaring that he had been misled and that all true subjects should support Stephen once more.

Matilda's next move was to march on Winchester. The crown might be out of reach, but the royal treasury was not; if she were to control that, with Stephen still in her custody, she might be able to regain ground in the quest for the crown. But this was also to prove an exercise that was futile and ultimately disastrous. Bishop Henry fled as they approached his city, running straight to Queen Matilda and her army to ask them for help. He had left his castle fortified and garrisoned behind him, so Matilda and her troops found themselves in a similar situation to that of Stephen in Lincoln: trapped between two sets of walls with an army approaching. They remained in Winchester just a little too long, and by the time the order was given to retreat, the queen's army was upon them. There was a running battle along the road from Winchester to Stockbridge as one side sought to flee and the other to stop them, and then a standing skirmish as Matilda's troops had to slow down to cross the River Test, which caused enough of a backlog for the queen's army to catch up.

Matilda made it through; she rode hard for Gloucester and arrived there half-dead from exhaustion. King David joined her, having narrowly escaped capture several times. But Earl Robert did not: he had stood his ground at Stockbridge to enable his sister to get away, and paid the price, 'buying his friends' freedom with the loss of his own'.[25] This was almost as serious as Matilda being captured herself: as a woman, she could not lead her armies into battle, so she needed her half-brother to do it for her. There was no choice but to agree to the demands of the queen, and exchange Robert for Stephen.

And so the war started again, with each side no better off than they had been at the start, and the people of England suffering as their lands and livelihoods were razed and ruined. Once Stephen was freed, Queen Matilda went back to her apartments and played no further active part in the war; Stephen may have been missing a trick here, for she was quite possibly a better general than he was. A later chronicler, writing in the thirteenth century, notes with hindsight that Empress Matilda 'had much more success making war on the king than on the queen'.[26]

The pendulum swung much further towards Stephen, almost fatally for Matilda, in 1142. Robert of Gloucester had been dispatched over the Channel to ask for help from Matilda's husband, Geoffrey; Geoffrey declined to assist, as he was busy using her name and her claim to the duchy to conquer Normandy, which had been an ambition for his family for some time. However, he kept Robert with him, which meant that Robert was not able to help when Matilda was unexpectedly trapped in Oxford by Stephen and his army in the autumn of that year. She was completely cut off, besieged for months and with food supplies sinking perilously low.

One freezing December night she took matters into her own hands and escaped in a fashion so daring it barely seems credible. Dressed in white for camouflage and with only three men to accompany her, she slipped out of a small postern gate that opened outside the city walls and picked her way across snowy open ground before walking right across the frozen Thames and slipping unnoticed through Stephen's very camp, tiptoeing 'through the king's pickets, which everywhere were breaking the silence of the night with the blaring of trumpeters or the cries of men shouting loudly'.[27] Astonishingly, she got away. 'A manifest miracle of God', says one chronicler,[28] while another cannot hide his amazement:

> In a wondrous fashion she escaped unharmed through so
> many enemies, so many watchers in the silence of the night
> [...] I do not know whether it was to heighten the greatness of
> her fame in time to come, or by God's judgement to increase
> more vehemently the disturbance of the kingdom, but never
> have I read of another woman so luckily rescued from so
> many mortal foes and from the threat of dangers so great.[29]

Matilda's position remained precarious; she did not have enough troops
or resources to force a decisive victory. But neither did she give up: of all
the lost heirs in this book, she is probably the one who pursued a claim to
the throne most doggedly. The war dragged on for another five years, by
which time there was a danger that there would not be much of England
left to rule, whoever won. Chroniclers made much of the depredations in
England, one writing that:

> The powerful oppress the weak by violence, and obtain
> exemption from enquiry by the terror of their threats.
> Death is the lot of him who resists. The wealthy nobles of
> the land, rolling in affluence, care little to what iniquities
> the wretched sufferers are exposed; all their concern is for
> themselves and their own adherents.[30]

And, in probably the most famous passage detailing the war, the *Anglo-
Saxon Chronicle* notes that things were so bad that it was said openly
that 'Christ and His saints slept'.[31]

Matilda forced herself to rethink, and two major factors influenced
her plan. First, Robert of Gloucester died in 1147. He had been her
chief supporter, and his death both deprived her of her principal
military commander and reminded her that none of them was getting
any younger. But the passage of time also had a flip side, leading to
the second factor in the equation: by 1147, Matilda's eldest son Henry
was 14 and could therefore be presented as a plausible candidate to the
throne in his own right.

Matilda was acutely aware of the opposition in England to female
rule, and she must, by this time, have realized that it was unlikely she
would ever wear the crown herself. But if not her, then the next best
thing was her son – and he was certainly preferable to Stephen's son

Eustace (of whom we will hear more in Chapter 3), who was by now around 17 and who had been groomed for the throne since his childhood. Henry was the legitimate grandson of Henry I – whose reign was now regarded in hindsight as a halcyon time of peace and prosperity – so he could be positioned as the true heir. Henry made several trips to England during his youth, and he and his lineage were known by the magnates. Matilda began to associate his name with hers on charters and grants, and slowly many of the lords came around to the view that everything had been a terrible mistake and that they should forget the last decade and compromise by agreeing that Henry was his grandfather's true and lawful heir. This was promising, but unfortunately for Matilda she soon also realized that the best way for her to promote her son's cause was to get out of his way completely. Thus it was that she took ship in the summer of 1148, never to return to England.

Matilda's story was, however, by no means over. Her husband Geoffrey had succeeded in his conquest of Normandy and had been named duke; rather gallingly, Matilda now found herself duchess of Normandy as Geoffrey's wife. The situation became more palatable in 1150 when Geoffrey resigned the title in favour of Henry, on the basis that he had technically been fighting on behalf of his son's hereditary right all along. With Henry much engaged in England, Matilda was able to act as his regent and, strangely enough, her rule in Normandy was accepted because she was now, quite properly and appropriately, acting on behalf of a man.

Sufficient numbers of English magnates came round during the next few years to make the question of the succession more urgent. In 1153 Stephen and Henry came to terms, the agreement being that Stephen would remain king for the rest of his life but that the crown should then pass to Henry, rather than to his own children. This understandably outraged his eldest son, Eustace, but it did bring hostilities between the two major figures to an end, for which most of England was profoundly grateful.

Stephen only survived another year after the agreement was reached, and in 1154 Matilda found herself the mother of the king of England. Henry was still only 21 and he relied upon her for advice and guidance in many matters. In some endeavours she was successful in persuading him to avoid folly: a planned invasion of Ireland was cancelled when Matilda pointed out the probable negative consequences. But in other areas she had less influence – her advice to Henry not to appoint Thomas Becket archbishop of Canterbury was ignored, with disastrous results.

With the benefit of hindsight, it is difficult to see that Matilda's reign, had she managed to have one, would have been anything other than a disaster. This is not because she was incapable of ruling: far from it. She had extensive international political experience and was both intelligent and shrewd; had her exact combination of abilities been housed in a male body, she would have made an excellent medieval king. No, the problem would have rested with the magnates, who would have used every conceivable excuse to squabble, to rebel, and to push back against her authority, in the belief that it was unnatural to have a woman in such a position of power. Matilda would have been placed in an intolerable lose–lose situation: any attempt to exert proper authority would have been met with accusations that she was aberrant and unwomanly, and therefore unsuited to rule; and had she endeavoured to soften her image by acting in a more traditionally acceptable feminine way, this would have led to her being considered a weak woman ... and therefore equally unsuited to rule. The only way in which she could possibly 'triumph' was in making sure that her son sat on the throne.

But Matilda's son, at least, did appreciate her. As Henry – who chose throughout his life to be known as Henry fitzEmpress rather than Henry fitzGeoffrey – aged and grew into his royal role he still relied upon Matilda and her vast diplomatic experience. She negotiated on his behalf with such powerful figures as the king of France and the Holy Roman Emperor, and she was at the time of her death in 1167 considered the elder stateswoman of Europe. Although she never did sit on the English throne, Matilda was arguably more successful than many others who will feature in this book. She lived a long life and died of natural causes; she saw the crown restored to her own line. This restoration had two further distinct consequences. Firstly, it set the precedent that although England was not yet ready for female rule, the crown could at least be *transmitted* in the female line, something that was to be of great consequence centuries later in the struggle between York and Lancaster, and then again under the Tudors. Secondly, and more immediately, the agreement of 1153 – which we must class as a victory for Matilda as well as Henry – sidelined others. Just as Matilda had been dispossessed when she had expected the crown, so had the outcome of the war she waged disinherited Stephen's children.

# Chapter 3

# Eustace, William and Mary of Blois

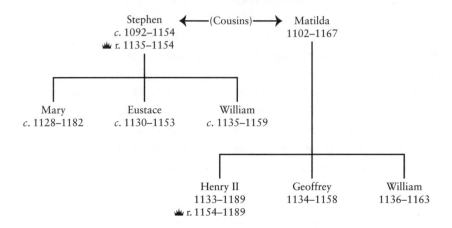

Eustace of Blois was not born 'in the purple'. At the time of his birth, his father Stephen was a count twice over – of Mortain in his own name and Boulogne in his wife's – but he was not a king and nor was he realistically considered a contender for the English throne. Neither would Stephen inherit his ancestral lands; he was the son of the late count of Blois but had two older brothers. His ambitions, therefore, seemed focused on the rich county of Boulogne, which controlled much of the lucrative cross-Channel trade in wine and wool, and the name he chose for his eldest son reflected this: Eustace had been the name of three recent counts including the previous incumbent, Stephen's father-in-law.

However, Eustace was only around 5 years old when his expectations were dramatically raised: his father's appropriation of the English crown meant that he was brought up to expect it as his birthright.[1] He was therefore given a royal education and, like other heirs, was associated with government from an early age; he was only around 7 when he gave homage to the French king for Normandy in 1137. A word of explanation on this custom might be useful here, as the subject will arise again in later chapters. The king of France was the overlord of the duchy of Normandy, and could therefore expect to receive homage from the dukes in the same way he received it from his other counts and vassals. However, the situation had been complicated by William the Conqueror's seizure of the English crown, since which time (with a few brief intermissions), the king of England and the duke of Normandy had been the same man. Although the holdings were separate, and it would be the duke paying homage, onlookers would still be treated to the sight of the king of England kneeling to the king of France. The English kings found this unacceptable, so various ways around it were found, including the practice of having their sons and heirs – often as young boys – perform the homage in their stead.

Eustace, like any heir to the throne, would need to have an advantageous marriage arranged for him. And here Stephen struck very lucky indeed; courtesy of a large sum of money that he gained by confiscating the worldly possessions of a number of English bishops, he was able to persuade the new young French king, Louis VII, to agree to a match between Eustace and Louis's only sister Constance.[2] She was somewhere between two and five years older than her new husband (we do not have firm dates of birth for either of them), but the difference was small compared with that of many other royal marriages. The wedding was celebrated in 1140 and Constance was brought to England to live at the royal court.

Stephen's defeat and capture at the Battle of Lincoln in February 1141[3] meant that all his carefully laid plans for his eldest son came crashing down. Far from being the heir apparent to the throne, Eustace was now faced with the prospect of becoming a mere count, and even that was soon thrown into doubt. His uncle Henry, bishop of Winchester, had deserted Stephen and declared for Matilda but – perhaps wishing to make some amends to his family – while they were in London in the summer of 1141 awaiting her coronation, he petitioned her for Eustace to be given his father's personal lands and titles 'as being his lawful property while his father was held a prisoner'.[4] In a move that was perhaps harsh, but nonetheless understandable in the circumstances, Matilda declined. Neither option, as it happened, was particularly beneficial to her. On the one hand, monarchs had to tread very carefully if they wanted to deprive anyone of their ancestral estates, as it could cause unrest and distrust among all the magnates, and therefore destabilize the realm; but on the other, she had spent many years in fear of a challenge to her position from William Clito, and presumably did not wish to give

Eustace the opportunity to make himself into another such danger in exile. Therefore her decision was something of a compromise: she did not imprison Eustace along with his father, but she deprived him of the resources with which to mount a rebellion against her.

Eustace's confused and unstable childhood took yet another turn during the same year when Stephen was released from prison and reinstated as king. Once again, he was the heir, and he would remain so for the foreseeable future. He was knighted in 1147, at which point he would have been around 17; and at the same time he was invested as count of Boulogne. Eustace's mother, Queen Matilda, was countess of Boulogne in her own right, but she was either persuaded or pressured into believing that the appropriate womanly thing to do was to hand over the reins of power to her son now that he was considered an adult.

Despite all this, Eustace could not feel himself to be safe: he had hardly reached his teens when he became aware of the serious threat posed to him by Henry of Anjou, the empress's son, and the rivalry would go on until it could be ended permanently one way or the other. The problem was that neither of them had an overriding claim to the throne that could extinguish the other's, but that each had sufficient grounds to make himself a contender. Eustace could claim to be the son of an anointed king, which Henry could not; but Henry could point to the fact that Stephen's coronation and rule were illegitimate in the first place. Thus he, Henry, was the true heir of Henry I, whose reign was not by this time in any dispute, despite its unorthodox beginnings (the unfortunate Robert Curthose had not been dead for many years, but he had been irrelevant for a long time before that, and Henry I's rule was in hindsight considered not only legitimate but a time of order and firm governance). The question would be solved, in the long run, not by legal wrangling but by might: whoever won the war – or whoever had a parent who won the war – would triumph.

Eustace never met his nemesis face to face, although it would appear that they had some near-misses. On one of his trips to England, in 1149, Henry landed in the south and then rode all the way to Carlisle in order to be knighted by his great-uncle King David of Scots. Stephen and Eustace heard of the event; Stephen travelled in haste to York but when Henry successfully bypassed him, Eustace tried to intercept him further south by laying no fewer than three ambushes through Herefordshire and Gloucestershire. Henry evaded them all and a furious Eustace reacted in a way which would become familiar over the next few years: he lost his temper and took it out on others. In this case he 'fell upon the lands of the noblemen who were with Henry, the son of the empress. There was no one to oppose him […] he caused much damage'.[5] At Salisbury there was worse in store for the common people; at this crucial harvest time of the year, Eustace's men 'took and plundered everything they came upon, set fire to houses and churches, and, what was a more cruel and brutal sight, fired the crops that had been reaped and stacked all over the fields, consumed and brought to nothing everything edible they found'.[6]

The war had by now been raging for over a decade, and both sides were resorting to ever more brutal tactics to try to end it. Stephen 'deliberated on the most effective means of shattering his opponents' and:

> At last it seemed to him sound and judicious to attack the enemy everywhere, plunder and destroy all that was in their possession, set fire to crops and every other means of supporting human life, and let nothing remain anywhere, that under this duress, reduced to the extremity of want, they might at last be compelled to yield and surrender.[7]

Eustace seemed to revel in this kind of warfare. Having already ravaged the land around Salisbury he turned to Devizes and attacked the castle there, and 'by ordering his men to set fire immediately to the houses everywhere, to kill those who came in their way and commit indiscriminately every cruelty they could think of, showed that a day of grief and weeping was at hand'.[8]

Henry returned to Normandy, and Eustace followed him there in 1151. By this time any hope that Eustace may have had of one day being duke of Normandy had been well and truly crushed. His father had spent so much time, energy and resource trying to hold on to his English crown that he had none left for defending the duchy. One by one the magnates there had been defeated by or had come to terms with Geoffrey of Anjou, who had spent years grinding his way inexorably towards victory. He had succeeded, had been recognized as duke, and in 1150 had handed over the duchy and its title to his son Henry, who was considered an adult following his knighting the previous year. Eustace evidently felt that he had to do something, but once he reached Europe, the alliance he formed with his brother-in-law Louis VII was ineffectual.

Louis accepted the Angevins' *fait accompli* and received Henry's homage as duke of Normandy, which meant that, in turn, Louis recognized the legitimacy of Henry's title.

Worse was to come for Eustace and his brother-in-law when in 1152 King Louis divorced his wife, Eleanor, only to see her remarry within weeks to none other than Henry, thus bringing the vast duchy of Aquitaine, which Eleanor held in her own right, under Henry's control. This was a blow to Eustace, as it enriched his foe greatly, and it also disadvantaged Louis: he had two daughters by Eleanor, of whom he retained custody, so he had been consoling himself with the fact that the elder of them would one day inherit Aquitaine. But if Eleanor were to have a son by Henry, that son would take precedence and Louis and his daughters would lose out.

Eustace was more than willing to form another coalition, and this time the partnership was strengthened by others. First came the brothers Theobald, count of Blois, and Henry, count of Champagne, who were Eustace's cousins – the sons of King Stephen's elder brother Theobald, who had held two French counties and left them to separate sons. To cement the relationship, Theobald and Henry were married off to Louis's daughters, despite the huge differences in age (the brothers were 25 and 22; the sisters 7 and 2). Also joining the alliance were Louis's younger brother Robert, count of Dreux, and Henry's younger brother Geoffrey fitzEmpress. This last may seem surprising, but Geoffrey, who was only fourteen months younger than Henry, had seen his brother gain Normandy, Anjou, Maine and Aquitaine, while he had to settle for just three castles left to him by his father; he was jealous, and evidently saw a greater future with Eustace than with Henry.

However, Geoffrey, Eustace and their allies were to be disappointed: the campaign was a failure. They had waited until Henry was at Barfleur, on the point of taking ship for England, before they invaded his lands behind his back; but they had underestimated both him and his mother. Empress Matilda was by now permanently based in Rouen, close to the French border from where the attack was launched, and she managed to get a message to Henry quickly enough to stop him sailing. He turned his troops around and returned with astonishing speed, forcing Eustace's coalition to retreat without engaging in battle. Eustace, deprived of the opportunity to relieve his feelings with violence, was left to gnash his teeth in frustration and return to England.

King Stephen, growing older, ever more weary of the war and worried for his son's future, tried another tactic to secure his future. Coronation, as we noted earlier, was irreversible; the main reason Stephen's own kingship had managed to stagger on for so long was that he was God's anointed, and that status could not be taken away. He therefore sought to make sure of his son's succession by pursuing the extraordinary step of having Eustace crowned king while he himself was still alive. This was a well-established custom in France, where the Capetians had been crowning 'junior' kings during their predecessors' lifetimes since the late tenth century, but it was unprecedented in England.

Stephen had been making subtle overtures to the pope for some time – or, to be more specific, to several popes, as there had been a rapid turnover during the previous few years[9] – but he had made little progress. During a brief six-month papacy Celestine II, on being applied to, had written to Theobald, archbishop of Canterbury, 'forbidding him to allow any change to be made in the position of the English crown, since the transfer of it had been justly denounced, and the matter was still under dispute'.[10]

Perhaps feeling that he was running out of time, Stephen took more direct steps. In April 1152 he summoned Archbishop Theobald and several other bishops to appear before him, and demanded that Eustace be crowned:

> But when he demanded of the said archbishop [Theobald] and the other bishops whom he had summoned there, that they anoint Eustace king and confirm him with their blessing, he was refused. Indeed, the pope in a letter had forbidden the archbishop to elevate the king's son as king. It was understood that this was because Stephen had seized the kingdom contrary to the oath [to support Matilda's claim].[11]

The result was predictable: 'Boiling with rage at this crushing humiliation, father and son ordered them all to be shut up [...] subjecting them to powerful intimidation, [they] urged them to do what they demanded.'[12] Archbishop Theobald evaded the king and escaped to Flanders, but the threat of violence hung over the others. What Eustace may have done, left to his own devices, must be left to conjecture; but Stephen, perhaps realizing that he could not afford to make an enemy of the Church, later released the bishops without harm.

It was all going horribly wrong for Eustace, and matters went from bad to worse very quickly. Just a month after this meeting, in May 1152, his mother died. This was a devastating blow both to Eustace and to Stephen, as she had been the rock they relied on; without her, Stephen would probably be still be rotting in prison after a decade in the empress's custody. Indeed, the loss of his wife seemed to knock out of the king any stuffing that might have remained after all this time. More and more magnates were siding with Henry of Anjou, seeing in him the best hope of ending the war, and Stephen could feel his fingers slipping as he sought to keep the crown.

When Henry returned to England in 1153, Stephen and Eustace raised their banners once more and brought troops to face him across the River Avon at Malmesbury. At this point the magnates on both sides, fed up with the never-ending war, simply refused to fight. 'The leading men of each army […] shrank, on both sides, from a conflict that was not merely between fellow countrymen but meant the desolation of the whole kingdom, thinking it wise […] to join all together for the establishment of peace.'[13] The parties were forced to negotiate, and the outcome of the talks was swift and simple: that Stephen would remain king for the rest of his life, but that he would then be succeeded by Henry. Eustace had been disinherited.

Now, although Henry was unquestionably in a strong position, the English magnates – and indeed Stephen himself – might not have supported this plan so speedily had they not had serious doubts about Eustace and his capabilities. If he had shown any indication that he might be a strong, just king who would bring peace and stability, they might have made more of an effort on his behalf, but the examples of his erratic and violent behaviour had become too frequent. Violence was of course an acceptable tactic at the time, but it needed to be used strategically; senseless and random brutality was a different matter as it made the perpetrator look unpredictable – something which, in a king, was dangerous for all concerned.

For Eustace, the agreement reached between Stephen and Henry in July 1153 was the last straw, and being disinherited by his own father, without even a semblance of protest, must have seemed like the ultimate betrayal. Eustace only knew one way to react to the situation: 'greatly vexed and angry',[14] he withdrew from Stephen's court, headed to East Anglia and indulged in an orgy of violence, wasting the lands of the abbey of Bury St Edmunds, the burial place of one of England's greatest saints. And then, quite suddenly, he died. There is no suggestion that this was due to a wound received in combat; rather, he appears to have had some kind of seizure. This was considered unusual for a man in his early twenties, and so contemporaries sought to explain it in more understandable terms.

One sympathetic source says he 'met his end from grief',[15] but others put it down to God's judgement, saying he was 'destroyed by the providence of God';[16] 'because he had plundered the land belonging to St Edmund'.[17] It was an unhappy end for an unhappy young man, the tragedy compounded by the fact that – in marked contrast to some of the lamentations over the untimely deaths of other young heirs featured in this book – the chroniclers heaved a unanimous sigh of relief. 'He was a man proven in military skill, but obdurate against the things of God, very harsh towards the incumbents of churches, very loyal towards those who persecute the Church [...] God Himself was already in His greatest kindness preparing the tranquillity of His realm.'[18] Or, more pithily, Eustace was 'an evil man, because wheresoever he came he did more evil than good'.[19]

Eustace was buried alongside his mother, who had done so much for him, at the family foundation of Faversham Abbey in Kent. He had no children; his wife Constance left England soon after his death, and by 1154 was married off again by her brother, this time to the count of Toulouse in Southern France.[20]

\*\*\*

Although his primary focus had always been his eldest son, Stephen had other children. Initially he and his wife had five: Mary, Eustace, Baldwin (another continental name, common in Boulogne's neighbouring Flanders), Matilda and William. Baldwin and Matilda had both died in infancy; Mary had been given to the Church in early childhood.[21] That left William. His exact date of birth is not known, but it is likely to have been at approximately the time of Stephen's coronation (December 1135), and therefore he might have mustered a claim to have been born 'in the purple', a supposition bolstered by the choice of an Anglo-Norman forename for him.

Eustace's death in August 1153 left William in the awkward position of being the only surviving legitimate son of the king, but not the designated heir to the throne. As we noted in the previous chapter,

Empress Matilda's claims, when she found herself in a similar situation, would have been immeasurably improved by her being a man.[22] But although William was now in a comparable position and was male, he made no claim – and nobody else seemed particularly interested in making one on his behalf.

This can be attributed to a number of causes. The English magnates were sick of the war and wanted to end it as quickly and as painlessly as possible; if they and Stephen were prepared to disinherit the king's eldest son to achieve this aim then they can have had no qualms at doing the same to the younger son. From William's own point of view, strange as it may seem in an age of deadly ambition, he seems simply to have had no desire to sit on the throne. He had not been brought up to expect it and so did not care about it as passionately or violently as Eustace. Additionally, he had spent his entire existence observing the troubles his father had keeping the crown on his head, and might have been happy to settle for a quieter life.

As it was, William benefited greatly from the succession arrangements. He had already become count of Boulogne on Eustace's death; he was heir to his father's county of Mortain; and he was married to Isabel de Warenne, a great heiress who had brought him the earldom of Surrey and the extensive Warenne lands in both England and Normandy. On top of this he was now offered the honours of Pevensey and Lancaster, and lands in Norfolk and East Anglia. He would be – by a long way – the richest magnate in the realm, and all he had to do was surrender a right to the throne that he never thought he would possess anyway. William agreed, and when his father died in October 1154, just a year after the treaty was finalized, nobody raised banners in his name. After all the years of war England was glad to have the crown on the head of Henry II.

However, Henry remained suspicious of William and his motives, as well he might. His and his mother's long animosity towards Stephen and all his family had not inclined him to be gullible, and given his own determined nature it was perhaps difficult for him to believe in the concept of a man without ambition. It is worth noting that although he had granted William extensive tracts of land, Henry had been careful to ensure that they were geographically dispersed, thus preventing him from forming a solid block that might give him enough concentrated resource to attempt any kind of rebellion. But just three years later, in 1157, William came into conflict with Hugh Bigod, the other East Anglian magnate of note, and Henry took advantage of the situation to step in, side with Hugh and confiscate all William's lands and estates in England and Normandy. He returned William's family lands – even a king had to step carefully when it came to depriving men of their patrimony, as it made everyone else nervous – but without the castles and fortifications.

William was discomfited at this, but was now in even less of a position to mount a claim for the throne than he had been before, being deprived of military means. He had the sop of being knighted by Henry in the summer of 1158, but although this might have improved his social standing among his peers, it did little for his financial situation. He decided to regain favour by working with Henry rather than against him, and joined the king's expedition to Toulouse in the summer of 1159.[23] Perhaps, too, the idea of engaging in knightly adventures was also more exciting than managing the complex administration of his lands.

However, the campaign was a damp squib. Count Raymond of Toulouse appealed to his overlord Louis VII, the king of France (who was by now his brother-in-law), for assistance, and Louis marched south with an army of his own. Of course, as Henry was duke of Normandy, Louis was technically his overlord as well, and Henry did not want to set his own vassals the example of rebellion, so he withdrew. William saw no fighting, and set off to return to England in the autumn of 1159. He had only reached Poitou when he fell seriously ill; he died there soon afterwards, aged around 24. William was denied the opportunity to lie with the rest of his family – Stephen had been buried along with Matilda and Eustace at Faversham – as he was not considered important enough for anyone to go to the trouble and expense of preserving his body. Instead he was buried in Poitou.

Like his brother, William had no children, and this had two consequences of note. The first was to increase Henry II's personal sphere of influence even further: the king married off the widowed Isabel de Warenne to his illegitimate half-brother Hamelin of Anjou (the son of Geoffrey of Anjou and the mistress he took during his separation from Matilda during the second and third years of his marriage to her), thus bringing huge swathes of land into his own family, and he retained Mortain and Lancaster for his own growing brood of children. The second consequence involved the rich county of Boulogne, which William had inherited via his mother. Who was to have that?

\*\*\*

There was one sole survivor of the short-lived English royal house of Blois: Stephen's eldest daughter, Mary. She had been a nun since childhood and she was, as far as we can gather, happy with her lot in life. She had lived in various communities; at the time of her brother William's death in 1159 she was abbess of Romsey in Hampshire.[24] But with a title and rich lands at stake, Mary was not to be left in peace. In what one outraged contemporary calls 'an unprecedented occurrence!'[25] she was abducted against her will from the convent by Matthew, the second son of the count of Flanders,[26] who married her and claimed the county of Boulogne in right of his new wife. Once they were bound together there was little Mary could do about the situation in practice, but she continued to rail against it and to petition the pope. She eventually succeeded in having the marriage annulled – although not until she had given birth to two daughters – and in 1169 or 1170 she re-entered religious life.

Mary never raised the possibility of a claim to the English throne. However, she evidently did retain some family feeling, for in a letter she wrote to Louis VII during the time she was countess of Boulogne she referred to 'the impetuous presumption of that fraudulent king', Henry II.[27] England was ever more firmly in Henry's grasp, and it would be a fool who would attempt to unseat him; besides, Mary was content with her religious vocation and had no wish to leave her convent again. Her daughters were King Stephen's only legitimate grandchildren, but they could never be considered as having a serious claim to the throne, either; the daughters of his daughter, and the children moreover of a professed nun whose marriage had been annulled. Nobody was going to put them up as candidates, and neither of them ever set foot in England.

Matthew, Mary's ex-husband, continued to exercise his rights in Boulogne but he overreached himself when he tried also to claim Mortain, thus raising Henry's ire; he sued for an annual payment instead.[28] Once Mary returned to Romsey Abbey Matthew ruled in right of his elder daughter Ida until his own death in 1173, upon which the two sisters were left to the guardianship of their uncle Philip, count of Flanders.[29]

After Mary's return to the cloister she lived peacefully for another dozen years, and her death in 1182 extinguished the royal house of Blois. Henry II could have no more trouble from that quarter; he could concentrate on the fortunes of his own sons. But this was to be a more complex and fraught experience than he could have thought possible.

# Chapter 4

# Henry the Young King

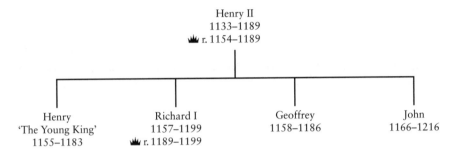

Henry II
1133–1189
👑 r. 1154–1189

| Henry | Richard I | Geoffrey | John |
|---|---|---|---|
| 'The Young King' | 1157–1199 | 1158–1186 | 1166–1216 |
| 1155–1183 | 👑 r. 1189–1199 | | |

Henry II had no intention of replicating the succession problems of his grandfather, and to this end he was fortunate in both his and his wife's fertility. They were married in May 1152 and their first child was born fifteen months later; another seven would follow.

The eldest, William, died in infancy, meaning that his next brother Henry (born in 1155) became heir to the throne while still in his cradle, the first of his Angevin line to be born 'in the purple', the son of a reigning king.[1] Keen as Henry II was to consolidate his position, Young Henry was introduced to the political game even earlier than most heirs: he was betrothed in 1158 to Margaret, daughter of the French king Louis VII.[2] The betrothal, or promise of marriage, of such young children (Margaret was not even a year old at the time) was not unusual at the level of royalty and higher nobility, but the actual wedding would normally be postponed until both parties were of suitable age. However, control of the lands promised as Margaret's dowry would not be passed over until the wedding took place, so King Henry organized it sooner rather than later: Young Henry and Margaret were married in 1160 when he was 5 and she was just 3.

This was irregular, to say the least. The Church set the canonical age of marriage at puberty – widely interpreted to mean 14 for boys and 12 for girls – and it also stipulated that both parties should consent to the union. Of course, for many young people (brides in particular) 'consent' was a nebulous term and it could be obtained in a number of ways, but with the parties in this case being not much more than toddlers, there was not even a pretence of their personal acquiescence – the children were pawns in the hands of their fathers and their fathers' ambitions. A number of contemporary chroniclers were shocked by King Henry's insistence on the wedding taking place so soon, with one saying that he pressed ahead with it 'although they were as yet but little children, crying in the cradle'.[3] That the union was political rather than personal in nature was further underlined by a clause in the marriage contract stating that if Young Henry were to die, Margaret would marry one of his brothers.

Margaret was taken from Louis's household and placed in King Henry's; she grew up in the royal nursery under the control of her mother-in-law, Eleanor of Aquitaine. Young Henry remained there only until he reached the age of 7, in 1162, at which point he was sent away to be educated by his father's chancellor, Thomas Becket.[4] They were at the time in Normandy; later that same year Becket brought the young prince to England to receive the homage of the English barons. By all accounts Young Henry enjoyed his time in the chancellor's household, which was a rich and extravagant one, and he would hold Becket in great esteem thereafter; but the arrangement was not to last long. In 1163 Becket was rather unexpectedly appointed archbishop of Canterbury, and his subsequent falling-out with Henry II meant that Young Henry was removed from his care.

Young Henry was the recognized heir to the throne, and the oaths of the English magnates were followed in 1163 by him accepting the homage of the Scottish king (for his English lands) and the Welsh princes.[5] However, following his own struggles and those of his mother Henry II was not satisfied: after all, he knew from Matilda that English magnates were perfectly capable of swearing to uphold an heir's rights and then reneging on their promise if it suited them. He had been planning the succession ever since his eldest son was born, having the magnates swear allegiance to the toddler William and the then new-born Henry as early as 1155.

Henry's fears for his sons' futures were well grounded. At the time of Young Henry's birth, King Stephen's surviving son, William of Blois, was still alive and a potential threat even though he had accepted the settlement offered to him. Henry II had already faced an open rebellion from his own younger brother Geoffrey fitzEmpress, who represented an ongoing danger; and he also had a second younger brother, William fitzEmpress. Geoffrey died in 1158 and William of Blois in 1159, but Henry II was seemingly still fearful. Therefore, in order to guarantee that the crown would pass to his own eldest son (something that had not occurred in England since 1035, let us not forget), he attempted to achieve what King Stephen had failed to do: to have his designated heir crowned king during his own lifetime.

It would seem that King Henry formed this plan as early as 1162, as orders were issued for a crown to be made while Young Henry was in England during that year.[6] However, by long-established custom, for the coronation to be valid it would have to be carried out by the archbishop of Canterbury, and given that Becket had gone into exile in 1164 this was, for the present, an insurmountable obstacle. The king was forced to shelve his plans for the coronation, although he did continue to associate his heir with the crown: Young Henry performed homage to Louis VII for Anjou and Maine in 1169, having already done so for Normandy in 1160.[7]

The postponement lengthened from months to years, as Henry and Becket could not be reconciled, but eventually the king lost his patience and made other arrangements: in June 1170 Young Henry was crowned and anointed at Westminster by the archbishop of York. The ceremony was a magnificent one, attended by most of the nobility and bishops of England, 'to the great joy of the clergy and people',[8] and it set Young Henry apart from other men: he was now the Lord's anointed, a monarch whose status was approved by God.

Henry II, then, had achieved his aim; nobody could possibly call into question his son's right to succeed him on the throne. However, he had succeeded only at great cost, in that he had alienated a number of influential international figures and stored up family problems that would become more apparent as the years went by. Firstly, of course, he had offended Archbishop Thomas of Canterbury, and by extension Pope Alexander III, who resented such a usurpation of Church authority; this was to return to haunt Henry later on.[9] Henry had also managed to insult Louis VII, as his daughter Margaret had not been crowned alongside her husband even though she had been in Normandy awaiting the summons to cross the Channel for the event. Louis interpreted this to mean she had been 'repudiated [...] to the disgrace and contempt of her father',[10] and went so far as to mount an attack on the Norman border. Henry II took steps to rectify the situation; after a period of negotiation and arrangement Margaret and Henry were crowned and re-crowned, respectively, at Winchester Cathedral in August 1172. By this time, of course, Becket was dead, murdered in his own cathedral of Canterbury in December 1170; the ceremony was conducted by the archbishop of Rouen.

As of his coronation in 1170, Young Henry was, in the eyes of his contemporaries, as much a king as his father. Although he was generally styled as *Henricus rex junior* ('Henry the junior king'), legally he had exactly the same status as Henry II, and this was going to cause a great deal of trouble. Young Henry apparently gave an early indication of his new self-importance at his own coronation feast. When Henry II personally served him at table, in order to emphasize his regal status, the archbishop of York commented on what an extraordinary experience it was to be waited on by a king; Young Henry's reply was that it was perfectly natural under the circumstances, given that he was the son of a king and Henry II was only the son of a duke.[11] The equality of status is illustrated by the syntax of contemporary chroniclers, who were forced into constant disambiguation such as 'the king of England, the father, leaving the king his son behind in England, crossed over into Normandy'.[12]

Now that he had achieved stability and succession for his dynasty, Henry II could start to plan for the future, and in particular the way his territories were to be divided among his offspring. He and Queen Eleanor had four surviving sons, and initially the plan was that they would be provided for in the traditional manner. Henry, aged 15 at the time of his coronation in 1170, would have the patrimony: England, Normandy, Anjou and Maine. Richard, 13, would have the lands brought into the family by his mother: Aquitaine and Poitou. Geoffrey, then 12, would gain his estates through marriage; he had already been betrothed to a rich heiress, in this case Constance, only daughter of the duke of Brittany. There followed an age gap, Henry's youngest son John being only 3 at the time of his eldest brother's coronation; there was some thought that he might be destined for the Church (he was sent to the abbey of Fontevraud for his education) but as he did not take vows at this stage the possibility lay open for him to be given a smaller grant of land or some cash.

As it happened, Young Henry's two next brothers were to establish themselves with lands and authority long before he did. Although Queen Eleanor was duchess of Aquitaine in her own right, she ceded the title to Richard in 1170 when he was just 13, and he was duly invested as duke of Aquitaine and count of Poitou.[13] Geoffrey's future was also assured: Henry had forced Conan, the duke of Brittany, to abdicate and cede his duchy to his daughter Constance as long ago as 1166, and the betrothal took place straight away, the prospective bride and groom being then 5 and 8 respectively. The wedding itself would take place in 1181, at which point Geoffrey would perform homage to his eldest brother for Brittany, as he was to hold it from him as overlord. But all through the 1170s Young Henry was effectively left to kick his heels: he could not inherit any of his promised lands or titles until his father died, and Henry II would not share power while he lived; moreover, despite sometimes being called 'the old king' he was not much more than twenty years older than his eldest son, and in robust and energetic health. 'A king without a kingdom is at a loss for something to do', notes a contemporary, and 'at such a loss was the noble and gracious Young King.'[14]

What, then, was Young Henry to do? He was adolescent, royal, rich and with little formal responsibility, so he gathered round him a large crowd of young men who were equally landless and bored, and they lived extravagantly, travelling round to tournaments and spending huge amounts of money. He did have one older head in his close entourage, Henry II having appointed the knight William Marshal, then in his mid-twenties, to his son's household in 1170 to see to his 'care and instruction' – that is, to train him in the military arts now that he was of a suitable age – but Marshal himself was a landless bachelor so he did not offer the kind of stability that Young Henry perhaps needed. He was a renowned warrior, however, and he did succeed in improving his charge's military skills. According to Marshal's biographer, 'he did so much for him [Henry] that, as a result of what he had learned, the young king's reputation increased, along with his eminence and the honour paid to him; he also acquired the quality of valour'.[15]

Young Henry's reputation for extravagance grew. At Christmas 1171 he apparently held a banquet so lavish that one room alone was filled with 110 knights all called William;[16] he spent a fortune maintaining both his retinue and his reputation for open-handed generosity. This was not always to his father's taste: 'He [Young Henry] travelled far and wide, he spent lavishly [...] when he had scarcely any money left, he informed his father to this effect, and, when his father heard of this, he thought to himself that his son was far too lavish.'[17] In 1173 Young Henry was knighted by William Marshal, which meant that he was now considered a man of full age.[18] He was 18, married, a knight, an adult; he wanted some of the authority that should accompany his status.

Henry II was normally very astute, but he seems to have had a blind spot when it came to his sons – Young Henry in particular – and he now made a bad situation worse. Firstly, he shut off the ready supply of cash ('the king sent a forthright message to the young king and his entourage: he should make out as best he could, for never more would he use any of his resources to make generous gifts, since the life his son led was far too lavish');[19] and secondly, he failed to use his son's coming of age as the opportunity to delegate any authority to him – indeed, he actually announced that he was shaving three important fiefs and castles off Young Henry's eventual Anjou inheritance to give to John, now aged 6. Young Henry protested vociferously against this proposal, evidently not wanting to see yet another younger brother advanced while he still had nothing; he 'would in no wise agree thereto, nor allow it to be done'; he was 'already greatly offended' that he had no lands or authority of his own, and now demanded that he should be given either England, Normandy or Anjou to rule in his own right.[20] But Henry II once again refused any sharing of power.

This was not to be borne. In an escapade probably more overdramatic than it needed to be, in March 1173 Young Henry escaped from his father's court at Chinon in the dead of night and rode for Paris. His father-in-law King Louis, happy to facilitate anything that might discomfit Henry II – who controlled more of France than Louis did and was therefore an ever-present threat – welcomed him. This was nothing less than a declaration of rebellion by Young Henry against his father, and Louis must have been rubbing his hands together in glee when they were shortly joined by both Richard and Geoffrey, sent to join their brother at the instigation of Queen Eleanor, now showing her own displeasure at her husband's behaviour. The coalition against King Henry was joined by Philip, count of Flanders, and Philip's brother Matthew, count of Boulogne; also by Louis's other long-term allies, his brother Robert, count of Dreux, and the men who were both his brothers-in-law and his sons-in-law, Henry, count of Champagne, and Theobald, count of Blois. On the face of it,

Young Henry seemed to be enjoying formidable support, but in his excitement he was perhaps not perspicacious enough to see that the primary purpose of many of these compatriots was not to fight *for him*, but rather *against his father*.[21] And they had ambitions of their own: Count Philip, for example, already controlled the key ports of Gravelines and Wissant, commanding the shortest possible crossings of the Channel, and now in return for his homage to Young Henry he demanded the county of Kent along with its strategically important castles of Dover and Rochester – which would give him not only a great income but also a very secure foothold in England from where he could plan his next move. The inexperienced Young Henry was showing himself to be, in political terms, entirely out of his depth in such company.

Contemporary commentators were split on the question of whether Henry II's treatment of his son caused or justified the rebellion. Some were sympathetic to Young Henry; one, addressing his remarks to the elder king directly, wrote: 'After this crowning and after this transfer of power you took away from your son some of his authority, you thwarted his wishes so that he could not exercise power. Therein lay the seeds of a war without love.'[22] But others thought that nothing could excuse such filial disobedience: 'Thus did the king's son lose both his feelings and his senses: he repulsed the innocent, persecuted a father, usurped authority, seized upon a kingdom; he alone was the guilty one.'[23]

Henry II sent envoys to Paris, but now the negative consequences of his decision to have Young Henry crowned – which had surely been entirely predictable – began to make themselves apparent. Louis refused to hear the envoys on the grounds that the Young King was in fact the anointed and legitimate ruler of England, Normandy, Anjou and Maine, the father having resigned his kingdom at the son's coronation; thus the messengers had no authority. This, of course, was a slightly incongruous claim coming from the king of France, where 'junior kings' had been crowned for some 150 years without usurping the authority of their seniors, but it was enough to needle Henry II. He had wanted to ensure the succession, and he had accomplished his aim only too well; how much he was already regretting the decision must remain a matter for conjecture.

However, Henry II had not attained his current exalted status without being prepared to take decisive action, and this he now did, massing his troops in Normandy and crushing any resistance in his path. Count Matthew of Boulogne was killed by a crossbow bolt at a siege in July;

his brother Count Philip of Flanders had to break off his own campaign in order to address the succession issues this caused in his own house, and Young Henry's campaign stalled.[24] Efforts at rebellion in Young Henry's name in England were likewise supressed, and an attempted simultaneous invasion from the north by King William of Scots was thwarted. The old king had therefore been victorious on all fronts, and when he approached Young Henry and Louis's army in person at Verneuil in Normandy, issuing an ultimatum that could have resulted in a major pitched battle, they withdrew, leaving Henry II's men to sack their camp.[25]

An initial peace conference between Henry II and his three eldest sons was held in September, but as 'it did not suit the purpose of the king of France that the king's sons should at present make peace with their father',[26] obstacles and objections were raised. Louis and Young Henry even planned an invasion of England in early 1174, but it came to nothing, as did an assault on Henry II's Norman capital of Rouen; later that year peace terms were agreed. As the elder king had the upper hand, there was still to be no significant autonomy for the younger, although a sop was offered: little brother John would have the lands he had been promised, but in return Young Henry was given two castles in Normandy to have now, along with £15,000 annually for his upkeep.[27] There was no choice for Young Henry but to accept the yoke – a gilded one, but a yoke nonetheless – and go along with his father's wishes. The elder Henry clung as tightly to power in this twentieth year of his reign as he had done in the first.

Peace held for a while and Young Henry accompanied his father on some royal duties in England. As he entered his twenties he not unnaturally became restless once more, and in 1176 he asked Henry II's permission to go on a pilgrimage to the shrine of St James at Compostela in Spain. However, Henry II was not keen to let his son travel so far from his authority – and particularly not through Gascony and Aquitaine, the Pilgrims' Way which would be the obvious route – and Young Henry, 'who did not find it in the slightest bit amusing to be so long confined in England', grew irritated again.[28] He was let off the leash as far as Normandy, however, where he headed immediately for the court of Count Philip of Flanders. For several years Young Henry did little but take part in tournaments, a circuit of which was well established in northern France. This suited him perfectly. He had no administrative responsibilities to fulfil and so could concentrate on honing his military skills and on spending the vast amounts of money necessary to keep up a reputation for chivalry and largesse, and to equip the retinue of impoverished young nobles who flocked to his glamorous side and fought for him under the captaincy of William Marshal.[29] Henry II, meanwhile, realized that this was as good an outlet as any for his son's pent-up energy, and happily provided a generous allowance to enable him to continue.

Young Henry's queen, Margaret, travelled with him as part of his entourage, and in early 1177 he received the excellent news that she was expecting a child. He perhaps entertained hopes that he would cement his own position and that of his line by producing a male heir; if so, they were raised when Margaret gave birth to a son, William, in June. However, the birth was both traumatic and premature; William died three days later and Margaret, although she survived, never conceived again. She and Henry may not have known of this future problem at the time, however, and he certainly made no moves for a divorce or annulment.

By 1179 Count Philip of Flanders was losing interest in his English protégé – who was still tourneying and still no nearer any real power – and beginning to transfer his attentions to Philip, King Louis's son and heir. Young Philip was now 14, and he was crowned as 'junior king' of France in the autumn of that year (with Young Henry in attendance at the ceremony). Ostensibly this put him in a similar position to Young Henry, but given that Philip's father was by now elderly and frail, he was likely to succeed to his throne much sooner than his counterpart despite being a decade younger. Count Philip then arranged for his 10-year-old niece, Isabelle (the daughter of his sister Margaret and her husband Baldwin, count of Hainaut), to marry Philip, thus ensuring his own influence over the future French royal court. His ambitions looked to have come to fruition less than a year later when Louis VII died in September 1180, leaving a 15-year-old boy in sole possession of the crown.

For once, both Henrys could agree: this situation was dangerous for them, and they needed to join forces. Their plan was in two parts: to prise King Philip away from Count Philip, and to exert influence over him themselves. In the first they were successful, encouraging conflict between the factions of Flanders (represented by King Philip's wife and her uncle Count Philip) and Blois (represented by King Philip's mother Adela and her brothers Theobald and Henry) as they squabbled for precedence and influence. Henry II could thus position himself as a peacemaker between all parties, and Young Henry as a friend to his young and inexperienced brother-in-law. However, their attempts to win over the new French king met with markedly less success than they had expected. Philip II, later known as Philip Augustus, would go on to become one of France's greatest kings during a forty-three-year reign; he was gifted with an extraordinary political brain, and – far from being easily led, even at this tender age – he showed a mind of his own, and it would be he who would later manipulate the family of Henry II to his own advantage.

And so Young Henry remained unsatisfied. To him it must have seemed as though his father would go on forever: still only in his late forties and demonstrating indefatigable energy,[30] refusing to let the slightest bit of power slip from his clenched fist. By 1182 Young Henry's frustration boiled over again. He was 27, a man in his prime, but still effectively a landless youth; he had spent the best part of a decade doing little more than marking time. Meanwhile, his brother Richard was duke of Aquitaine and count of Poitou, while Geoffrey was duke of Brittany and count of Richmond; both were governing, ruling – and enjoying the income and the prestige that came with it.

There was little that Young Henry could do about it. He briefly left his father's court and went to Paris again, declaring his semi-serious intention to go on crusade, which put Henry II in something of a quandary: although he did not want to cede any power to his son now, he nevertheless wanted to ensure his safety so that he could inherit later, according to plan. Therefore the potential dangers of a trip to the Holy Land must be avoided. Henry II decided that the answer in the short term was to throw cash at the problem, and Young Henry was wooed back by an increase in his allowance to an astonishing £110 Angevin per day – almost three times the amount he had enjoyed before, which was already generous.[31] That he could be so easily bought probably says something about his character: although he was constantly badgering to have some of his promised territories under his own control, it is likely that he was concerned with enjoying the revenue and status that came with ruling, rather than looking forward to taking on the administrative burdens of governance.

But he was still kicking his heels and was no doubt glad when an opportunity for direct action presented itself. Richard, as we have noted, was ruling Aquitaine, but he was ruthless and not well-liked by the magnates there:

> The nobles of Aquitaine hated their lord, Count Richard, on account of his great cruelty. They planned to drive him by force from the duchy of Aquitaine and the county of Poitou, and greatly desired to transfer the principality to the good and benign Young King [...] for he was amiable to everyone, of handsome countenance, and especially famous for his military glory, to such an extent that he appeared second to none. He was self-effacing, responsive and affable, so that he was loved with very great affection by those both near and far.[32]

As far as Young Henry was concerned, this was an opportunity not to be missed, so he looked for an excuse to join the coalition against his brother. Richard, obligingly, seized and refortified the castle of Clairvaux as part of his crackdown on rebellious barons. As this castle was on the border between Poitou and Anjou, Young Henry was able to argue that it came under his jurisdiction, thus enabling him to proclaim his open support for the barons. 'And therewith', says one contemporary, 'that strife began which was not resolved until everyone all round had the worst of it.'[33]

Henry II found himself obliged to step in to arbitrate. He called a peace conference early in 1183, but once again his seeming inability to understand the characters of his sons hindered him. Richard should retain Aquitaine, said the king, and (as a member of the family firm) he must be supported by the rest of them against his magnates. However, as part of the deal he should do homage to Young Henry, his eventual overlord, for the duchy. Richard – by now in his mid-twenties and a proud and violent man – refused. As far as he was concerned, Aquitaine was his inheritance from his mother, and nothing to do with his brother at all: once Henry II died, Aquitaine would loosen its ties with England and Richard would hold the duchy in his own right while recognizing the tacit overlordship of the king of France. Agreement could not be reached; Richard withdrew; the negotiations broke down. Young Henry, seizing on the excuse of insubordination (he was a king, after all), decided that Richard needed to be punished; he summoned his younger brother Geoffrey and invaded Aquitaine.[34]

There are two important things to note at this point. The first is that, according to the chronicler quoted above, the nobles of Aquitaine would prefer Young Henry to Richard as their lord, but the subtext is that they would prefer him because he was a softer touch – which does not say a great deal for Young Henry and his perceived abilities. And the second is that his dazzling reputation for chivalry had been gained amid the glitz and glamour of the tournament circuit, where appearance and reputation were more important than actual skill. While he had been winning prizes there, Richard had been engaged in real war, against tough opponents, in sometimes difficult terrain and circumstances, for years. Glamorous, generous, spendthrift Henry was no match for battle-hardened, violent Richard, and this soon became apparent. Richard and his men rode quickly and effectively around Poitou, crushing resistance, capturing rebels and then making an example of them. In a pointed gesture he brought a group of prisoners to the River Vienne outside Limoges, where Young Henry and Geoffrey were staying at the time, and had some executed by drowning or the sword. Others were blinded.

Henry II, who had been in Normandy apparently happy to leave his sons to fight it out for themselves, rode south to the region. He arrived near Limoges but Young Henry, suspecting that his father might in this instance have a preference for Richard, would meet him only while armed in his hauberk, a sign of distrust. This then shifted his position: not only was he fighting against his brother, but he was now technically in rebellion against his father as well, a dangerous position to be in. Both Henry II and Richard moved to assail Limoges; King Philip of France, sensing an opportunity to sow discord among the Plantagenets, evened the odds by sending a supply of mercenaries to his brother-in-law.[35]

Young Henry was in need of further resource to pay for more men and supplies, for his father had – not unnaturally under the circumstances – cut off his allowance. Either he or Geoffrey, probably the latter,[36] decided that the best way to obtain it was to embark on a series of plundering expeditions in the lands around Limoges, and this they did, burning and killing as they went. However, this was not appreciated by the locals – he was, after all, ostensibly there to help them in their campaign against Richard's harsh overlordship. When he returned after one such expedition, he found the city gates shut against him. There was little to be done except to withdraw in high dudgeon; he then embarked on a further plundering campaign around Aquitaine, although it is not clear whether this was an attempt to get more money to bolster his position, or as revenge, or simply because he did not know what else to do. He was perhaps aware that events were spiralling out of his control and that he was ill-equipped to deal with the situation he had created.

And then further disaster struck: in late May 1183 Young Henry fell ill. The cause was probably dysentery, a common disease among soldiers on campaign: 'He was attacked first by a fever, then by a flux of the bowels, which reduced him to the point of death.'[37] It was not long before it became apparent that his end was near, and he sent a message to Henry II to ask for a meeting. But he had cried wolf once too often, and Henry II suspected a ruse; in answer to his son's increasingly desperate pleas for forgiveness and for him to come in person, he merely sent a ring, together with the promise that the two of them could be reconciled in due course. By the time the severity of the situation had been made clear to him, it was too late.

As Young Henry lay on his deathbed he had enough time to reflect on his actions and to repent. Like many noblemen who found themselves faced with their own mortality and the prospect of being judged by the Almighty, he embraced religion:

> Laying aside his fine garments, he placed upon him haircloth, and fastening a cord around his neck, said to the bishops and other religious men who stood around him: 'By this cord do I deliver myself, an unworthy, culpable and guilty sinner, unto you, the ministers of God, beseeching that our Lord Jesus Christ [...] will, through your prayers and his ineffable mercy, have compassion upon my most wretched soul.'[38]

He then ordered his men to lay him on a bed of ashes. And it was there, in fever and delirium – and apparently seeing a vision of his old tutor, the now Saint Thomas Becket – that he died on 11 June 1183, at the age of 28. 'Grieving broke out in the hall', says the biographer of William Marshal (Marshal was present at Young Henry's death), 'so great that there could not be greater, for never had God allowed to be brought into this world a knight so worthy to be mourned.'[39]

As part of his last testament, Young Henry had stipulated that his entrails should be buried at Limoges but that his body should be taken to Rouen to lie with his ancestors. This may sound macabre, but such a division of the body after death was not unusual at the time: on a symbolic level, it allowed a noble with many landholdings to be interred in several of them, thus enhancing their prestige equally; and, more practically, it meant that if a body needed to be preserved ahead of long-distance transportation, those parts most likely to rot were removed and buried first. But such was Henry's popularity, the glamour of his name, that as his cortege stopped en route at Le Mans the citizens there seized his coffin and buried it in their own cathedral. No doubt they were hoping to profit from the many visitors who would arrive to see the tomb of such an illustrious personage. Henry II, by now fully aware of the truth of the situation (on hearing of his son's death, 'bursting into tears, he threw himself upon the ground and greatly bewailed his son')[40] and regretting that he had not been to see Young Henry before his untimely death, intervened. This was one area at least in which he could attend to his son's wishes; he had the body exhumed and reburied in Rouen.

Young Henry was extremely popular in his day, but would he have made a good king? The short answer must be 'probably not'. Of course, unlike many other putative heirs, if he had survived his predecessor, he would not have had to fight for his inheritance – no doubt could possibly have arisen that he should succeed, for the crown was already on his head. And his popularity might have lasted a little way into his reign, for he was charming, persuasive and generous. However, as we saw in earlier chapters, these were not necessarily the attributes of a good medieval king, who needed firmness of purpose and a certain ruthless streak. Indeed, the esteem in which he was held by contemporaries may have been enhanced precisely *because* he was not ruling over the people who praised him, not being forced into making decisions that might have undesirable consequences. Given Young Henry's known propensity for lavish spending, it seems likely that he would have enjoyed the trappings of being a king while everything slowly went to rack and ruin around him for want of attention to the tedious details. His epitaphs do tend to concentrate on superficialities or make excuses for his rash behaviour:

> He was of the most handsome countenance, of the most
> pleasing manners, and the most free-handed in his liberality
> [...] no landed inheritance had as yet been assigned him,
> although he had an annual allowance from his father in
> money [...] but this was little to satisfy the largeness of

his heart. In military matters, he was so eminent as to be unrivalled [...] he had been seduced by the advice of wicked men to rebel.[41]

Young Henry's death may have been a personal tragedy for Henry II,[42] but it probably saved England from many years of turmoil. He did leave one lasting legacy: after such disastrous consequences, the experiment of having the heir to the English throne crowned during his (or her) predecessor's lifetime was never repeated. The theory, in terms of ensuring the succession, was not matched by the practice of having two kings in one kingdom – it might have worked when Young Henry was a boy looking up to his father, but young boys grow up to be ambitious men. It was said of Henry II's sons that 'their father rejoiced more in the flower than in the fruit, more in the herb than in the ear, more when they were boys than when they had advanced to manhood',[43] and this is probably a fair reflection of Young Henry's unfulfilled life.

\*\*\*

Henry II reigned for another six years, dying in July 1189; by that time he had lost another son, Geoffrey having been killed in a tournament in 1186. There was no question who would succeed to the English throne. Young Henry's marriage to Margaret had, as we noted above, produced a single child, the William who died shortly after birth in 1177, so his line was extinct; Richard had therefore been recognized as heir from the time of his elder brother's death. No voices were raised in protest at his accession in 1189: not only was he the clear hereditary heir, born 'in the purple', but he was a man in his prime and one with a fearsome military reputation. So, for the first time since the Conquest, the English crown passed uncontested from father to eldest surviving son. It seemed as though a new dawn was breaking, but the peace was not to last.

# Chapter 5

# Arthur and Eleanor of Brittany

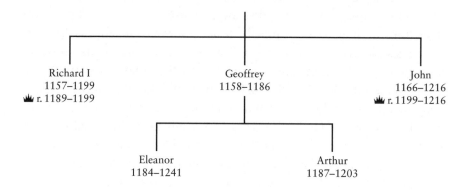

Geoffrey, duke of Brittany, died in August 1186 from injuries sustained in a tournament. He left a 3-year-old daughter, Eleanor; a pregnant widow, Constance; and – unwittingly – the seeds of another battle over the throne of England that was to end in bloodshed and murder.

If Constance's second child had been another girl, the family claims might have been forgotten or swept away, but in March 1187, on Easter Sunday, she gave birth to a boy. He was the heir to the duchy of Brittany, but he was also Henry II's only legitimate grandson in the male line and therefore a figure of great potential importance. Henry pressed for the baby to be named after him; but Constance, who was duchess in her own right, who had been forced into the Plantagenet marriage as a powerless young girl and who wanted greater independence for her Breton homeland, called her son Arthur. This pleased her subjects as they saw in the historic allusion a representation of their desire to be free of King Henry's influence.[1] It also piqued the interest of Philip Augustus; before Constance's marriage to Geoffrey, Brittany had owed its overlordship to France rather than to England, and he was keen to get it back.

Henry II died in 1189 and, as we noted in the previous chapter, the accession to the throne of his elder surviving son, Richard, was uncontested. However, Richard was at that time unmarried and with no legitimate children, which meant that, until he had sons of his own, young Arthur was heir presumptive and destined to be a pawn in the hands of those with ambitions. The terms 'heir presumptive' and 'heir apparent' will occur frequently in this book from now on, so it is worth clarifying them here, as they have distinct meanings. An heir *presumptive* is the person who is currently the heir, but who might legally be displaced by someone else (for example, the younger brother or daughter of a king, who might be supplanted by the later birth of a son). An heir *apparent* is the person who is currently the heir and whose position cannot be altered by subsequent births – normally the king's eldest son.

Both Arthur and Eleanor passed their infancy with their mother, as was usual at the time. But the common fate of those with royal blood was to be pushed on to the political scene at an early age, and King Richard had no hesitation in using them both for his own ends. In 1190, while on his way to the Holy Land, he needed to reach an accommodation with Tancred, king of Sicily; part of the agreement they reached was that Arthur would marry one of Tancred's daughters. The offer to the Sicilian king came with a hefty incentive, for Richard declared publicly that Arthur was to be his heir, thus raising the possibility that Tancred's grandchildren would one day rule over England and its associated territories.

However, there was more to this proposal than met the eye. Firstly, the ages of the parties concerned meant that they were still under threat from the dangers of infant mortality, so the match might never come to fruition.[2] Secondly, Richard had been experiencing problems with his younger brother John, and was worried that his absence from England – potentially of long duration – would provide John with the opportunity to cause trouble. Naming Arthur as heir may have been an attempt to force John to behave himself. And thirdly, Richard expected to have children of his own. It was noted by contemporaries that the arrangement was 'in case of his dying without any lawful heir'[3] and, unknown to Tancred, Richard was about to marry Berengaria of Navarre. He was in his early thirties and already had at least one illegitimate son; she was a decade younger, and there was no reason to suppose that their union would not produce a line of sons and daughters.

For the moment, though, Arthur and Eleanor remained of significant importance to the king. On his way back from the crusade Richard was captured and imprisoned by Duke Leopold of Austria, and as part of the negotiated terms of his release he arranged for Eleanor to marry Leopold's son. She was actually on her way there in 1194 when news of Leopold's death reached her party; the arrangement fell through and she turned back. Richard kept her in his custody and reserved to himself the right to dispose of her future marriage, regardless of Constance's opinions on the matter.

The siblings were also of great interest to the king of France. This, as we noted above, was still Philip Augustus, now some twenty years into his reign and a vastly experienced political figure. Described as 'that wily King Philip, who knew only too well how to play the high and mighty',[4] he had over the years managed to set Henry II against his sons and various of the sons in turn against each other, to his own benefit. Now he saw in Arthur a chance to sow additional discord between Richard and John and the opportunity to further his own ambitions. In his position as overlord of Brittany he tried to claim wardship of Arthur, and he opened negotiations to marry Eleanor to his own son and heir Louis.

The one person on whom Arthur and Eleanor could rely to act in their best interests was their mother, Constance. She was in a precarious position herself: after being widowed, she had been obliged by King Richard to marry one of England's most powerful earls, Ranulf of Chester, but she objected strongly to the union, remaining in Brittany while he lived in England, and she never allowed her subjects to recognize him as duke in her name. A woman of determination, she spent ten years trying to have her second marriage annulled, while simultaneously lobbying for custody of her children and attempting to bolster Arthur's position by associating him with her rule in Brittany. When Eleanor returned from her aborted journey to Austria – still aged only 10 – Constance's will prevailed and her daughter was, temporarily at least, returned to her.

The guardianship of Arthur was more difficult to retain, for he was in political terms the more important of the two siblings. When Richard returned from his captivity he demanded that Arthur be handed over to him, but – following an extraordinary episode in which Constance was kidnapped and held captive by her estranged husband Ranulf, probably at Richard's order[5] – she and the Breton lords decided that the safest place for the boy was with King Philip. Arthur was therefore sent to Paris, where even Richard could not reach, and he was brought up in the household of Philip's son and heir Louis, who was of similar age.

By 1197 Arthur had survived the perils of early infancy and his mother could more justifiably associate him with her rule in Brittany, issuing charters that included both of their names. But the spectre of French control threatened to become overwhelming, and the lure of the English throne was great: in 1198 the 11-year-old Arthur, ostensibly in his own name but in reality guided by his mother, renounced his fealty to Philip and agreed to be guided by Richard in his dealings with the French king. Of paramount interest in this arrangement were the facts that Richard was by now past 40, that he had been married for seven years and that the union had produced no children. After coming to terms with Richard, Arthur was permitted to remain with his mother and sister; the evidence of charters puts the family of three together in 1199. Constance had finally succeeded in having her marriage to Ranulf annulled and she was by now married again, to one Guy of Thouars, a Poitevin nobleman.

King Richard's sudden and unexpected death in April 1199, at a minor siege in the Limousin, part of Aquitaine, sent shockwaves across England and western Europe. The immediate question, of course, was who was to succeed him on the throne of England – his nephew or his brother?

Unfortunately for all concerned, both John and Arthur had a good claim, but neither was overwhelming enough to blot out the other. They were close and direct descendants of Henry II, being his son and his grandson – so far, so straightforward – but after that things got more complicated. On the grounds of primogeniture (which gave precedence to the offspring of a king's sons in the order of those son's births) Arthur's claim was better, as his father Geoffrey had been older than John; moreover, Richard had designated him heir back in 1190. However, there was some evidence that Richard might have changed his mind on his deathbed to favour John,[6] given that the two of them had been reconciled following Richard's return from captivity, and, to add to the mix, primogeniture was still not an exact science. There was much debate as to whether the claims of the younger son of Henry II should take precedence over the claims of his grandson who, although descending from a senior line, was the son of a father who had never ruled. There were different customs in different territories, and now opinion was dangerously split. The barons of Anjou, Maine, Touraine and (unsurprisingly) Brittany favoured Arthur, while those of England and Normandy preferred John. And finally, there was the not insubstantial consideration that John was 32 and Arthur just 12.

The entire debate is summed up in a lengthy passage in the biography of William Marshal.[7] The actual dialogue is probably fictional, or at least highly stylized, but it summarizes the situation in which the barons of all parts of the Plantagenet empire found themselves at the time. According to this text, news of Richard's death had reached Marshal in Rouen late on the eve of Palm Sunday 1199, just as he was about to go to bed. 'In a state of violent grief' he immediately went to call on the archbishop of Canterbury (who was also in Rouen) so that they could discuss the matter in private before the news was disseminated more widely.[8]

At first the conversation seems to indicate that neither of the potential candidates was seen as a particularly good choice. 'The king is dead?' exclaims the archbishop:

> What solace is there for us now? None, so help me God! With him gone, I can think of nobody to choose to rescue the realm or come to our aid in anything. The realm is now on the road to destruction, grief and destitution. We can be sure it won't be very long before we see the French rush upon us to take everything we have.[9]

The archbishop then goes on to suggest that Arthur ought to be king, but Marshal replies that this would be a 'bad decision' because Arthur has 'treacherous advisors', he is 'unapproachable and overbearing' and 'he does not like those in our realm'. He suggests that John is the preferred choice, because he 'is nearest in line to claim the land of his father'. The archbishop is persuaded, and agrees that 'the son is indisputably closer in the line of inheritance than the nephew is, and it is right that that should be made clear'.[10]

There are numerous interesting points in this passage, not least that – in the eyes of Marshal's biographer at least – it is up to the great men to 'choose' a king (the word occurs several times in the conversation). We have already noted that succession to the English throne at this time was not automatic on the death of the incumbent, but here the agency seems to be vested in the barons, not the candidates. The depiction of Arthur as 'unapproachable and overbearing' smacks of hindsight (given that Marshal later went on to serve John and therefore his biographer needed to justify his actions), but it is probably unfair given that Arthur was only 12 at the time. So too is the accusation that he did not like those in England, although this is perhaps less a personal comment and more a recognition that Arthur had in fact never been there. The nobles might therefore have worried that his accession would result in a Breton-based overturning of various English customs and practices that currently favoured them. And they were certainly right to suspect Arthur's advisors; the situation was ripe for exploitation by King Philip of France.

Richard died on 6 April 1199. By coincidence, John was actually staying with Arthur when news reached them, so the race to succeed him started from the same point.[11] As had been the case for hundreds of years, all that was really needed to claim the English throne was a decent blood claim, quick enough wits to seize it and sufficient resource to hold on to it; the candidate who could react the fastest and most effectively would be victorious. Here John had the advantage; with the support of William Marshal and others he moved quickly to capture the Angevin royal treasury at Chinon. Ensuring control of the vast resources of the treasury was always an astute first move for a claimant to the throne, as it meant he could afford to defend his claim and could offer patronage and/or bribes to nobles who chose to accept him. It had worked for Henry I in 1100 and Stephen in 1135, among others, and it would work for John now.

Constance, not to be outdone, appealed to King Philip and began raising troops; her army seized Angers, the capital of Anjou, and there a group of barons declared Arthur king on Easter day (18 April). The Normans, however, had no wish to be ruled by a Breton, so they in their turn proclaimed John as king in Rouen on 25 April. Philip, meanwhile, 'at once sent him [Arthur] to Paris under charge of a guard, and received into his care all the cities and castles which belonged to Arthur',[12] but John forestalled him by crossing the Channel and having himself crowned and consecrated at Westminster on 27 May 1199. This, naturally, made Arthur's task (or indeed Philip's, as we might call it at this moment) harder: if Arthur were to take the English crown himself, he would have to wrest it from John rather than just picking it up while it remained unassigned.

Arthur's tender age prevented him from taking direct action on his own behalf, but King Philip was just warming up, and now he made both military and political moves in support of his ward. He knighted Arthur and accepted his homage for Anjou, Maine, Touraine and Brittany – and Normandy.[13] This nominally placed all of those lands in his overlordship, so he was entitled to seize them from John (who was, by Philip's acceptance of Arthur's homage, now technically considered a usurper in those French lands). Philip moved in with his troops and took control of the towns and fortifications in those areas while keeping Arthur in Paris.

While the men were fighting and the children being kept out of the way, the political dimensions of the war were spearheaded by two women. Duchess Constance was busy negotiating with the nobles of Maine and Touraine, offering lands and patronage in return for their continuing support for Arthur, while John was fortunate to have in his camp his redoubtable mother, Queen Eleanor. Eleanor was by now in her late seventies, but still ruling Aquitaine; King Richard's death had caused no specific upheaval there as she was duchess in her own right. But the resources of the duchy were huge, and much would depend on which side the dowager queen decided to support. She chose her son over her grandson, and now made a tour through Poitou, the northern part of Aquitaine, securing for John the support of the nobles and the Church as she went.

The conflict continued through the spring and summer of 1199, until the two parties met in August to negotiate. Philip asked John to cede Poitou to Arthur on top of his other four territories (with Philip as his overlord, naturally), but he was aware by this stage that the momentum was with his opponent. Those in England and Normandy held firmly for John based on the fact of his coronation and their own best interests; and with Aquitaine in support, the smaller areas still holding for Arthur were in danger of being surrounded. An invasion of Anjou and Maine from both north and south would cause irreparable damage, and might even endanger Brittany itself. Initially Philip vacillated. In all probability he had originally declared his support for Arthur not because he liked the boy, but rather on the basis that conflict between the Plantagenets would be good for France; France naturally had to remain his highest priority.

It was the Treaty of Le Goulet, sealed in May 1200, that ended this phase of the war. Under its terms Philip recognized John as Richard's lawful heir, which meant that Arthur was to lose Anjou, Maine and Touraine. He would remain duke of Brittany, but would hold it from John; John, meanwhile, would recognize Philip as his overlord for Normandy. Arthur therefore gave homage to John 'with the sanction and advice of the king of France'[14] and Philip (perhaps unsurprisingly) came out on top at the expense of both the others. The final flourish on the new agreement between the two kings was that Philip's son and heir

Louis would be married to John's niece Blanche of Castile, for whom John provided a lavish dowry in both cash and land.[15] This put paid to any of Constance's lingering hopes that her daughter might one day be queen of France; it also benefited Philip, for he was to keep the dowry castles and territories in his own hands until such time as the marriage should be consummated – which, given that the parties were both 12, would not be a for a while.

Arthur, his own hopes of the English crown dashed, spent the next year or so partly at the French court as one of Louis's companions, engaging in the knightly training that was *de rigueur* for boys of his class and age, and partly in Brittany with his mother, stepfather and their two young daughters. He suffered a terrible loss when Constance died in September 1201; she had been the rock on which he had depended for the whole of his life, and her authority was unquestioned in Brittany.[16] However, Arthur was now 14 and of an age to start taking a more active part in his own affairs, and he had not relinquished his ambitions. For the present he needed to maintain a fine balancing act between the two kings, furthering his own interests while avoiding being a mere pawn in theirs; but this was a difficult task for an inexperienced young boy caught between two unscrupulous political predators, and it was almost inevitable that he would slip up. At Easter 1202 John summoned Arthur to do homage to him once more; Arthur, perhaps fearing a trap, instead went to Philip. The French king now had before him a young man of potential rather than a child, so he reshuffled his priorities and proposed a marriage between his infant daughter Marie and Arthur. This would give Arthur greater resource with which to pursue his claim, but it would put him even more firmly under Philip's thumb.

Events had moved on while Arthur had been occupied with his knightly training. John had spent the last couple of years alienating many of his continental vassals and was now deeply unpopular. Of major significance was that he had prevented an alliance between the Poitevin Hugh de Lusignan, count of La Marche, and the heiress of the neighbouring county of Angoulême by the expedient of seizing the girl and marrying her himself.[17] This broke up a potential block of land and influence, and also insulted both Hugh and, by extension, the Poitevins in general. Meanwhile, John was also facing rebellions against his rule in Normandy. Both the Normans and the Poitevins appealed to King Philip, as their ultimate overlord; Philip summoned John, as his vassal, to appear before him; John declined. Philip, therefore, announced that John's lands were confiscated, invaded Normandy, and sent Arthur to Poitou, where a rebellion had broken out in his name.

This was the chance Arthur had been waiting for to prove himself. He was 15, a knight and a duke, and considered himself the lawful king of England. It was time to fight for his birthright. When he arrived in Poitou the lords there 'welcomed him with great joy and made him their leader',[18] but his first act was a disastrous one. His elderly grandmother Eleanor of Aquitaine was at the castle of Mirebeau (on the border of Anjou and Poitou) and Arthur moved to assail it. His forces took the town, but the castle inside it had separate defences and Eleanor was able to retreat there and send a plea for help to John. He, no doubt realizing the potential seriousness of the situation, responded personally; in what was to be the greatest – and in truth the only – real military triumph of his career he made astonishingly good time from Normandy, marching his troops 80 miles in just forty-eight hours.

They arrived on the night of 31 July/1 August 1202 and attacked early in the morning, entering the town through an unsecured gate and falling on Arthur's unprepared forces.[19] There was fierce fighting in the streets and Arthur had nowhere to go, trapped between the oncoming army and the walls of the castle still holding out behind him. The Poitevins had no time even to arm themselves properly and were no match for the king's men;[20] the defeat was total. 'What shall I tell you?', asks one contemporary of his readers. 'The Poitevins were totally defeated, and Arthur and all the Poitevins were captured; not a single nobleman escaped.'[21] Arthur was taken by William de Braose, one of John's adherents, who handed him over to the king. In total, John took over 200 prisoners, thus quelling the revolt completely.[22]

It is unclear whether Arthur's sister Eleanor was with him at Mirebeau and was captured alongside him, or whether she was already in John's keeping as part of a wardship arrangement. What is definite, however, is that she was in John's custody immediately after this event, so he had both of them, and their claims to his crown, at his mercy. His retribution was swift, and the siblings were parted for what was to be the final time. Eleanor, then aged 18, was sent to England to be imprisoned. A young, single woman of royal blood was dangerous, for if she married she would transfer her claim to the throne to her husband and any subsequent children. The 15-year-old Arthur, meanwhile, was kept in captivity on the other side of the Channel. Immediately after his capture he was confined at Falaise castle in Normandy, and initially John made noises about being open to negotiations over his release; but this was never a serious prospect and in the event it never transpired. In January 1203 Arthur was transferred to Rouen; he disappeared into the dungeons there and was never seen again.

\*\*\*

What happened to Arthur is one of the great unsolved historical mysteries. There is little doubt that he was murdered, but exactly how, when and under what circumstances remains a matter of debate. The contemporary chroniclers, some better informed than others, agree on some points and disagree on others. All seem to concur that Arthur was kept in harsh conditions – this was no comfortable confinement in a luxurious apartment – and that he was dead within less than a year. After that their stories diverge, although some common elements appear.

Roger of Wendover, normally a loquacious commentator, simply notes that Arthur 'suddenly disappeared' and leaves it at that.[23] Ralph, the abbot of Coggeshall in Essex, gives more details in his chronicle: according to him, John gave orders that Arthur should be blinded and castrated (which would render him incapable, in contemporary eyes, of ruling, as well as precluding the possibility of heirs), but this seemed barbaric to Hubert de Burgh, the man charged with keeping Arthur in Falaise, so he stopped those who were about to perform the deed. However (says Ralph), Hubert then thought it might be a good idea to *tell* the Bretons that Arthur was dead, so that their rebellion would collapse due to having no focal point. However, this backfired as it enraged the Breton lords, who swore vengeance on John; Hubert then backtracked to say that Arthur was still alive, but nobody believed him. This all seems unnecessarily complicated, and still does not explain what ultimately happened to Arthur, although Ralph does go on to mention a rumour that he was drowned after his transfer from Falaise to Rouen.[24]

The two accounts that correspond to the greatest extent are those of William the Breton, a chaplain and chronicler based at the French royal court, and of the annals of Margam Abbey in South Wales. William claims that John had Arthur put in a boat, that he rowed him out into the

Seine, stabbed him and then dumped his body overboard.[25] The Margam annals give even more precise detail:

> After King John had captured Arthur and kept him alive in prison for some time, at length, in the castle of Rouen, after dinner on the Thursday before Easter [3 April 1203], when he was drunk and possessed by the devil, he slew him with his own hand, and tying a heavy stone to the body cast it into the Seine.[26]

The correlation of John's personal involvement and the use of the Seine for disposing of the corpse is significant, especially given the geographical distance between Paris and Margam – it is unlikely that the authors of the two accounts colluded. Moreover, John is known to have been in Rouen on the date given by the Margam annals, and – crucially – the patron of Margam was the same William de Braose who had captured Arthur and handed him over to John, and who was also in Rouen at the relevant time. That William de Braose knew something that might compromise John was made clear almost a decade later: after falling out with John, William was ordered to hand over his sons as hostages and his wife, Matilda, made the mistake of saying out loud and in public that she would never surrender her children to the man who had murdered his own nephew.[27] John's vengeance, perhaps born of a guilty conscience, was terrible: Matilda and her eldest son were imprisoned and starved to death, while William was hounded and hunted through England, Ireland and France before dying, a broken man. If he did know what happened to Arthur, and later spoke of it, it is not implausible that the Margam account is the closest to the truth.[28]

Arthur never set foot in England. Although he had a better blood claim to the throne than John, it was unlikely that the nobles there would support him, and no king could rule without the support of his barons (as John was to find himself, to his cost, in due course). If King Richard had survived longer, if he had taken Arthur under his wing and designated him properly as his heir, if he had brought him to England to familiarize him with the county and its governance, if he had gained the respect of the barons, there might have been a chance … but that is a lot of 'ifs'. As it was, his campaign was doomed to failure almost from the start and certainly after the death of his formidable mother, the one person who was truly on his side and who had the determination to fight unceasingly on his behalf.

There is perhaps an argument that the claim should never have been contested in the first place, that Arthur could and should have been content to inherit Brittany. But this misunderstands both the realities of twelfth- and thirteenth-century politics and the character of John. Arthur's mere existence was a threat to him; however quietly he tried to live, there would always be some disaffected baron who could rebel against John by raising banners in the name of Arthur, whether Arthur was personally involved or not. Whatever he did, John would have come for him eventually, so the only thing to be done (which Constance recognized from the moment of her son's birth) was to act pre-emptively, find a powerful ally and take the fight to the enemy while walking the tightrope between the kings of England and France. The only way for Arthur to be safe was to eliminate John and take the crown himself, however unrealistic a goal that might have seemed. He had to try, but he was forced into trying before he was old enough, tough enough or experienced enough; these were all major reasons why he failed, a failure that led directly to his dark and probably unpleasant fate.

\*\*\*

Whatever the precise manner of his demise, Arthur was certainly dead. He was almost as certainly dead by murder, and this probably happened before the summer of 1203. Rumours began to circulate very soon after the alleged event:

> An opinion about the death of Arthur gained ground throughout the French kingdom and the continent in general, by which it seemed that John was suspected by all of having slain him with his own hand; for which reason many turned their affections from the king from that time forward.[29]

Philip Augustus took full advantage of the situation: every time John made overtures at peace during their subsequent war (during which he lost the whole of Normandy to the French king), Philip would taunt him by saying he would not talk until John produced Arthur, knowing full well that he could not. As the years went by any remaining doubts about Arthur's death or John's culpability disappeared, and it was stated publicly at the French court in both 1213 and 1215 that John had murdered his nephew.[30]

Arthur's widely assumed death left his sister, Eleanor, as the principal threat to John's crown, and her fate is yet another sad reminder of how little power most women had over their own destiny at this time. As we saw earlier, a couple of marriages had been lined up for her when she was just a child; she might, in the autumn of 1202, have wished that one of them had come to fruition in order to keep her out of John's hands. As it was, she was never to be allowed to marry, for if she did then her husband could potentially make a bid for the throne in her name. After being captured at Mirebeau she was taken to England and away from any potential Breton support, first to be lodged at Corfe castle in Dorset, and then later moved to a succession of fortresses as far flung as Burgh in Westmorland and Bristol in Gloucestershire.[31] She was more fortunate than her brother in that she was kept in tolerable apartments rather than a dungeon, and money was spent on her upkeep. She appears to have had a reasonable diet and to have been provided with clothing,[32] but this was no compensation for the lack of freedom as the years, and her youth, passed.

One glimmer of hope appeared in 1214, the twelfth year of her captivity, when John attempted to regain some of the French lands he had lost to King Philip. In coalition with the Holy Roman Emperor Otto, another of his nephews (the son of John's eldest sister Matilda, who had married Henry the Lion, duke of Saxony), he launched an invasion of Poitou and brought Eleanor with him, perhaps hoping to drum up support in her name and set up some kind of puppet regime. However, her captive status had rendered her ineligible in the eyes of her contemporaries to succeed to her inheritance; the duchy of Brittany was now held by her half-sister Alix (the eldest of Constance's daughters by Guy of Thouars) and her husband. Nobody was particularly interested in raising banners in Eleanor's name, and John's campaign was a total failure. He was defeated by Philip's son Louis at La-Roche-aux-Moines, near Angers, and his allies were simultaneously crushed at the battle of Bouvines by Philip himself.

John returned to England, dragging Eleanor with him, and she was once again confined, this time never to emerge. She outlived John, eventually dying in 1241 at the age of 57 after spending all thirty-nine years of her adult life as a prisoner of state, her only crime being that she was born her father's daughter.

\*\*\*

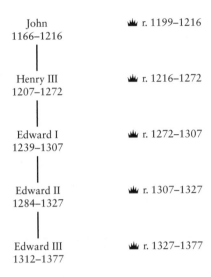

John
1166–1216

👑 r. 1199–1216

Henry III
1207–1272

👑 r. 1216–1272

Edward I
1239–1307

👑 r. 1272–1307

Edward II
1284–1327

👑 r. 1307–1327

Edward III
1312–1377

👑 r. 1327–1377

We now come to a slight hiatus in our tale, because after the death of King John in 1216 the crown passed from father to eldest surviving son four times in a row over the course of a century. However, this being medieval England, the seemingly smooth line of succession masks all kinds of hidden troubles.

At the time of John's death his barons were in revolt against him, and half the country was under the control of the man they had invited to replace him, Louis of France (the son of Philip Augustus, later Louis VIII, who had defeated John in 1214).[33] Louis was a direct descendant of William the Conqueror, and his wife Blanche, in whose name he was ostensibly pursuing his claim, was John's niece; but still this would have been quite some diversion from the previous line of succession, with many others being higher up the hereditary queue. As it transpired, John's death was the best thing to happen to his cause, for the barons grew tired of the honest and upright Louis and decided that John's 9-year-old son would be easier to control. He was crowned as Henry III.

Henry's reign saw England once more plunged into civil war as many magnates threw their weight behind Simon de Montfort and his reforming agenda; however, Simon was defeated and Henry's death in 1272, after the longest reign since the Norman Conquest, not only resulted in the peaceful accession of his eldest son Edward I, but the first time that a new king of England was proclaimed upon the death of his predecessor, rather than upon the occasion of his own coronation.

Edward was on crusade when he heard of his father's death, but there was no scramble to usurp him and he was able to make his way home in his own time in order to be crowned. He did not reach English shores until August 1274, but his reign is usually dated from 1272 because of this precedent.

The line of succession almost took another twist under Edward I, for his long-suffering queen, Eleanor of Castile, was obliged to give birth to at least fourteen – and possibly as many as sixteen – children before the couple could produce a surviving son, Edward. They had ten or eleven daughters (of whom only five survived to adulthood), and three or four sons who died in infancy or childhood.[34] After Eleanor's death, Edward I married again and fathered in his old age two more sons as insurance for the succession; they were nearly forty years younger than his eldest daughter.

In the event the youngest child of Edward's first marriage survived to become Edward II, but after a twenty-year reign he was overthrown by his wife, Isabella of France, and her lover Roger Mortimer. This was not strictly a departure from the line of succession as, rather than seeking to rule in their own names, they proclaimed Edward and Isabella's son as Edward III. He was for a number of years an unwilling child puppet king before he in turn overthrew them to take the reins of government into his own hands.

After several turbulent centuries Edward III finally brought firm government and stability to England during his fifty-year reign. He ensured the succession in abundant fashion by fathering eight sons, of whom five survived to adulthood. The eldest, also named Edward, grew up to be everything a medieval prince should be, so Edward III could grow old safe in the belief that the peace would be long lasting.

He was wrong.

# Chapter 6

# Edward the Black Prince

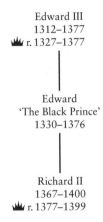

Edward III
1312–1377
👑 r. 1327–1377

Edward
'The Black Prince'
1330–1376

Richard II
1367–1400
👑 r. 1377–1399

Edward was the eldest of the thirteen children of King Edward III and his queen, Philippa of Hainaut. Although he is known to posterity as the Black Prince, in his own lifetime he was known as Edward of Woodstock, after the place of his birth.[1] He was born in June 1330, at an uncertain time when Edward III was not actually in control of his own kingdom; England was still being ruled by his mother Isabella of France and her lover, Roger Mortimer. But the young king was becoming more sure of himself and his position, and perhaps the birth of his own son and heir contributed to his decision to seize the initiative; it was in October 1330 that he clandestinely entered the castle at Nottingham and captured them both, resulting in Mortimer's execution and Isabella being confined in a convent for the foreseeable future. Edward III was now secure on his throne, so his baby son could grow up in a stable environment and with no questions over his place in the royal succession.

The family dynamic was an unusual one – or certainly it would be considered so today – due to the ages of the parties involved. At the time of Edward's birth his father and mother were just 17 and 15; he would remain close to them not only in age but in outlook throughout his life. The next three siblings who followed him were two girls, Isabella and Joan, and a boy who died in infancy; this meant that he grew up with no brothers who were close to him in age. The four other sons in the family who survived to adulthood – Lionel of Antwerp, John of Gaunt (anglicized from Ghent), Edmund of Langley and Thomas of Woodstock – were respectively eight, ten, eleven and twenty-five years younger than him. Thus it was that young Edward could later be named as England's regent before any of his brothers were out of their cradles, and he was fighting at Crécy as his father's companion-in-arms while they were still in the royal nursery. This is one of the reasons why he was, throughout his life, considered somewhat apart from them, England's great hope.

The honours came both soon and quickly for the heir to the throne: Edward was created earl of Chester in 1333 and earl of Cornwall in 1336. The king was still not satisfied, though, and in 1337 he upgraded Cornwall to a royal duchy, the first of its kind in England; 'duke of Cornwall' is a title borne by male heirs to the British throne to this day. At a time when kings led their own armies into battle, military training was a significant part of Edward's childhood, and we know that he owned a complete set of armour by the time he was 7. He also needed a political education, and when Edward III crossed the Channel to Flanders in 1338 it was his 8-year-old son who was left as regent and 'guardian of England'; he would assume the same responsibility again in 1340 and 1342. Of course, he had older and wiser heads to guide him, but he was officially the ruler of England during this time, the head of the royal household, and all government business was in his name. Edward appears to have taken his responsibilities seriously; a letter to his mother, dating from 1338, has survived, in which he informs her that the collection of England's wool (needed to send financial aid to the king) is completed.[2]

In 1343, at the age of 12, Edward was invested as prince of Wales, a fairly recent title that had been created for his grandfather Edward II.[3] By this time the royal nursery held three infant brothers, so the dynasty was deemed secure enough for Edward to continue his training for the throne by accompanying his father on his overseas trips. Edward III was at this time making a claim for the crown of France, and he embarked on a major military expedition across the Channel in the summer of 1346; Edward, who had just turned 16, went with him. The background to this conflict is complex, but to summarize in brief: the French king, Philip VI, was the first king of the Valois dynasty, a first cousin of his predecessor Charles IV; he had inherited the throne after the direct father–son line of the Capetians finally ended after more than three centuries. Charles IV and his two older brothers (Louis X and Philip V) had reigned one after the other, leaving between them six daughters and no surviving sons. Edward III of England claimed the French crown via his mother, Isabella, who was the sister of the three deceased kings, but his claim was spurious: if inheritance of the throne via the female line were permissible, the claims of the daughter of Louis X and then the daughters of Philip V and Charles IV would have taken precedence over their sister and her children.[4] As it was, the crown followed the male line and ended up on the head of Philip VI – he had been on the throne since 1328 so King Edward had, in any case, left it rather late to dispute the succession.

Still, dispute it he did, and whatever the rights and wrongs of the situation the reality was that he had the will, the resources and the support to mount a credible threat. Young Edward, already a prince and later to be king of England, could set his sights on the eventual acquisition of a double crown. This was no doubt a positive incentive as he stood on the deck of his ship as it crossed the Channel in the summer of 1346.

The campaign did not, as it happened, get off to the best start: a contrary wind meant that they landed in Normandy rather than Gascony, their intended destination far to the south. However, the situation improved for young Edward when the king knighted him the day after their arrival – a great honour and one that marked the start of his career as a soldier. Now considered a grown man, Edward was immediately removed from the shelter of his father; he was given command of the vanguard (the advance part of the army) as it made its way through France. This was an exalted and responsible position, but it was dangerous, for it meant riding and camping in more exposed positions some miles ahead of the main force.

King Edward's method of waging war was direct and to the point: he embarked on a campaign of slaughter, rapine, plunder and burning. Contemporaries did not seek to minimize the damage when describing what happened, and passages similar to the ones below may be found in several sources. At first, the French town-dwellers and rural peasants were taken by surprise. The English army didn't need to go looking for supplies [...] for the people, taken unawares, had hidden nothing away. It's no wonder they were in a state of shock: they'd never experienced war or even seen a man-at-arms, and now they were seeing people slaughtered without mercy, houses set ablaze and pillaged, the land laid waste and burnt.[5]

The same chronicler's accounts of the sacking of towns are repeated over and over again in a similar manner as the English continued on their path of destruction, as in this representative example:

This great town was taken with little effort and sacked and pillaged from top to bottom. No man alive would ever believe the wealth of booty plundered there [...] a great many of the wealthy burghers were taken prisoner and sent to England to be ransomed, and a lot of the common folk were killed [...] and a good number of fair townswomen and their daughters were raped.[6]

Other writers concur. 'The English amused themselves by burning everything', wrote one; 'they made many women widows and many poor children orphans.'[7]

This was not indiscriminate slaughter, or the result of undisciplined troops running wild – it was a deliberate policy of terror and destruction from Edward III, carried out in order to goad Philip into battle. And contemporaries saw nothing wrong with it: a member of King Edward's household wrote dispassionately in a letter, of the sack of Caen, that 'between 120 and 140 noble and valiant knights were killed and captured, of whom about a hundred are still alive; and five thousand squires, citizens and commons were taken or killed. So far, our affairs have gone as well as possible.'[8] And the same chronicler who detailed the atrocities above is positive in his depiction of Edward III:

Some people, when they hear this story read, may wonder why I call the king of England 'the noble King Edward' but the French king simply 'King Philip of France' [...] I do this to honour the one who behaved most nobly in this story, and that is King Edward, who cannot be honoured too highly

[…] none of this can be said of King Philip of France, who allowed his land in many parts to be ravaged and laid waste.[9]

Yes: in the tough world of the fourteenth century, having your lands attacked and burned was considered more dishonourable than being the one who actually ordered the mass rape and murder.

This was a salutary lesson for the young prince, at the forefront of his father's army and carrying out his orders. It seems likely that for this, his first command of a large force, Edward was only nominally in charge and that real authority lay with the earls of Northampton and Warwick, who accompanied him, but there is no doubt that he was personally involved in the events of the campaign and its atrocities. There is no doubt, either, about Edward's personal involvement in the encounter that would take place on 26 August 1346, and that would make his name.

The French forces, led by Philip VI, had been tracking the English army, and they caught up with them on the north bank of the River Somme. A pitched battle was now inevitable, and King Edward selected a site just north of the forest of Crécy to deploy his men. They faced south and down a slope, which was a tactical advantage. The vanguard, commanded by the prince, was at the front; he placed himself in the very centre along with his earls and household knights. This was the scene of the fiercest fighting, and Edward was hard pressed. However, he stood his ground, as all chroniclers of the event agree:

> In this desperate battle, Edward of Woodstock, the king's eldest son, aged sixteen, displayed marvellous courage against the French in the front line, running through horses, felling knights, crushing helmets, cutting lances apart […] he encouraged his men, defended himself, helped fallen friends to their feet, and set everyone an example.[10]

Eventually the French retreated, leaving the English in possession of the field. Young Edward's military reputation was made. His courage in the face of danger impressed those on both sides, and the stories were soon exaggerated and romanticized in the telling. For example, an early account notes that when the prince was hard pressed, 'someone ran or rode to the king his father, and asked for help'; the king sent some twenty knights but when they reached Edward they 'found him and his men leaning on their lances and swords on mounds of dead men, taking deep breaths and resting'.[11] But later this was embellished:

> And because of the danger in which those responsible for the prince found themselves, they sent a knight to King Edward […] the king asked the knight, 'Is my son dead or stunned, or so seriously wounded that he cannot go on fighting?' 'No, thank God,' replied the knight […] the king answered, 'Go back to him and to those who have sent you and tell them not to send for me again today, as long as my son is alive. Give them my command to let the boy win his spurs.'[12]

This is not to detract from the very real bravery of a boy of 16, but it does show that a military reputation was important, and that such a reputation could become inflated in the telling.

It was also here at Crécy that Edward's later reputation for chivalry had its roots. As a nobleman and a soldier he could admire bravery in others even if they were on the opposing side, and there was one combatant who had shown perhaps even more courage than he. King John of Bohemia (whose daughter was married to King Philip's eldest son and heir) had fought on the French side despite being blind; he had charged into the thick of the press with his horse's reins tied to those of his companions. They were all killed together, their bodies found the following day with the reins still entangled. Despite King John's enemy allegiance this was the kind of action, and the kind of heroic death, that could be admired. John's heraldic device was the ostrich feather; Edward adopted it as a badge of his own.[13]

The prince remained with his father throughout the rest of the campaign, including at the siege of Calais, during which the townspeople starved and Edward himself fell ill with some kind of camp fever. It was while they were at Calais that they learned of an invasion of the north of England under the Scots king, David II, who had acted under the terms of the 'Auld Alliance', an agreement between Scotland and France, dating from 1294, under the terms of which each realm agreed to invade England if England should attack the other. They need not have worried, however; in their absence an army raised by the archbishop of York had defeated the Scots at the Battle of Neville's Cross, resulting in David's

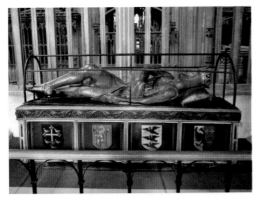

*Above*: The tomb of Robert Curthose in Gloucester Cathedral. (Courtesy of Wikimedia Commons)

*Right*: William the Conqueror, with a list of his sons in birth order: Robert Curthose appears at the top to show that he is the eldest. (Courtesy of the British Library)

*Above left*: Cardiff Castle, where Robert Curthose was imprisoned by his younger brother Henry I until his death in 1134.

*Above right*: A line drawing of the effigy added to William Clito's tomb some years after his death. (Courtesy of Wikimedia Commons)

*Left*: Henry I mourns the loss of his heir, William Adelin, in the *White Ship* disaster of 1120. (Courtesy of the British Library)

*Below*: Henry I with his wife Edith/Matilda (top), his son William Adelin (left) and his daughter Matilda (bottom). (Courtesy of the British Library)

Arundel Castle, where Empress Matilda landed in 1139 to begin her campaign for the English throne.

King Stephen; in contrast to other kings depicted in this manuscript he is shown with no children, as they were disinherited under the terms of the Treaty of Wallingford in 1153. (Courtesy of the British Library)

*Above left*: Westminster Abbey, where English monarchs are crowned by the archbishop of Canterbury. None of those featured in this book were able to achieve this, although some came closer than others.

*Above right*: Four kings of England: Henry II, Richard I, John and Henry III. Henry the Young King is depicted in an insert in the middle, as though the artist did not quite know where to put him. (Courtesy of the British Library)

A marginal image of the English crown being pulled in two different directions, symbolizing the civil war between Henry the Young King and his father, Henry II. (Courtesy of the British Library)

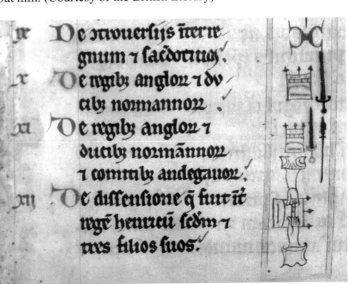

Corfe Castle, where the unfortunate Eleanor of Brittany was imprisoned for much of her life.

*Above left*: A genealogical depiction of Henry II's children and grandchildren. Arthur and Eleanor of Brittany are the two central figures in the bottom row; their uncle King John is furthest to the right in the line above. Henry the Young King is second from the left in the upper row. (Courtesy of the British Library)

*Above right*: Edward III entrusts his eldest son, Edward the Black Prince, with the duchy of Aquitaine. (Courtesy of the British Library)

*Left*: The Black Prince wearing robes signifying his membership of the Order of the Garter. (Courtesy of the British Library)

A representation of the descendants of Edward III, who is the crowned figure depicted in the lower left part of the drawing. The Black Prince issues from the lowest of the three branches to the right of the king, and his brother Lionel of Antwerp from the highest; Lionel's line continues through his daughter Philippa, his grandson Roger and his great-grandson Edmund Mortimer (who is the small figure just above Philippa's head). The marriage of Anne Mortimer with Richard of Conisbrough unites two branches of the tree; from them stem Richard, duke of York and his son Edward IV (the figure in plate armour at the top). In the centre of the image, Henry IV cuts off the branch that holds Richard II. (Courtesy of the British Library)

*Above left*: The remains of Sandal Castle, from where Richard, duke of York sallied forth to meet his death in 1460. (Courtesy of Julian Humphrys)

*Above right*: Micklegate Bar, where the heads of Richard, duke of York, his son Edmund, earl of Rutland and his brother-in-law Richard, earl of Salisbury, were displayed following their defeat at the Battle of Wakefield. (Courtesy of Wikimedia Commons)

*Left*: A later memorial stone erected to commemorate the death of Richard, duke of York in 1460. (Courtesy of Julian Humphrys)

*Below left*: Detail of a genealogy of Henry VI; he is the figure in the lowest circle being crowned by two angels. The English half of his ancestry is held up by Richard, duke of York. (Courtesy of the British Library)

*Below right*: Tewkesbury Abbey, where the survivors of the Battle of Tewkesbury sought sanctuary in 1471, and from where they were taken and executed. (Courtesy of Julian Humphrys)

*Above left*: A plaque in Tewkesbury Abbey commemorating the resting place of Edward of Lancaster. (Courtesy of Julian Humphrys)

*Above middle*: Ludlow Castle, from where Richard, duke of York was forced to retreat to Wales and Ireland in 1459. York's grandson Edward V passed most of his chidhood here, and was in residence in 1483 when he heard that he had acceded to the throne. (Courtesy of Julian Humphrys)

*Above right*: Edward V, from a fifteenth-century painted wooden panel. The crown floats above his head to denote that he was never crowned king of England. (Reproduced by kind permission of the Dean and Canons of Windsor)

Middleham Castle, where Edward of Middleham passed most of his short life. (Courtesy of Julian Humphrys)

Edward, earl of Warwick (far left) and Edward of Middleham, prince of Wales (far right) along with the prince's parents, Richard III and Anne Neville, and the earl's sister Margaret, countess of Salisbury. (© National Portrait Gallery, London)

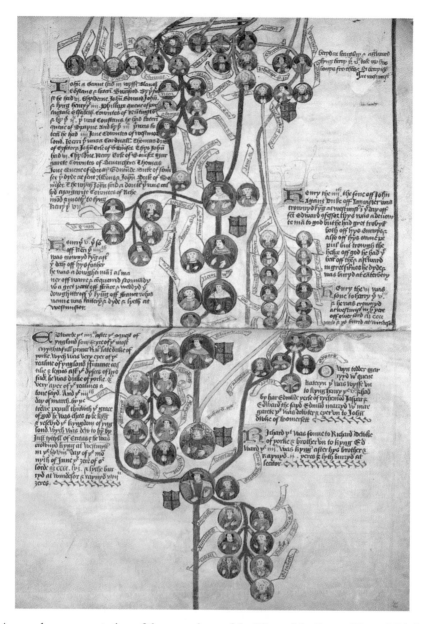

A complex representation of the genealogy of the Wars of the Roses. Henry VI is in the middle circle just above the central page fold; his wife Margaret of Anjou is to the left of his picture, and his son Edward of Lancaster squeezes in before the page fold. Edward IV is the crowned figure immediately below Henry, with his eight children branching from him. His son Edward is not given the title or status of king; he is the child to the right of the second row. The path of the crown leads straight from Edward IV to Richard III, and the accompanying text says that Richard 'was kyng after hys brother'. Richard's son Edward of Middleham, meanwhile, is not depicted at all. The artist has made a valiant attempt to show that Henry VII (in the lowest central circle) was related to the royal line, but obviously had difficulty doing so. (Courtesy of the British Library)

capture. The Edwards, father and son, returned to England in November 1347, triumphant and admired. But a deadlier foe, one that could not be fought with swords, was soon to assail them.

The plague later known as the Black Death had entered Europe from Sicily in October 1347, reaching France in early 1348 and crossing the Channel in the summer of that year. The plague made no distinction between rich and poor: among the dead were the king of Castile and the queen of Aragon, while in France both the king and his heir lost their wives.[14] The royal family of England did not escape; Edward's sister Joan of the Tower (then aged 14) was on her way to marry the heir to the throne of Castile when she contracted the plague and died near Bordeaux in July 1348, to the great grief of her parents.[15] The disease then reached England and swept through it; by the end of September two of Edward III's young sons, the toddler Thomas of Windsor and the new-born William of Windsor, were also dead.

At the time it must have seemed like the end of the world, but eventually the plague departed, having killed somewhere between a third and a half of the population of England, and leaving the rest in deep shock. But life, for the survivors, had to go on. In the absence of another *bona fide* war to engage their attention, both Edward and his father occupied themselves in chivalric pursuits. They took part in many tournaments together – let us not forget that the king, although he had an adult son, was still only in his mid-thirties himself – and the Order of the Garter was founded to celebrate both the triumph at Crécy and the companionship in arms of king, prince and nobles.

Edward now had a household of his own and, in a sign of things to come, he was a lavish spender. He wished to live in a style he thought appropriate for the heir to the throne, and this was coupled with the fact that one of the markers of chivalry was largesse; in order to sustain one's reputation it was necessary to be seen to give extravagant gifts and to live a life of conspicuous consumption. His accounts from this period list the purchases of a gold cup as a gift for the king; jewellery for the queen and Edward's sisters, and further jewels for members of his household. Perhaps surprisingly – and certainly in contrast to many others featured in this book – he was still unmarried; many international matches had been proposed over the years, but for one reason or another they had all fallen through. The existence of a clutch of younger brothers perhaps reassured him and his father that there was no particular hurry –

finding the right match was more important. During the next few years Edward continued with his bachelor lifestyle, spending most of his time on his various estates in Cornwall and Chester. He needed to make sure they could finance his wants and needs, which were becoming ever more elaborate, and there were some complaints that his methods of raising money were harsh. Landowners' revenues had decreased due to the sharp drop in population caused by the Black Death, but it seems that Edward wanted to squeeze the same amount of money out of fewer people and less resource. His stewards were relentless in the pursuit of income, to the extent that one was murdered in Cheshire in the summer of 1353.

Edward also had estates in Aquitaine, the southern part of which was still held by the English crown.[16] A series of truces with France that had held since 1346 were shortly to come to an end, so King Edward wanted his heir to be in position to take advantage of any opportunities that might arise. The prince – perhaps tiring of his life as landowner and administrator – was by no means averse to the thought of potential military action, and he sailed in the late summer of 1355, landing at Bordeaux in September. At the same time the king sent Henry of Grosmont, duke of Lancaster, to Normandy with an army. Henry, whose lineage will be of importance in later chapters, was not in the direct line of succession, but he was of royal stock several times over, being descended from both Henry III of England and Louis VIII of France. He served Edward III loyally, and became England's second duke when his earldom of Lancaster was upgraded in 1351. He was also earl of Derby and earl of Leicester, and thus the richest peer in England.

Edward wasted no time once he landed, marching from his own territory into the hostile Languedoc lands held by John of Armagnac. Here he put into practice the techniques of warfare that had been drilled into him since an early age: you attacked your noble enemy first by depriving him of economic resources. That is, you burned his lands and terrorized and killed those who lived on them:

> He [Edward] set out from Bordeaux, entered that part of Gascony that supported the French, and advanced right across it, burning and destroying a swathe five leagues wide […] they proceeded to Carcassonne, where they found riches vast beyond all belief; everything was plundered, and fair townswomen and their daughters were raped. They stayed

in the lower town for three days to complete their pillage
and destruction [...] they continued their march, setting fire
to the fine houses and markets as they left Carcassonne, and
made their way to the city of Toulouse, burning and laying
waste the land left and right.[17]

And so it goes on, and on. To add to the cruelty it was harvest time, so
the burning of crops meant that any locals who managed to survive the
slaughter might well end up dying of starvation anyway. Yet Edward is
still 'the valiant prince of Wales',[18] and letters home from members of
his household display no shame in telling of such conduct:

You will be glad to know that my lord [Prince Edward] has
raided the county of Armagnac and taken several walled
towns there, burning and destroying them [...] and then he
went through the lordship of Toulouse and took several good
walled towns and burnt and destroyed them, laying waste
the surrounding countryside [...] my lord was in the field
against his enemies for eight weeks and only took eleven
rest days. It seems certain that since the war against the
French king began, there has never been such destruction in
a region as in this raid.[19]

Armagnac, however, refused to be drawn into battle, so Edward turned
back towards his own lands in Aquitaine, where he spent the winter, no
doubt more comfortably than those remaining in the regions he had laid
waste. He began his campaign anew in the spring of 1356 and continued
throughout the summer, moving north along the Loire. By this time the
French king, John II (the son of Philip VI, who had died in 1350), had
mustered the main royal army, and his force met Edward's just south of
Poitiers on 19 September 1356. John's host was formidable, a roll-call
of the highest names in France: the king himself; his brother Philip, the
duke of Orléans; his eldest son, the dauphin Charles;[20] two of his younger
sons, Louis and Philip; other dukes and counts; and Sir William Douglas,
an experienced Scottish knight whose king was still in English captivity.

It was ten years since Prince Edward had 'won his spurs' at Crécy;
in the meantime, he had gained in experience without losing any of his
personal skill or courage. Once again he placed himself in the centre of his

line to engage in hand-to-hand fighting; thanks to good communication systems he was able to react to changing situations across the field.[21] Once again, Edward fought bravely, 'hewing at the French with his sharp sword, cutting lances, parrying thrusts, bringing the enemy's efforts to nothing, raising the fallen and teaching the enemy what the true fury of war meant'.[22] Once again, the result was victory. And what a victory: the king of France himself was taken prisoner, along with his youngest son, Philip. Despite his capture, Philip was given the nickname 'the Bold' for his part in the battle – at just 14 years of age he had remained by his father's side in the thick of the press, even when it was clear that all was lost. His brothers and his uncle got away, enabling the dauphin Charles to form an emergency regency in his father's absence.

In another echo of the earlier battle, tales of Edward's chivalrous behaviour were embellished in the telling. King John was in his personal custody and was naturally treated with honour, as befitted an anointed monarch; but the prince's reasons for not joining him at the dinner table after the battle developed over time. To start with it was a simple matter of him slipping away to attend a wounded companion who had been found and carried off the field, and asking John 'not to consider it an unworthy action of his in leaving him at dinner, because he had gone to attend a man near death'; later it was an ostentatious display of chivalry, with the prince 'steadfastly refusing to sit down with the king in spite of all his entreaties' because 'he was not yet worthy to sit at the table of so mighty a prince and so brave a soldier as he had proved himself to be on that day'.[23]

Several months elapsed while negotiations for a truce took place and Edward and his captives finally sailed for England in May 1357. His triumphant entry into London at the end of May was probably the high point of his life, and quite possibly the apogee of medieval English monarchy as a whole. A respected and admired king, still in his prime at the age of 45, had been on the throne for thirty years and had quelled all opposition; his adult heir was a glorious and victorious warrior; he had other sons and there was no doubt about the succession; the kings of France and Scotland were both in his custody.[24] The names of King Edward and Prince Edward were renowned throughout Europe as noble paragons of chivalry.

The problem with reaching a peak, of course, is that there is only one way to go.

\*\*\*

Both Edwards undertook another excursion to France in 1359, the king's intention being to have himself crowned at Reims, but this was unsuccessful thanks to the efforts of the dauphin Charles, who very effectively organized resistance to delay and then halt their progress so that they never reached their goal. The campaign stalled and King Edward was bogged down in negotiations until the summer of 1360, while the prince – constrained by the talks not to fight – kicked his heels. He did come out of the resulting Treaty of Brétigny well, though; Aquitaine was henceforth to be a sovereign state, no longer subject to the overlordship of France, and Edward was to rule it as its prince.

While these negotiations were going on, in the summer of 1360, Edward turned 30. He was still unmarried – a situation almost unheard-of at this time for the heir to the throne. He had one illegitimate child,[25] but his position required him to marry and to produce legitimate heirs so that the Plantagenet line could continue. Moreover, the plague returned in 1361, bringing fear and taking two of his teenage sisters (meaning that no fewer than five of his siblings had been lost to the disease over the years) as well as grandees such as the duke of Lancaster. Who knew who might be next? And so, in the autumn of that year, he married; but he did it in almost the most unorthodox way possible.

The arguments that could be raised against his choice of bride were legion. Joan, countess of Kent, was an English noblewoman rather than a foreign princess, so no international alliance was formed by the match. She and Edward were closely related: as the granddaughter of Edward I she was a first cousin of her bridegroom's father, a relationship well within the prohibited degree.[26] She was 33 and a widow with four young children. And finally, her previous marital history was, to say the least, unconventional.

Joan had been brought up in Queen Philippa's household (her father having been executed after the deposition of his half-brother, Edward II, when Joan was just 2) and when she was barely or not quite into her teens, she had contracted a secret marriage with one Sir Thomas Holland. However, he went abroad shortly afterwards and the king – unaware of these events – arranged a formal marriage for her with William Montacute, the earl of Salisbury. Joan, probably afraid to reveal the earlier union in fear of the possible consequences, went ahead with it and was sent to live with her new husband. When Holland returned to England after an absence of several years he confessed to their wedding and petitioned to have his 'wife' returned to him. He was supported by Joan, who – much to Salisbury's chagrin – asked for her second marriage to be annulled and the first to be considered valid. The matter was arbitrated by Pope Innocent VI, who ruled that the first union must take precedence and Joan returned to Holland; she lived happily with him and their growing brood of children until his death in 1360.[27]

This, then, was the woman that the prince of Wales, the heir to the English throne, the most eligible bachelor in Europe, had chosen as his bride. The only possible explanation is that the decision was personal, rather than political; after all, they were of a similar age and had known each other since childhood. He would later address her as 'my dearest and truest sweetheart and beloved companion' in letters, and a contemporary would say that he 'married a lady of great worth, with whom he had fallen in love'.[28] The situation remained fraught with complications as Salisbury was still alive and might theoretically have a claim on any further children Joan might bear. But the prince was insistent. King Edward might not have been overly pleased at the prospect, but after papal dispensation (necessary due to the parties' close blood relationship) was secured, he gave his consent and even attended the wedding.

In 1362 the prince and princess of Wales became also the prince and princess of Aquitaine, and they moved their household across the Channel. And it was at this point that Fortune's wheel began to turn, sending Edward downwards. He was, as everyone knew, a great warrior, but he was not in Aquitaine to make war. Instead he needed to administer and govern, and at this he proved markedly less adept. He was used to giving autocratic commands to soldiers, expecting them to be instantly obeyed; this was not necessarily the best way of dealing with the nobility of Aquitaine. He was uninterested in finance except insofar as it meant he could continue to fund a lavish lifestyle. And, now that he had a wife whose expensive tastes matched his own, and the costs of the large household necessary for the prestige of a ruler, they needed a great deal of money. In 1362, £200 was spent on a single set of jewelled buttons for Joan; later that year an embroiderer was paid £715 for clothes for Edward, Joan and Joan's children.[29] And this was before the military and administrative costs were factored in. But Aquitaine was supposed to be self-supporting (that is, Edward could expect no financial aid from England) so the prince would have to raise his own revenues.

His Aquitanian agents were as unyielding as those on his English estates had been ten years previously, and much hardship was caused.

There was some good news for the couple during these years. Edward and Joan had been 31 and 33 respectively when they married, so a large family was not to be expected, but they were given a boost by the arrival of two sons, Edward in 1365 and Richard two years later. But again, this turned into an excuse for conspicuous display and expenditure: at the celebrations for the baptism of little Edward in March 1365, 154 lords and 706 knights were hosted at the prince's expense and thousands of horses were stabled; over £400 was spent on candles alone.[30]

Meanwhile the French king was fast making up the ground that had been lost at Poitiers. John II had by now died, to be succeeded by his son Charles V, who was – not without cause – known as 'the Wise'.[31] He had seen Edward's growing unpopularity in Aquitaine and had capitalized on it by encouraging resistance. Then, in 1366, he scored another diplomatic coup. To the south of Aquitaine, over the Pyrenees, lay the kingdom of Castile. England and Edward were allies of its king, Peter I 'the Cruel'; Charles sent an army under his renowned general Bertrand du Guesclin to support Peter's half-brother Henry of Trastamara, and they succeeded in overthrowing Peter and placing Henry on the throne. Peter appealed to Edward for help, and Edward obliged, marching early in 1367. In the short term the campaign was a success: Edward won a resounding victory at the Battle of Nájera, du Guesclin was captured and Peter was reinstated on the throne.[32] The prince's military reputation was enhanced once more, a decade after Poitiers and two decades after Crécy. But in the longer term it was a disaster. Edward had incurred huge expenditure – around 2.7 million crowns, nearly the same as the ransom of King John that had crippled France for years – and he expected Castile to reimburse him. But Castile was much poorer than France, and when Peter failed to pay up, Edward had no recourse: he had been fighting effectively as a mercenary and thus had no right to levy a tax on either Peter's subjects or his own.

Moreover, he was ill. The heat of summer in the unfamiliar southern climate brought on a sickness that may have been malaria or dysentery, or a combination of both. He would gain nothing further by remaining in Castile, so he was forced to cut his losses and cross back over the mountains to Aquitaine. The success he left behind him was not to last; in 1369 Peter was murdered by Henry who took the throne (permanently this time) as Henry II.

Edward was broke, and he was never to recover his health; bouts of crippling illness would strike him ever more frequently throughout the remainder of his life. A series of defections of Aquitanian nobles to the French king forced him into one more campaign, as he moved to attack the city of Limoges in 1370, but he was so ill he had to be carried on a litter – a great fall for the once-mighty prince and the victor of Crécy and Poitiers. The city fell to Edward, but the chronicler Froissart accuses him of a great atrocity there:

> Then the prince [...] with all the others and their men burst into the city, followed by pillagers on foot, all in a mood to wreak havoc and do murder, killing indiscriminately, for those were their orders. There were pitiful scenes. Men, women and children flung themselves on their knees before the prince, crying 'Have mercy on us, gentle sir!' But he was so inflamed with anger that he would not listen. Neither man nor woman was heeded, but all who could be found were put to the sword [...] more than three thousand persons, men, women and children, were dragged out to have their throats cut.[33]

Other sources make no specific mention of this,[34] and some modern writers have cast doubt on the massacre having taken place at all, but – atrocious as it seems – it would not have been particularly out of character for Edward, given his previous documented behaviour during the chevauchées (plundering expeditions) of the 1340s and 1350s. Whatever the truth of the matter, Edward was to be swiftly punished by Fortune: after the sack of Limoges he returned to his wife in Bordeaux to find that his elder son and heir Edward had died, aged just 5. The future of his dynasty now lay solely on the shoulders of 3-year-old Richard; Joan was 42 and unlikely to bear any more children for her sickly husband. Edward, too ill to cope, resigned his command of Aquitaine and sailed for England.

Worse was to come. There he found that his father, now approaching 60, was also in poor mental and physical health. Queen Philippa had died in 1369, and Edward III was being disproportionately influenced by a 21-year-old mistress, Alice Perrers, who had borne him three children – their dates of birth proving that the relationship had started well before the queen's death – and who was manipulating the king to gain both wealth and influence. Prince Edward was in little condition to intervene or to help, and the monarchy was a sad shadow of the magnificence of 1357. Edward was able to do a little work on government business, though he was forced to remain in and around London as he was not well enough to travel. The realm was essentially being run by his younger brother John of Gaunt, by now duke of Lancaster via his marriage to Blanche, only surviving child and heiress of Henry of Grosmont, who had died of the plague in 1361. This left John as the richest man in England after the king, and the most senior adult male member of the royal family after the king and the prince of Wales (King Edward's second son, Lionel of Antwerp, had died in 1368).

Somehow, Prince Edward managed to survive for six years after his return to England, although recurring and ever more serious bouts of his illness confined him to bed for much of that time. He weakened and eventually died in June 1376, shortly before his forty-sixth birthday; not gloriously in battle, but in his bed, worn out and racked with pain. He predeceased his father, and therefore never inherited the crown of England.

The grief in England was extreme, partly for what Edward had been and partly for the dire situation caused by his early demise; as one chronicler wrote, 'on his death, the hopes of England utterly perished'.[35] The prince was, with much ceremony, interred beside the high altar of Canterbury Cathedral. Edward III lingered another year, bedridden, before dying in June 1377.

Would Edward have made a good king? His record in Aquitaine is against him, suggesting as it does that he might not have turned out to be quite the paragon of kingship that many observers expected: he was bellicose, extravagant and seemed uninterested in peaceful governance. He might have found his popularity starting to decline when his continual demands for money for personal expenditure could not be met. On the other hand, his accession would have caused no controversy and no conflict, a situation much to be envied during the Middle Ages in England: he had been recognized as heir to the throne since his birth, he was respected and revered by his contemporaries and no rival candidate could possibly have appeared to challenge him.

In an age when military prowess and ostentatious chivalric display were much-admired qualities, Edward would have benefited from the esteem and loyal support of his nobles. His companions-in-arms would have gone anywhere and done anything for him, and that was a strong basis for kingship. Moreover, had he outlived his father he would have been a week past his forty-seventh birthday at the time of his accession – easily, at that point, the oldest man ever to succeed to the throne in England – and the realm would have benefited from his experience and the associated stability. As it was, it would have to face the chaos of a boy king and a regency, as the crown passed not to Edward but to his 10-year-old son Richard.

# Chapter 7

# Edmund Mortimer

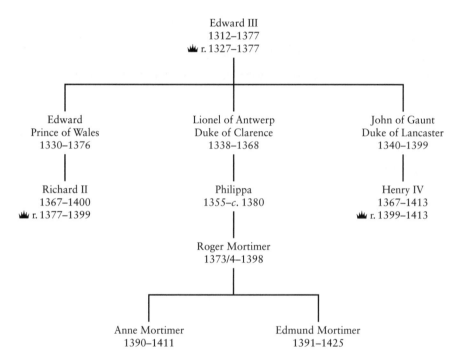

Edward III
1312–1377
r. 1327–1377

Edward
Prince of Wales
1330–1376

Lionel of Antwerp
Duke of Clarence
1338–1368

John of Gaunt
Duke of Lancaster
1340–1399

Richard II
1367–1400
r. 1377–1399

Philippa
1355–c. 1380

Henry IV
1367–1413
r. 1399–1413

Roger Mortimer
1373/4–1398

Anne Mortimer
1390–1411

Edmund Mortimer
1391–1425

The young Richard II, of course, had many capable uncles to help him rule. However, as it transpired this turned out to be part of the problem rather than the solution, and things only got worse as the years went by. This is the point at which the royal family tree and the line of succession start to become very complicated, but as the birth order of Edward III's sons and their respective offspring would be of vital importance in the years and the wars to come, it is worth including a recap here.

At the time of Richard II's accession in the summer of 1377 he was 10 years old, and his family situation was this. The eldest of Edward III's sons, Edward of Woodstock, prince of Wales, had predeceased his father; this is why Richard followed his grandfather on to the throne. The second brother, Lionel of Antwerp, duke of Clarence, was also dead – although he had left descendants, of whom more in a moment. The third, John of Gaunt, duke of Lancaster, was 37; he was a politician of great experience who had effectively been running the government for some years during the illnesses of his father and older brother. John had married twice: first to Blanche of Lancaster, by whom he had three surviving children, Philippa, Elizabeth and Henry of Bolingbroke. Young Henry was 10, the same age as King Richard. By his second wife, Constance of Castile, John had one daughter, Catherine; and finally he had four illegitimate children – three sons and a daughter – by his mistress Katherine Swynford. After Constance's eventual death John would marry Katherine, an act that was to have far-reaching dynastic consequences; we will hear more of this later.

The fourth son of Edward III was Edmund of Langley, earl of Cambridge and later duke of York, who was 36 at the time of his nephew's accession. In marked contrast to his brother John of Gaunt he seemed to have little interest in government, and although he had taken part in a few military expeditions and held various official positions, he seems to have lacked ambition and preferred to spend his time on his own lands, engaging in hunting and hawking.[1] Edmund was married to Isabella of Castile, and they had three young children, Edward, Constance and Richard.[2] The fifth and final brother was Thomas of Woodstock, earl of Buckingham and later duke of Gloucester; he was at this point 22, much younger than any of his surviving siblings, and had played little part in the military adventures of his father and brother. He would later marry Eleanor de Bohun, and their surviving children were Humphrey, Anne and Joan.

Young King Richard was thus amply supplied with uncles and cousins, but once again the family dynamic was affected by the ages of the parties concerned and the rapidity with which some branches reproduced. Lionel of Antwerp, who had been next in line to the throne after the Black Prince until Edward produced children of his own, had been only 14 when he married Elizabeth de Burgh, countess of Ulster in her own right, and 17 when his only surviving daughter Philippa was born. Philippa herself was married at 13 and a mother at 15, meaning that Lionel (although he did not live long enough to know them) had grandchildren older than his brothers' children.

Of particular interest to our dynastic tale are Philippa's two sons, Roger Mortimer, 4th earl of March (born in 1373 or 1374) and his younger brother Sir Edmund Mortimer, born in 1376.[3] This Roger – as the senior descendant of the second son of Edward III – was never officially proclaimed as such but was considered to be, *de facto*, heir presumptive to Richard II until such time as the king had his own children. Richard, as we mentioned above, was only 10 at the time of his succession so no children could be expected for some while, but it was taken as a matter of course that he would in the fullness of time marry and father sons to continue his line. There were also great hopes that he would emulate his father and grandfather in their military prowess.

All these hopes were to be disappointed. Richard inherited his father's love of luxury and extravagant living, but without the martial capability or the knack of inspiring loyalty in those around him – the exact reverse of what was needed for a successful medieval king. In 1382 Richard married Anne of Bohemia, the granddaughter of King John the Blind, who had been killed at the Battle of Crécy and whose bravery was admired by the Black Prince. Richard and Anne were both 15 at the time of the wedding and thus pregnancies and births might be expected before long, with the prospect of a large family to ensure the succession, but their twelve-year marriage (ended when Anne died of the plague in 1394) produced no children. This left Richard as a childless king of 27, a worrying situation, so his advisors urged him to marry again, and soon; he obliged, but, as 'a matter for wonder' chose as his bride Isabella of France, eldest daughter of Charles VI.[4] There was nothing wrong with an alliance with France – English kings often married French princesses – but the problem in family terms was that she was just 6 years old, and thus no heirs could be expected for at least another eight or nine years, a potentially dangerous situation.

This all had significant consequences for Roger Mortimer and for his own son Edmund, who had been born in 1391; every day that passed without Richard fathering a child bolstered his position as heir presumptive to the throne. However, the speed at which events moved in the second half of the 1390s brought about results that nobody could have predicted a few years earlier and the situation ended up looking quite different.

King Richard had been antagonizing his nobles for some years, and his behaviour became more erratic after the death of his first wife. He was on particularly bad terms with his (admittedly slightly overbearing) uncles, and Thomas of Woodstock, duke of Gloucester, was the first to suffer the consequences. He was arrested in July 1397 and died mysteriously in prison while awaiting trial – probably murdered to avoid the spectacle of a king's son being tried in public for treason.[5] A contemporary had previously linked him with the Mortimers:

> He had a great-nephew, the son of the daughter of an elder brother of his called Lionel [...] the duke of Gloucester would have liked to see this great-nephew of his on the throne of England in place of King Richard, who he said was unworthy to reign.[6]

But Richard still felt threatened by the enormously wealthy and powerful Lancaster family, specifically John of Gaunt (now an elder statesman approaching 60) and his 30-year old son Henry of Bolingbroke. Henry was exiled in 1398; John died in 1399 and Richard confiscated all his estates, thus disinheriting and enraging Henry. This could have been a boost for the ambitions of Roger Mortimer, but he had been killed in a skirmish in Ireland in 1398 leaving little Edmund, then aged 6, as his heir. Had Roger survived longer – an adult male as the head of the Mortimer/Clarence line rather than a small child – then the situation in England might have been very different. As it was, the tensions escalated and life became increasingly dangerous for the young boy who was now earl of March and earl of Ulster as well as heir presumptive to the crown and the focus of attention from those who disliked both Richard and the house of Lancaster. Edmund was descended from royalty many times over via the various branches of his family, making him even more of a potential threat to those on the throne or claiming it.[7] Matters came to a head in the autumn of 1399 when Henry of Bolingbroke invaded England, deposed Richard and declared himself Henry IV.

Henry's claim to the throne violated hereditary principle – which had become the defining characteristic of the succession since the time of Henry III – so he had to be careful how he presented it. An early idea was that he could ignore his descent from Edward III completely and rely on his Lancaster heritage (via his mother and her father Henry of Grosmont) by fabricating the complete fiction that Edward I had been the *second* son of Henry III, while his own ancestor on his mother's side,

Edmund Crouchback, had been the elder. However, this was roundly ridiculed and soon dropped.[8] Next came the idea that he was descended in the direct *male* line from Edward III: he was the son of Edward III's son, whereas Edmund Mortimer, although descended from an older son, traced his claim through a woman, his grandmother Philippa. However, this was in direct contradiction to an earlier disposition. Edward I, who had lost several sons in infancy and childhood,[9] had in 1290 settled that if he were to die without surviving male issue, his daughters and their heirs would succeed – in order of seniority – in preference to his brother and his brother's sons. Edward III had never renounced his grandfather's disposition: partly this was because he had numerous sons and so presumably thought that the question would not arise, and partly as it was not in his own wider interests to do so.[10] Henry IV was therefore not the nearest heir by hereditary right, so he needed to bolster his position in other ways. A claim of conquest – he had, after all, invaded and seized the crown from its present owner – would not help much, as it would undermine his claim to have succeeded legally. Thus he fell back on two positions: first, that Richard had resigned the crown to him personally, and second, that he was an adult male of royal descent.

England had just endured one long minority and had no stomach for another so soon. This seems to be indicated in the speech given by the archbishop of Canterbury in parliament, in which he 'highly lauded the duke of Lancaster [Henry] and his *strength* and his *understanding*', and made a point of quoting the biblical verse 'a *man* shall reign over my people'.[11] Edmund's claims were thus put aside in favour of the greater good. Like others before him, he found his age to be a disadvantage, and he also suffered from the rapidity with which his line had reproduced: had he been the underaged *son* of Lionel of Antwerp, rather than his underaged great-grandson, greater consideration might have been given to his rights.

As it was, no voices were raised at this point in support of Edmund's claim to the throne. But Henry IV – as was common for kings unsure of their own position, and particularly those who had gained their crown by usurpation – remained suspicious, and Edmund and his younger brother were taken into royal wardship (for which we can read 'custody').[12] After all, he would not be 7 years old forever. And any illusions anyone might have had that Edmund's position was not a dangerous one were shattered by Henry IV's ruthless violence towards others who might conceivably threaten him: Richard II was murdered in his prison cell in 1400,[13] some months after Henry's accession, and then attention turned to Sir Roger Clarendon.

Clarendon was the illegitimate son of Edward, the Black Prince. Although he had not been brought up as a royal or with any related expectation, he was recognized as a member of the family both by his grandfather Edward III, from whom he received an annuity, and by his half-brother Richard II, for whom he was a knight of the king's chamber. He was older than Richard – somewhere around 50 in the year 1400 – and an experienced fighter prone to violence, so he could feasibly be considered more of an immediate threat to Henry IV than a 7-year-old boy of better birth. In 1402 Clarendon was accused of plotting against Henry and of spreading rumours that Richard II was still alive (but not of trying to seize the throne himself); he was imprisoned in the Tower of London and then taken to Tyburn, where he was hanged and beheaded.[14]

To begin with, Edmund and his younger brother Roger were kept at Windsor, but any hopes of a peaceful childhood were soon shattered. Henry IV was campaigning in Wales when the boys' uncle, Sir Edmund Mortimer, defected to the Welsh under Owain Glyn Dŵr; he married Owain's daughter and promptly declared against Henry by announcing that his nephew Edmund was the rightful heir to Richard II. This move was not unpopular in Wales, for young Edmund, via one of his many royal lines, was a descendant of Llywelyn ap Iorwerth, the great Welsh prince of the thirteenth century. There was also support elsewhere for the scheme; one of the elder Mortimer's allies was his brother-in-law Henry 'Hotspur' Percy, high-profile son of the earl of Northumberland and a magnate of great resource. However, Percy was defeated and killed by Henry IV's forces at the Battle of Shrewsbury in July 1403, a loss that dented Mortimer's campaign for the time being.

Sir Edmund's plans were resurrected in 1405 when an attempt was made to kidnap both boys; it was masterminded by Constance (daughter of the late Edmund of Langley, who had died in 1402) and she also implicated her brother Edward, duke of York. She managed to get Edmund and Roger away from Windsor, and they rode for Wales with the intention of joining Sir Edmund; had Mortimer senior succeeded in taking his nephew into his personal custody it would have bolstered his campaign considerably. But the small party had only made it as far as

Cheltenham when they were caught; Constance was arrested, her brother Edward detained in the Tower, and the boys returned to Windsor. This was deemed not sufficiently secure and they were moved to Pevensey, almost as far away from Wales as England could afford. As children, they were deemed innocent parties in the scheme, and no further punishment was imposed. The consequences for the adults involved, meanwhile, were mixed: Edward, duke of York, was released a few months later and reinstated to his estates; his sister Constance was temporarily imprisoned at Kenilworth but also released in 1406. Sir Edmund Mortimer, young Edmund's uncle, was not captured but he had little success pressing any further claims thereafter. He died in straitened financial circumstances in 1409; his widow and children were taken to London and placed in the Tower, where they all appear to have died in 1413, although it is not clear whether this was by disease or by design.

While he remained underage, Edmund was not in control of his own lands or estates; these were passed around to various of Henry IV's retainers and, due to a combination of greed, negligence and conflict, their worth was soon greatly reduced. As it happened this worked in Edmund's favour, as a lack of personal resource made him less of a threat to Henry IV. Remarkably, given the circumstances, he not only survived his childhood but it was agreed in 1408 that he would be allowed to marry, as long as he did this 'with the king's assent and the council's advice'.[15] This was a signal marker of Henry's decreasing suspicion; had he felt that Edmund was a great menace he would not have permitted him the opportunity to father any children through whom his claims might be transmitted.

With little definitive evidence it is difficult to explain why Henry should have been so merciful to Edmund, when he had not been to many others. As we saw in earlier chapters, youth was no protection against violence for those with a blood claim to the throne. Perhaps Henry's clemency was in part due to Edmund's blood claim being less immediate, and therefore perhaps less 'real', to contemporaries: after all, Lionel of Antwerp had been dead for forty years and there can have been few people at court in the early 1400s who remembered him. But this might not have been enough on its own, so we are left to conclude that there must have been something about Edmund personally that allayed Henry's fears. Although he remained in Henry's custody, he would have been educated to a level commensurate with his rank and perhaps this allowed others to see that he did not demonstrate the bellicosity or ambition common in other noble youths of his age. And, of course, he would have taken care to tread carefully in his dealings with Henry, walking – as he was no doubt obliged to do – a tightrope between the manner and self-confidence expected of a nobleman who would in due course be fit to have control of his own estates, yet at the same time posing no threat to his overlord. This is necessarily all speculation, but it might go some way to explaining how he survived.

In 1409, when Edmund was 18, he and Roger were transferred to the custody of Henry of Monmouth, who was the eldest of Henry IV's four sons and his designated heir. Henry was only in his early twenties himself, and he and Edmund appear to have struck up a friendship that lasted into later life; Edmund showed no outward signs of disaffection with his position (or, at least, none that were strong enough for any contemporary chroniclers to comment on). Henry of Monmouth held the erstwhile titles of the Black Prince – prince of Wales, duke of Cornwall, duke of Aquitaine and earl of Chester – and his position, and that of the house of Lancaster, seemed unassailable. When Henry IV died in 1413 there was no question at all over who should succeed him, and Henry V was proclaimed and crowned with no apparent dispute, no voices raised in support of Edmund's claim. Indeed, so secure did Henry feel that he released Edmund from custody, knighted him, declared him of age and allowed him to inherit his estates. It was at around this time that Edmund's younger brother, Roger, died; nothing is heard of him after this date.

Their relationship continued amicably for the next two years, but in January 1415 Edmund tried Henry's patience when he took advantage of his permission to marry: he chose as his bride Anne Stafford, granddaughter of Thomas of Woodstock, duke of Gloucester and youngest son of Edward III. The two lines of descent from King Edward were therefore united, and any children of the match would be of royal blood several times over. Henry could not dissolve the union, which had received papal dispensation, but he did levy an enormous fine of 10,000 marks – this impoverished Edmund for the rest of his life, and he had still not finished paying off the debt when he died.

From the available evidence, it would seem that Edmund's choice of wife had been a matter of personal preference, rather than any furthering of political ambition, of which he still appeared to have little. But his royal blood could not go away, and Henry, as it turned out, was too complacent. Edmund might be loyal to him, but there were others in his realm who were ready to rebel against him using Edmund as their puppet. Matters came to a head in the summer of 1415 as three nobles with a grudge decided to make their move.

The 'Southampton plot', as it became known, was the brainchild of three men. The first was Richard of Conisbrough, earl of Cambridge, who was the younger son of Edmund of Langley, and thus the brother of both Edward, duke of York and Constance, whom we met earlier in this chapter; he was also Edmund Mortimer's erstwhile brother-in-law, having been married to the late Anne Mortimer, Edmund's sister. The second was Sir Thomas Grey, whose son was betrothed to Cambridge's daughter, and the third was Henry, Lord Scrope, whose uncle had been executed for his part in an earlier plot against Henry IV. Their somewhat far-fetched intention was to depose Henry V and replace him on the throne with Edmund – probably not because of any particular admiration for Edmund, but more because they wanted rid of Henry and therefore needed a plausible candidate (preferably one they felt they could manipulate) to replace him.

The conspirators were soon apprehended, and the record of their trial spells out their plans in detail:

> At the town of Southampton, and in divers other places in the realm of England [they] falsely and treacherously conspired, and confederated themselves together, that, having gathered to themselves many others, both of the retinue of the lord king and of his liege subjects, to take Edmund, earl of March, to the parts of Wales, without licence of the lord king, and procured to elevate him to the sovereignty of the realm of England [...] and make a certain proclamation in the said parts of Wales, in the name of the aforesaid earl of March, as heir to the crown of England, against the said present lord king [...] And moreover that they themselves would take divers castles of the present lord king in Wales, and hold and defend the same castles by force of arms against the present lord king, besides falsely and treacherously proposing and imagining many other treasons, felonies, conspiracies and confederacies,

namely finally to destroy and kill the same present lord king, Thomas, duke of Clarence, John, duke of Bedford and Humphrey, duke of Gloucester, his brothers.[16]

Surprisingly, it was Edmund himself who informed Henry of the plot; he did so on 31 July 1415, saying that he had only just learned of it. It remains unclear to what extent this is true, or whether he had initially considered going along with the plan and then thought better of it. It is perhaps just about possible that Edmund's annoyance with the king at the huge marriage fine imposed on him – maybe he felt Henry intended to ruin him? – may have made him discontented enough to listen to Cambridge. However, this would have been a very dangerous course of action indeed, and it is out of keeping with the cautious path he had trodden thus far in his life. It is probable, then, that he was merely to be the pawn of the conspirators, rather than one of them.

Contemporaries certainly seemed to believe in Edmund's innocence. '[God] delivered the just from the ungodly and revealed the Judas-like iniquity and treason of these evil men through the lord Mortimer, the earl of March, whose innocence they had assaulted as part of this murderous design', says one; and another notes specifically that the plotters were '*discovered by* the earl of March', without mentioning the possibility of his actual involvement.[17] And King Henry believed his friend and kinsman; not only was Edmund not arrested along with Cambridge, Scrope and Grey, but he was appointed as one of those who would sit in judgement on them. It is extremely unlikely that Henry would have acted thus had he entertained any serious suspicions of Edmund's involvement in the plot.

The king's retribution was swift, and all was over within a week of him hearing the news. The trial of the three conspirators took place immediately at Southampton, where Henry was gathered with his army ready to embark for France.[18] The three were unsurprisingly found guilty and sentenced to death: Grey was beheaded on 2 August and the others three days later. On 7 August Edmund was granted a pardon for any part he might conceivably have played. This must have been a formality for, as we noted above, Henry must have really believed in Edmund's innocence; if not, he would have had no qualms in executing him, and the ties of kinship between the two men would not have kept Edmund's neck off the block. The earl of Cambridge, after all, was an even nearer relation to the king.

Henry and his army sailed on 11 August, Edmund accompanying him at the head of his own retinue of sixty men-at-arms and 160 archers. The Southampton plot had one dynastic consequence of note, which was to become evident on the French campaign: Richard of Conisbrough, earl of Cambridge and second son of Edmund of Langley, had been the heir to the duchy of York, his elder brother Edward having no children. When Edward was killed at the Battle of Agincourt in October 1415 the title duke of York thus passed to Cambridge's son Richard, then 4 years old. Young Richard was Edmund Mortimer's nephew, as his late mother Anne (who had died in childbirth or shortly afterwards in 1411) had been Edmund's sister.

Edmund remained in the king's company for the first part of the campaign in France, but he was struck down by dysentery at the siege of Harfleur and, along with many others including Thomas, duke of Clarence, the king's brother and heir, was invalided back to England. Disease was always a danger in a siege camp and this outbreak appears to have been particularly virulent:

> But because the dysentery, which had carried off far more of our men, both nobles and others, than had the sword, so direly affected and disabled many of the remainder that they could not journey on with him any further, [Henry] caused them to be separated from those who were fit and well and gave them leave to return to England, and these [...] numbered about five thousand.[19]

Dysentery could be a death sentence, but Edmund survived his illness; he returned to France in 1416 along with John, duke of Bedford (the second of Henry V's three younger brothers) to relieve Harfleur. He now seemed to be one of Henry's most trusted lieutenants. In 1417 he had charge of a fleet to patrol the seas, and the following year he was appointed king's lieutenant in Normandy. When Henry V married in 1421, to Catherine, daughter of the French king Charles VI, Edmund carried the sceptre at her coronation.[20] Edmund then returned to France with Henry and was with him when he fell mortally ill.

Henry V died in August 1422 at the age of just 36, leaving as his heir the 9-month-old son he had never met, who was proclaimed Henry VI. A very long minority beckoned, and appropriate arrangements had to be put in place. Thomas, duke of Clarence, the king's next brother and long-time heir, would perhaps have been the obvious choice to act as guardian to the young king, but he had been killed in March 1421 at the Battle of Baugé. An attempt by Humphrey, duke of Gloucester and Henry V's youngest brother, to be named sole regent was overruled in favour of a council, which would comprise a number of peers and be headed by John, duke of Bedford as 'keeper of England'. As a near relative of baby Henry, and a substantial magnate in his own right, Edmund was appointed to this council, but some lingering suspicions about his own claim to the throne – put forward by the now embittered and hostile Gloucester, among others – raised their heads again. Edmund's own extreme youth had prevented any effective claim to the throne in 1399, as Henry IV made much of the fact that he, as an adult man, was more suited to take the crown, but with a baby now on the throne, might this be his opportunity?

Once again, Edmund made no public move, but he was evidently considered more of a threat to Henry VI than he had ever been to Henry IV or Henry V. In March 1423 he was appointed king's lieutenant in Ireland – where he had lands of his own, being earl of Ulster as well as earl of March – ostensibly as the new regime needed a representative there, but no doubt also to move him out of the way and to put the Irish Sea between him and Westminster. His term of office was to be nine years, which would make him a virtual exile from England and English politics.

Edmund would need to take a large retinue with him and such an expedition took time to assemble; it was the autumn of 1424 before he set sail. And there in Ireland, perhaps as intended, his story ended abruptly; he died of the plague at his family seat of Trim castle in January 1425, at the age of 33.

Epitaphs of Edmund are few. He was sometimes called 'the Good', and his family chronicle describes him as 'severe in his morals, composed in his acts, circumspect in his talk, and wise and cautious during the days of his adversity'.[21] However, this is likely to be a positive spin on the actions of a family member about whom there was not really much to say – not when compared with the notable lives of a number of his Mortimer predecessors, anyway. It is also a statement of the obvious: throughout Edmund's life a number of his peers and relations were executed for real or imagined threats to the Lancastrian dynasty, and this meant that being 'composed in his acts' and 'circumspect in his talk' was a necessary survival strategy.

It is perhaps possible that we are doing Edmund a disservice here. Perhaps he was constantly under pressure from friends and family members such as his uncle Sir Edmund Mortimer or Richard, earl of Cambridge, to claim his rights. Perhaps he faced them down and should therefore be given more credit for strength of purpose. To be honest, though, it is more likely that the judgements of modern historians, that he was 'the least notable and distinguished of the five Mortimer earls of March', that he was of mediocre ability and 'lack[ed] the capacity for political leadership' are accurate.[22] However, this is the principal reason for his survival in a dangerous age, so he can hardly be blamed for it.

Edmund Mortimer is probably the least well known of all the lost heirs in this book; so anonymous, so absent from his own narrative, that it is difficult to work out what he himself thought of his situation; the best we can do is speculate based on his actions. He seems to have had no particular desire for the throne, or at least not one that was strong enough to make him seriously contemplate rebelling against Henry IV or Henry V. Instead he wandered through life a little aimlessly, trying not to make trouble, but trouble followed him around. His royal blood and the claim it entailed could never be entirely suppressed, and he was always in danger of being used as a figurehead for revolt, a puppet in the hands of those with ambitions of their own. The fact that Edmund somehow managed to live even as long as he did while so many of his peers lost their heads is evidence of his success at being a nonentity.

However, although Edmund might be a shadowy figure in his own story, his existence was the lynchpin around which the bloody events of the fifteenth century were to hang.[23] The Lancastrians had seemed secure on the throne under the ruthless Henry IV and the much-admired Henry V, but the accession of the baby Henry VI changed the situation at a stroke. At first it seemed merely another long minority – a problem to be endured, but not one that was insurmountable. But as Henry VI grew up it became clear that he was totally unsuited to his kingly role, and there were many in England who cast about them for an alternative. Edmund Mortimer was dead, his younger brother likewise; neither of them had produced any children, so the Mortimer/Clarence claim to the throne passed to the son of their elder sister Anne: Richard, duke of York.

# Chapter 8

# Richard, duke of York

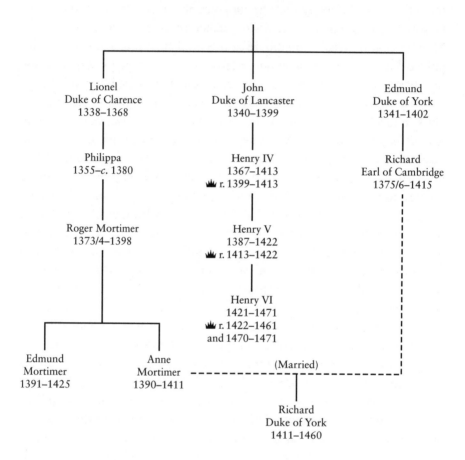

The life of Richard Plantagenet – the dynastic surname by which he chose to be known – did not get off to the best start. He never knew his mother, who died in childbirth or shortly afterwards, and he was just 4 years old when his father was executed for treason. As an orphan of noble status, his wardship belonged to the crown; he was sold off to the highest bidder and sent to live in the household of a stranger.

However, the situation – personally tragic as it was for a small child – was not quite as ruinous for his future as it could have been: the sentence of attainder (the loss of title and possessions) passed on Richard of Conisbrough was for him alone, and it did not bar his descendants from inheriting his lands and titles. Young Richard thus became titular earl of Cambridge in August 1415, and then duke of York and earl of Rutland following the death of his paternal uncle at Agincourt later that same year. Ten years later the demise of his maternal uncle Edmund Mortimer also left him the rich earldoms of March and Ulster, meaning that at the age of 14 he held lands throughout England, south Wales and Ireland and was the greatest magnate in the realm after the king.[1]

Richard was also, by this time, betrothed. His wardship – including control of his vast landholdings and of his marriage – had been bought by Ralph Neville, earl of Westmorland; Ralph had fathered twenty-two children (eleven sons and eleven daughters, by two marriages), of whom nineteen were living, so with such a large family to provide for he needed to make a return on his investment. He therefore in 1424 secured the future of his youngest daughter, the 9-year-old Cecily Neville, by arranging her marriage to Richard. It is not entirely clear when the actual wedding took place, but it had certainly happened by October 1429, when the parties were 18 and 15. As well as a wife, this union gave Richard links to the extended Neville family and numerous brothers-in-law who were to be of great importance in his later life.

Ralph Neville died in October 1425, leaving Richard's wardship to his widow, Joan Beaufort, who was the daughter of John of Gaunt via his mistress (and later wife) Katherine Swynford; we will discuss the Beaufort family more fully later in this chapter. However, with the ranks of noblemen of royal blood thinning out, Richard was soon called away to higher duties. In 1426 he was knighted by John, duke of Bedford (Henry VI's uncle and 'keeper of the realm' during the king's minority), and in 1428, when he reached 16, he was summoned to take up residence in the royal household, which he did.

The succession arrangements at this point, the autumn of 1428, were murky. The subject had been addressed by Henry VI's grandfather, Henry IV, quite early in his reign when he was trying to secure the future of his Lancastrian dynasty; he had overturned previous custom and ordained that the crown would pass in the male line to his sons and their heirs; this was ratified in two statutes of 1406.[2] Just to be clear, a *male-line* descendant was distinct from a simple *male* descendant in that the latter, although male, might trace his claim via a female ancestor. Richard, duke of York, was a male-line descendant of Edmund of Langley (the son of Edmund's son), but only a male descendant of Lionel of Antwerp (the great-grandson of Lionel's daughter). This distinction and its application to the succession narrowed the field of potential candidates quite considerably, cutting out – for example – the Stafford family, who were the children of Thomas of Woodstock's daughter, and the Hollands, the grandchildren of Henry IV's sister.

The new arrangement did, of course, bolster Henry IV's own position – as he claimed to take precedence over Edmund Mortimer because he was of Edward III's male line and Edmund was descended from Philippa of Clarence – and he would at that point have felt confident in his dynasty's male future, for he had four healthy sons and no doubt expected a number of grandsons. In a twist of dynastic fate, however, they produced only one legitimate child between them: Henry VI. Henry had been born in December 1421 and was still only 6 – a long way off being able to have children of his own, and also not quite safe himself from the dangers of child mortality, so the situation was precarious. The next two men in line were his surviving uncles, John, duke of Bedford, and Humphrey, duke of Gloucester, who were both married but childless. Bedford and Gloucester had also had two sisters, Henry VI's aunts, but one was dead and the other the queen of Denmark, and in any case now barred from the succession.

The previous generation was equally unhelpful in providing male-line heirs, for the legitimate siblings of Henry IV had been two sisters and a half-sister; no brothers. In order to find the next in line, should Henry VI die in childhood or fail to have children of his own, it was thus necessary to go back even further to the sons of Edward III and their descendants. These were by now rather sparse, at least in the male line. There remained no living descendants in the male line of the Black Prince, Lionel of Antwerp or Thomas of Woodstock, which left John of Gaunt and Edmund of Langley; their only legitimate male-line descendants were Henry VI and Richard, duke of York, respectively.

The situation was complicated, however, by the existence of the Beaufort family. As we noted in the previous chapter, John of Gaunt had fathered three sons and a daughter by his mistress, Katherine Swynford, whom he had later married. Upon that marriage the couple's children had been legitimized – thus saving them from the stigma of bastardy –

but it was specifically noted that they and their descendants were barred from any claim to the throne.[3] But their royal blood and their affinity to the Lancastrian house meant that they had risen high, and some of them were figures of great influence at Henry VI's court.

The four children of John of Gaunt and Katherine Swynford were John, Henry, Thomas and Joan; they were given the surname Beaufort after one of John of Gaunt's holdings in France. Joan, as we noted above, was countess of Westmorland. Thomas had been duke of Exeter but had died childless in 1426. Henry was a clergyman, bishop of the rich see of Winchester and also a cardinal. John had died in 1410 but left a family of children; the two who will concern us most here are John, earl (and later duke, after Henry VI upgraded the title) of Somerset and his younger brother Edmund. The younger John was at this time a prisoner of the French; he had been captured at the Battle of Baugé in 1421 while still in his teens and would not, as it transpired, be released until 1438. He would go on to father one daughter, Margaret Beaufort, but his years in captivity had taken their toll and he would die in 1444 – officially of illness but possibly as a result of suicide.[4] Some of his lands passed to Margaret but the ducal title went to his brother Edmund. Edmund, meanwhile, was rumoured to be having an affair with the widowed queen mother, Catherine of Valois; while there may or may not have been much truth to it, the rumours were sufficient to result in a parliamentary statute restricting the marriage of dowager queens of England.[5]

The upshot of all this complex genealogy was that Richard, nominally with a better claim to the crown than Henry VI himself under the old inheritance system via his Clarence/Mortimer heritage, actually found himself considered heir to the throne (after Bedford and Gloucester, who would both die with no legitimate children) even under the new rules. He was a youth of great importance, and he was soon closely involved in affairs of the realm.

In 1429 Richard was present at Henry VI's coronation at Westminster Abbey, and was created a Knight of the Bath; in 1430 he was one of the group of noblemen that accompanied Henry to France for the 8-year-old king's coronation there.[6] In 1432, when he was 21, Richard was declared of age and allowed to take possession of his own estates; the following year he was admitted to the Order of the Garter, the chivalric brotherhood founded by Edward III and the Black Prince. In 1436 he was appointed to replace the late John, duke of Bedford, as lieutenant of France: the royal commission says that France should be ruled by 'some great prince of our blood and lineage', and these were by now few and far between.[7] Before he could get there Paris was recaptured by Charles VII, but on his arrival in France Richard did manage to stop any further advance of the rival French king, and he ensured the safety of Rouen during a campaign in the autumn of 1436. Not a single contemporary lauds him as a brilliant or inspiring warrior in the mould of, say, Edward the Black Prince, but conversely he was a competent strategist, an able delegator and an efficient administrator.[8]

Richard spent the next few years engaged in various duties in both France and England. He and Duchess Cecily also – and somewhat belatedly, given how long they had been married – began a family. A daughter, Anne, was followed in 1441 by the couple's eldest son, whom they named Henry in honour of the king, but unfortunately the infant did not survive long, possibly not even long enough to be baptized, a serious consideration at that time. Two more sons, Edward and Edmund, followed in 1442 and 1443.

It is perhaps worth addressing here an idea that has become prevalent in recent years; that is, that Edward was not in fact the son of Richard, duke of York, at all. The 'evidence' usually cited for this is that Richard and Cecily were apart from each other at the point forty weeks before the birth, that Edward's baptism was rushed and not overly lavish, and that Edward did not resemble Richard physically. These can all be debunked fairly easily. Firstly, we can have no idea whether Cecily's pregnancy lasted exactly forty weeks (even today anything from thirty-eight to forty-two is considered normal), nor whether she and Richard – who were both in France although residing in different places – might have met up anyway. Secondly, the Yorks had recently lost a son who may not have been baptized; who could blame them if they rushed to make sure their next did not suffer a similar fate? And thirdly, it is perfectly possible for sons not to resemble their fathers. Richard was apparently slight and dark, while Edward was to grow to 6 feet 4 inches tall, but he might well have inherited his height from his ancestor Lionel of Antwerp, who was reputed to be of giant stature.[9]

While Richard was busy with his duties and his family, Henry VI was growing up, and it became clearer by the year that he in no way resembled Henry V in character or aptitude. He supposedly reached his majority at the end of 1442 but was not able to take a firm grip on the reins of government, remaining a pawn in the hands of those who sought to influence him; he is often described as 'childlike', 'naïve' or 'simple'.[10] Richard was not at this time in the king's close circle of advisors, being busy in France, and this was to his disadvantage. He was also not, unfortunately for him, the author of a string of notable military victories: this would doubtless have appealed more to the crowds back home than news of efficient governance. And meanwhile, a rival faction was gaining ground at his expense.

Cardinal Henry Beaufort, the last surviving son of John of Gaunt, was by now in his late sixties and a figure of great influence at his great-nephew's court. This was not merely because of his position in the higher echelons of the Church, but also because he had lent the crown a great deal of money and the king was therefore in his debt. The cardinal used his position to push forward his Beaufort nephews, first John (before his untimely death in 1444) and then Edmund, the new duke of Somerset. In the absence of both the duke of York and the duke of Gloucester, the Beaufort faction was the most powerful royal-related clique around the throne.[11]

Richard returned to England in September 1445; he was – rather ironically given what would happen in later years – considered to be a pillar of the Lancastrian regime, the unspectacular but dependable lieutenant. He also frequently proclaimed and demonstrated his loyalty to Henry VI. Henry was, on a personal level, probably hard to dislike; he was a gentle, peace-loving man whom Richard had known since he was a child, and perhaps he felt protective of his younger cousin, however unsuited to kingship the latter might have been. However, Henry's character did not make for a strong king or an effective hand on the tiller of state, and he continued to be easily influenced. While Richard had been on the other side of the Channel, the duke of Somerset and others had made the most of the chance to whisper in the king's ear, and Richard, on his return, found his management of Normandy being questioned. His lieutenancy of France, instead of being renewed at the end of its current term, was given to Somerset.

By the late 1440s Richard found himself the heir presumptive to the throne, following the death of Humphrey, duke of Gloucester. But the Beauforts were in a strong position and gaining, and with so few male-line royal descendants, who now remembered their disbarring from the line of succession nearly half a century previously? Moreover, during the late 1440s and early 1450s three new players appeared on the scene, none of them friendly to Richard. The first was Henry's queen, Margaret of Anjou, whom he married in 1445 when he was 23 and she had just turned 15. This was an unpopular choice in England as, although Margaret's father held titular claims to the crowns of Naples and Aragon, he was in practice an impoverished nobody who could give his daughter no dowry. All Margaret's standing came from the fact that she was the niece of the queen of France; her uncle by marriage, Charles VII, had arranged her match with Henry as he was not keen to supply one of his own daughters for the purpose.[12] However much the noblemen of England might grumble, the marriage took place and they could not undo it. It was to be hoped, at least, that the couple would produce a large family so that there would be no doubt of the future succession.

The other two new faces were Edmund and Jasper Tudor, half-brothers to the king, who were brought to court and given the earldoms of Richmond and Pembroke respectively. As we noted earlier in this chapter, the rumoured affair of Queen Catherine, the queen mother, with Edmund Beaufort had led to a new statute restricting the marriage of queens dowager. Catherine went on to disregard this statute when she married – in secret and probably in 1429 – Owen Tudor, a Welshman from a prominent but untitled Anglesey family. They had two sons, Edmund and Jasper, and possibly other children, before Catherine died in January 1437. Owen Tudor was imprisoned and later released, and King Henry took it upon himself to provide for the education and welfare of his half-brothers. They were valuable men for him to have around his court: they shared his blood, but only on his mother's side and so were therefore no threat, and they owed everything they had to him, so their loyalty was guaranteed. Rewards and patronage came their way, and in 1455 Edmund Tudor married his ward, the 12-year-old Margaret Beaufort, only child of John, late duke of Somerset; she was pregnant with Edmund's child when he died the following year. Jasper took both children – the mother and her new-born son – into his care.[13]

After losing his lieutenancy of France to the duke of Somerset, Richard was granted that of Ireland, to which realm he was therefore expected to travel. It is difficult to decide whether this was meant as some kind of reward, or a consolation prize, or whether it was simply to get him out of the way: after all, Ireland had proved to be a graveyard for the last three Mortimer earls of March in a row. Whatever his own personal feelings on the matter, Richard went. Once again he was efficient in his governance and he became popular in Ireland:

> And great thank there and love of all the land he had among the Irish always, and all the Irish began to obey him. He ruled that land full well and worthily, as did before his noble ancestors.[14]

This experience was to stand Richard in good stead later on, as we shall see.

Henry VI, meanwhile, remained at the mercy of his advisors, who were fast plunging everything into ruin. To cut a long story short, Normandy had fallen to the French and the crown was bankrupt. This could not, in contemporary eyes, possibly be the fault of the king himself; the blame must lie with those around him. It may seem strange to us that there was no overt criticism of Henry VI; he was, after all, nearing 30 and therefore could not in any sense of the word still be considered a minor. Why could he not take responsibility for his government's actions? But this is to misunderstand the reverence in which kingship was held at this time; as far as contemporaries were concerned, Henry VI had been appointed by God and could therefore not be at fault. Richard, from his vantage point in Ireland, could only observe as his king's losses accrued.

By 1450 he could stand it no more, and he returned from Ireland in September of that year. But such was the propaganda put about by his enemies – for enemies they must now be considered – that Henry became convinced that Richard was travelling to London in order to depose him. He sent emissaries to the duke to ask him to stand down. A contemporary takes up the tale:

> The duke replied, commending himself to the king's good grace and saying that he had never rebelled against the king and would obey him always. He asserted that his uprising had been directed against those who betrayed the king and the kingdom of England and that he was not against the king and desired nothing but the good of England. He wished to tell the king of those who were encompassing the destruction of his two kingdoms, that is to say, England

and France. And these men [included] Edmund, duke of Somerset, who had been responsible for the shameful loss of all Normandy.[15]

Richard must, by this stage, have been feeling frustrated. He was still the heir to the throne (Henry and Margaret's marriage having produced no children in five years), and he must have known that he would make a better job of being king than poor Henry. Although not spectacular, he had made a success of his stints in France and in Ireland, and certainly more so than any of the other lords available at this time. While he remained 'only' a duke, a supporter of the king but not the holder of royal power in his own right, he would always be subject to the whims of the king and to the malicious intentions of those who influenced him. But there appeared to be nothing Richard could do, and he certainly made no attempt at this stage to make a bid for the throne: once again he reiterated his loyalty, seeking only to reduce the influence of others on Henry – while perhaps hoping to increase his own – and retaining the position as heir that he held by right of his descent from Edmund of Langley. This position was becoming more secure with every year that passed without Queen Margaret bearing a child, although Richard was perhaps thinking in terms of the future of his dynasty rather than himself. He was, after all, a decade older than the king so had to work on the basis that Henry might outlive him; he therefore looked to secure the future of his own sons, Edward and Edmund, who were by now the 8-year-old earl of March and the 7-year-old earl of Rutland respectively. In this his main worry would have been that the duke of Somerset – himself descended from John of Gaunt and thus a nearer relation to the king – would eventually succeed in persuading Henry to name him as heir.

Such an eventuality became more likely in March 1452 when Somerset – with the help of the queen, who was his close ally and no friend to York – had Richard seized and taken to London as a prisoner. He was not thrown into a cell, but he was forced to take a public oath of loyalty to the king. This would not, in general terms, have been something he would resent, given his previous willingness to do the same; the humiliation stemmed from the fact that it looked to others as though he was doing it under duress and only because Somerset and the queen had forced him to.

In 1453 events took several momentous turns. First, in the spring of that year, the queen announced that she was with child – something of a miracle, or so it seemed. Then news reached England of a catastrophic defeat at Castillon in France.[16] In the summer the king fell into a stupor, a catatonic state, and was completely unable to function: he could not move or speak, although he apparently remained conscious enough for attendants to feed him so that he did not die of starvation. This was a new manifestation of his mental illness that might have been caused by schizophrenia or catatonic depression, though of course it is impossible to diagnose at such a distance. Henry's condition was unsurprisingly not properly understood at the time, but what became abundantly clear as the months went by was that he was not going to recover anytime soon, if ever.[17]

This was an unprecedented situation for the English monarchy; kings might have been ill before but this had been either temporary or due to old age, and there were procedures in place to deal with such eventualities. But an adult in his prime years who was totally incapacitated for an indefinite period – while showing no signs of actually dying – was both unique and dangerous. Eventually it was decided that some action was necessary, and now was Richard's moment. He had already acted as the king's lieutenant, his deputy, in both France and Ireland – why not in England? He was the obvious candidate, a prince of royal blood and a man of great political experience. After deliberations through the winter, parliament agreed and Richard was appointed 'protector and defender of the realm' in March of 1454. This was 'for the duration of the king's illness, until such time as Prince Edward should come of age', and so potentially for the long term.[18] He would have to step carefully, ruling but without assuming (or appearing to assume) kingly sovereignty. Richard accepted the position and promised to rule consultatively, and 'for a whole year [...] he governed the whole realm of England most nobly and in the best way'.[19] However, in one respect he could not restrain himself: he deprived Somerset of his offices and committed him to the Tower.[20]

As may be gathered from the terms of the appointment quoted above, while the discussions about Richard's role were ongoing in the autumn of 1453 a huge event had occurred: in October Queen Margaret had given birth to a son – as luck would have it on the feast of St Edward the Confessor, Henry's favourite saint. It was clear from the date of birth that she had conceived before Henry went into his catatonic state, but it was rumoured that the king was not the father, the prime suspect being none other than Margaret's close ally Edmund Beaufort, the duke of Somerset, who seems to have had a predilection for neglected queens. The subject of Prince Edward's paternity will be discussed more fully in the next chapter.

Margaret's new status as the mother to the heir to the throne put her in a very strong position, once they had both survived the initial period of danger, but she then overplayed her hand by asking to be named regent during her husband's incapacity, with full royal power: 'She desireth to have the whole rule of this land [...] she may make the Chancellor, the Treasurer, the Privy Seal, and all other officers of this land,' as one commentator put it.[21] But the magnates of England were not about to let a woman, and a French woman who was the niece of Charles VII of France at that, rule over them, so Richard secured his position as protector rather more easily than perhaps he might have expected. He reiterated his support for Henry VI and indicated his willingness to recognize the baby prince's claims over and above his own.

The birth of a son to the king pushed Richard out of his place in the succession. However, for the child to be officially designated heir he needed to be recognized as such by his father, and although the baby was brought to the king on several occasions he showed no flicker of recognition:

> At the prince's coming to Windsor, the duke of Buc[kingham] took him in his arms and presented him to the king in goodly wise, beseeching the king to bless him; and the king gave no manner of answer. Nonetheless the duke abode still with the prince by the king; and when he could no manner of answer have, the queen came in, and took the prince in her arms and presented him in like form as the duke had done, desiring that he should bless it; but all their labour was in vain, for they departed thence without any answer or countenance.[22]

Despite the lack of official recognition from Henry VI, young Edward was declared prince of Wales and earl of Chester in March 1454. Margaret's importance was secure, and although Somerset remained in the Tower for now, his own situation was improved by having his close ally in an enhanced position.

The standoff continued throughout 1454, although, as we noted above, it was generally considered that Richard ruled well. And then, on Christmas Day 1454, having been in his uncommunicative, catatonic state for eighteen months, Henry woke up. 'The king is well amended,' wrote a contemporary, and the now 14-month-old Edward was brought to him again:

> The queen came to him and brought my lord prince with her. And then he asked what the prince's name was, and the queen told him Edward; and then he held up his hands and thanked God thereof. And he said he never knew it until that time.[23]

This was a victory for Margaret: Richard of York was relieved of his post as protector of the realm and Edmund of Somerset was released from the Tower, his animosity towards his rival now even more deeply engrained.

There were now two distinct factions among the highest nobility, with others unable to ignore the rift and therefore having to choose sides. Richard's greatest allies were his brother-in law Richard Neville, earl of Salisbury, and Salisbury's son, another Richard Neville, the earl of Warwick.[24] Somerset and the queen enjoyed the support of Henry Percy, earl of Northumberland and a long-standing rival of the Nevilles.[25] King Henry, meanwhile, was his usual peace-loving self. After he woke up 'he said he is in charity with all the world, and so he would all the lords were',[26] but the situation had deteriorated past the point of no return. Armed conflict now seemed inevitable: a battle not for the crown itself but to control the person of the king.

Queen Margaret and the duke of Somerset made the most of their greater proximity to Henry, whispering in his ear. Richard and his compatriots, in a last-ditch attempt to avoid bloodshed, wrote a letter to Henry assuring him of their loyalty and expressing their sorrow that his bad advisors had spoken against them, but Somerset prevented it being delivered to the king.[27]

Two groups of armed men moved closer to each other. In May 1455 the king's army, led by Somerset and Northumberland – and, somewhat incongruously, including Henry himself – quartered themselves in the town of St Albans and blockaded the routes into it. However, the forces of York, Salisbury and Warwick found a way in, and fighting ensued in the streets. The engagement is generally known as the First Battle of St Albans, but it seems to have been something of a targeted strike: although the overall number of casualties was low, the duke of Somerset and the earl of Northumberland were both killed. Richard came upon King Henry – who had been slightly wounded in the neck by an arrow – in the town. He had the king, and the kingdom, at his mercy, but once again he did not take advantage of his position; he submitted to the king and re-declared his loyalty. Richard and Henry set off for London, with a chronicler careful to note that 'the duke of York brought him unto London as king and not as a prisoner'.[28]

Of course this reverence, however genuine it might have been on a personal level, was politically something of a blind – effectively Richard had the king in his custody, and indeed he sought to be named protector once more, an appointment that was secured in November 1455. When Henry was ceremonially crowned again to re-emphasize his position, it was Richard who handed the crown to the bishop to put on the king's head; the symbolism could hardly have been more obvious. Henry was, moreover, tired and ill again, the stress of the last few months on top of his previous long bout of illness becoming too much for him. This time he did not fall into a catatonic state but he withdrew from public life for a while to rest, which gave Richard the opportunity to govern more freely in his name. The extent to which he encouraged Henry to consider himself ill enough to retire is not known.

But once again, Richard's continuing respect for the holy institution of kingship and for the anointed person of Henry meant that he could never be secure: the king was still in nominal control, he could overrule his 'protector' at any time, and he would be swayed by whoever spoke to him last. And so it transpired: in February 1456 Henry had one of his occasional bursts of energy and decided to take the reins of government back into his own hands. The protectorate was dissolved.

Henry, in his own naïve way, made an effort to ameliorate the situation. His one overriding wish was that everyone should just be friends, and he could not seem to see that this was simply not possible in the circumstances; the rivalry between the factions was too intense. Still he persevered, and in March 1458 he organized a very ill-advised public 'Loveday'. The citizens of London were treated to the sight of a procession in which the king was followed by representatives of both sides, in pairs and holding hands: Queen Margaret walked with the

118

duke of York; the duke of Somerset (now Henry Beaufort, Edmund's eldest son) with the earl of Salisbury; the earl of Northumberland (now another Henry Percy, eldest son of the previous incumbent) with the earl of Warwick; and others in descending order. The feelings of the sons of the men killed at St Albans, as they walked with those responsible for their fathers' deaths, can only be imagined; and we can only surmise what Richard and the queen might have had to say to each other as they processed hand in hand. A later chronicler, looking back on the event with the benefit of hindsight, captured a flavour of the atmosphere:

> Their bodies were joined by hand in hand, whose hearts were far asunder: their mouths lovingly smiled, whose courages were enflamed with malice: their words were sweet as sugar, and their thoughts were all envenomed: but all these dissimulating persons tasted the vessel of woe.[29]

Any actual reconciliation was, of course, superficial at best and more likely to be non-existent. Once again, the queen's faction (now including Henry Beaufort and Henry Percy, both out for blood in revenge for their fathers' deaths at St Albans) had Henry's ear. They conspired both implicitly and overtly against the duke of York and his compatriots until, in a reverse of the events of several years previously, they declared that York, Salisbury and Warwick were now the 'evil counsellors' around the king who must be destroyed. At a parliament held in Coventry in June 1459, at which none of the three was present, they were all accused formally of treason.

York, Salisbury and Warwick now had to look to themselves, and in October they mustered at Richard's castle at Ludlow, along with York's sons Edward, earl of March and Edmund, earl of Rutland (now 17 and 16 respectively). Strangely, given the danger, Duchess Cecily was also there with the couple's two youngest sons, George and Richard; perhaps Duke Richard felt that they would be safer behind the stout walls there than they were at their normal residence of Fotheringhay.[30] Richard and the four earls stationed their troops in Ludford Meadow, with the bridge and the castle behind them. However, some defections and the strength of the royal army – which included Henry himself under the royal banner – facing them made their position untenable. The five men retreated from the field on the evening before battle was expected to commence, returning to the castle; it was decided that there was no choice but to flee. Had they been defeated or captured by the royal forces their lives would undoubtedly have been forfeit.

Richard and his son Edmund rode through Wales and took ship for Ireland; Edward of March, with his uncle Salisbury and his cousin Warwick, went to Calais, the last remaining English territory on the other side of the Channel, which was held by Warwick's men. Cecily was left to face the wrath of the king, the queen and the hostile army, with only 10-year-old George and 7-year-old Richard for company. It must have been a truly terrifying experience. They were apprehended and brought before the king; fortunately for them (for it could have turned out very differently) Henry declared that they personally had not offended against him, and they were merely placed in custody. Their jailor was to be one of Cecily's many sisters, Anne Neville, duchess of Buckingham, so – although the duke of Buckingham was one of the king's adherents – we may assume that they were treated with at least some dignity.

Richard and Edmund reached Ireland safely. The duke was popular there, thanks to his efforts and even-handed rule in the late 1440s; he and his son remained there out of harm's way for nearly a year. Indeed, there may have been some question over whether Richard might not stay permanently, setting himself up as sole ruler of Ireland at a time when Henry's chaotic regime could exert little influence there. But this would do little for his sons, his brother-in-law and his nephew. All of them had been attainted in their absence, and the attainder (unlike the one passed on Richard's father back in 1415) was total – York, Salisbury, Neville and all their heirs were deprived of every single title, estate, castle and manor they owned. They were now penniless outlaws, and both honour and self-interest demanded that Richard do something about it.

The stakes could not really get any higher, so there was not much to lose. The two separated parts of the group managed to communicate with each other and planned an invasion of England. Richard's son Edward landed with both Nevilles first, in Kent, in the early summer of 1460. Once more they professed their loyalty to Henry VI and their intention only of ridding the court of evil advisors; they won support in London and the south-east and defeated royal forces at Northampton in July. Once more they captured the king, and once more they submitted to him.

However, either this was all a ruse or the earls of March, Salisbury and Warwick were unaware of Richard's true intentions. He took longer to reach England, but when he arrived later in the summer he headed for London, giving those who marched with him 'banners with the whole arms of England without any diversity, and commanded his sword to be borne upright before him'.[31] The significance of bearing the arms of England 'undifferenced' (that is, without any marks of cadency) was huge, for only the king had the right to do so; the carrying of an upright sword also denoted the presence of a monarch. The shockwaves continued when Richard reached Westminster where, to a stunned silence, he marched up to the throne itself and laid his hand upon it. He had finally had enough, and now he was about to do the one thing he had resisted for so long. A few days after this event he had the lord chancellor (who happened to be George Neville, the son of Salisbury and the brother of Warwick) declare to all that he was the true king via his Mortimer ancestors and their descent from Lionel of Antwerp, the older brother of John of Gaunt from whose line the Lancastrians came.[32] He was not the heir to the throne, but the rightful king.

Given that he had made this declaration in parliament, parliament had to provide a response to it, and the general reaction was one of panic and indecision. They recognized Richard's strong position – and the consequent possible danger to themselves if they stood against him – but they still could not countenance the idea of deposing the useless but amiable Henry, the Lord's anointed who had been king since before he knew what the word even meant. They ended up with the sort of compromise – ratified as the Act of Accord – that suited nobody: Henry would remain king for the rest of his life, but his heir would be Richard, duke of York rather than Edward, prince of Wales. In addition, Richard would have 10,000 marks per year to keep himself and his family in a manner befitting the heir to the throne.

The situation bore some slight resemblance to the one we explored in Chapter 3, by which King Stephen agreed to disinherit his son Eustace in favour of Empress Matilda's son Henry, who later became Henry II. The reaction was similar too, although the parties were different. In the earlier case Eustace had been a grown man who took up arms at hearing of his dispossession; little Edward, having just passed his seventh birthday, was unable to do the same, but he did have the benefit of an enraged mother who would defend him and his rights to the utmost.

Margaret, as we mentioned earlier, was not overly popular among the English nobility, but her position now attracted sympathy. The magnates were no doubt worried about their own families; if the son of the king himself could be dispossessed, how many others might lose their inheritance? Margaret had been in Wales (under the protection of Jasper Tudor) and then in Scotland, but now she marched south with the military support she had been able to acquire. We will say more on Margaret and her actions at this point in the next chapter.

Richard, together with his son Rutland and his brother-in-law Salisbury, removed to Sandal Castle in Yorkshire, but it was by now winter and not a good time for provisioning a large group of men. He had to keep dispersing troops on foraging missions to feed them all as Margaret moved closer; eventually they were surrounded. Among those in the queen's army were the young earls of Somerset and Northumberland, hoping for their revenge at last. On 30 December 1460, for reasons that remain unclear to this day, Richard sallied out from Sandal to meet the queen's army in battle. Perhaps he had been misinformed about the number of her troops and did not realize how heavily he was outnumbered. Or perhaps he knew that provisions were running out and he needed to make a move before they all lost their strength from starvation. In either case, the result was disaster.

Richard's life, as we noted at the beginning of this chapter, had not begun well. It ended worse; his men were cut down in their hundreds, and both he and his 17-year-old son Edmund were killed in the engagement, which became known as the Battle of Wakefield. The earl of Salisbury was captured and executed the following day. All three of their heads were severed after death – a notable departure from the accepted customs of war at this time – and placed on spikes on Micklegate Bar in York. The queen additionally ordered that Richard's head be adorned with a paper crown to mock his royal ambitions. It was a sudden, tragic and humiliating end for the man who had tried everything he could before claiming the throne for himself and who would certainly have made a better king than the hapless Henry VI.

Margaret's triumph, however, would not last long. Edward, earl of March (and now both duke of York and claimant to the throne in right of his father), maddened by rage and grief, was unstoppable. He was victorious at the Battle of Mortimer's Cross – appropriately in the ancestral heartlands of his Mortimer ancestors – in February 1461, and was welcomed into London and declared king. The following month he underlined and ensured his triumph with a victory over the Lancastrian forces at Towton, still the bloodiest battle on English soil.[33] One chronicler saw in this divine justice:

> King Henry himself and his wife Queen Margaret were overthrown and lost that crown which his grandfather Henry IV had violently usurped and taken from King Richard II, his first cousin, whom he caused to be wretchedly murdered […] Men say that ill-gotten goods cannot last.[34]

Right seemed to have been restored; the crown had for three generations been temporarily diverted to the house of Lancaster but now it was back in its lawful hands. Once again Henry VI managed to survive, but Edward placed him securely under lock and key in the Tower. With the innocent and bemused monarch in his custody Edward felt safe as he set about imposing his authority and starting his reign. But of course, in so doing he started yet another cycle of violence by disinheriting another young boy, who would in due course set out for revenge.

# Chapter 9

# Edward of Lancaster

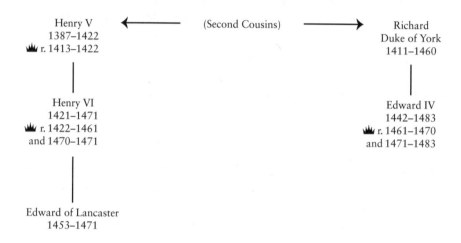

Henry V
1387–1422
r. 1413–1422

(Second Cousins)

Richard
Duke of York
1411–1460

Henry VI
1421–1471
r. 1422–1461
and 1470–1471

Edward IV
1442–1483
r. 1461–1470
and 1471–1483

Edward of Lancaster
1453–1471

> In this troublous season, on the thirteenth day of October,
> was the queen delivered at Westminster of a fair son, which
> was christened and named Edward […] whose mother
> sustained not a little slander and obloquy of the common
> people, saying that the king was not able to get a child, and
> that this was not his son.[1]

Gossip about high-profile women, and particularly high-profile women who unexpectedly become pregnant, is nothing new; Margaret of Anjou was one of many to suffer it. In the normal course of events we might therefore dismiss such rumours as idle chatter but the specific circumstances of Edward of Lancaster's birth mean that we should examine the question of his paternity a little more closely.

The case that Edward might not have been Henry VI's son is based on a combination of factors. First among them is the fact that Henry VI had a well-publicized aversion to physical contact and the female body. A contemporary notes that he 'avoided the sight and conversation of women, affirming these to be the work of the devil, and quoting from the Gospel that "he who casts his eyes on a woman so as to lust after her has already committed adultery with her in his heart"'. However, this evidence has sometimes been interpreted selectively. Henry was a pious man who adhered strictly to the dictates of the Church, and while the Church naturally frowned on physical intimacy between those who were not married, it not only condoned but actively encouraged it between husbands and wives – the primary purpose of noble marriage was, after all, to conceive children. The quote above actually continues: 'Those who knew him intimately said that he had preserved his virginity of mind and body to this present time, and that he was firmly resolved to have intercourse *with no woman unless within the bonds of matrimony*.'[2] So, although Henry may have avoided other women, he almost certainly had conventional marital relations with Margaret after their wedding.

A second argument, following on from the first, is that Margaret had not conceived in the previous eight years of their marriage, and that she would not do so again. Was it merely coincidence that the all-important conception happened at the time of her (and her ally Somerset's) greatest danger, when the duke of York was in the ascendant and Somerset's influence seemingly waning? For what could put them more firmly in the driving seat than the queen being the mother of the heir to the throne, and Somerset his godfather? We may set against this several points, not least Margaret's own morality. She has been much criticized both by contemporaries and by subsequent commentators, but none of them ever described her as flighty or flirty – indeed, quite the opposite. Her religious devotion did not reach the heights of Henry's, but she would have been well aware of the Church's rules on marital fidelity. Moreover, she would also have known that adultery, when committed by a queen, was not just a moral crime: it was treason. The penalties were severe, and if proven (that is, 'proven' to the satisfaction of the king) such adultery would have resulted in a hideous death for both parties.

And then there is the duke of Somerset to take into consideration. His career was spent furthering his own interests; however high the stakes might have seemed, he would surely not have risked such a catastrophic course of action. An affair with the reigning queen, by one of the realm's most influential magnates, was a very different thing indeed from the dalliance with the widowed dowager Catherine of Valois in which he may or may not have engaged as a youth. Such a liaison, when coupled with the enormity of trying to pass off a bastard as the legitimate heir to the throne, would have been monumentally stupid; it is therefore unlikely given Margaret's and Somerset's characters and situations.

We are left to conclude, then, that Edward *was* the child of the king and queen and that his conception occurred providentially – after all, some couples who have struggled to have a child do conceive spontaneously and surprisingly and there is no reason to suppose that Henry and Margaret were not among these. Indeed, there was immediate precedent close to the king: the duke and duchess of York had a large family, but they had not started it until they had been married for at least ten years. Henry and Margaret's subsequent failure to produce any more children can probably be put down to the very little time they spent together during the remainder of Margaret's childbearing years. Thus we can conclude that the rumours about young Edward's paternity were just that: rumours and gossip. Margaret was a woman who was both foreign and generally disliked, and the easiest way to slander such a woman was to insinuate that she was guilty of adultery. Possibly the allegations were encouraged by the Yorkist faction; after all, Duke Richard had been heir presumptive to the throne before the baby's birth and had now been pushed down the hereditary queue. But it was of little matter – in the eyes of everyone who mattered, the baby was the true heir to the throne.[3]

As we saw in the previous chapter, baby Edward was not immediately accepted by his ill father after his birth, but was named prince of Wales anyway; any lingering doubts about his status were dispelled fourteen months later when he was recognized formally by the now recovering king. In theory he could henceforward be treated in the same way as the other acknowledged royal heirs we have met throughout this book: a household was formed for him and a council was constituted to oversee his affairs. But these were not normal times for anyone, least of all the heir to a disputed throne, and Edward's childhood was to be unstable in the extreme.

The early part of Edward's life was, unsurprisingly, dominated by his mother. She was unwilling to let such a precious child (and asset) out of her sight, and he travelled with her everywhere rather than being left in the care of nurses at one royal residence. This was unusual, but then Margaret's position was both unusual and difficult. The role of a queen consort was partly to produce an heir, which she had done, but it was also to act as an assistant and helpmeet to her husband; if the king was a strong, authoritarian figure this role could be well defined, but how was Margaret to approach being a helpmeet to a king such as Henry VI? His hapless incompetence forced her into a more active role, one that led to her being portrayed as the voracious 'she-wolf' of legend, but it is difficult to see what else she might have done. Somebody needed to take charge, to safeguard the interests of Henry and Edward, and if Henry could not then Margaret would have to. Fortunately, it was a role to which she was well suited, as one chronicler noted:

> The queen having a wit, more than the common sort of women have, and considering the estate of her husband, the condition of her self, and the peril of her only son, thought it necessary to pluck the sword of authority out of their hands.[4]

Margaret's absolute priority was her son and her son's future; she would do anything to defend him. Unfortunately for her, Richard, duke of York was also reaching a point of similar desperation about his own and his family's future, and their differences were by now so irreconcilable that armed conflict was inevitable. The catastrophic loss of the duke of Somerset at St Albans in 1455, and the subsequent capture of the king, put Margaret and Edward in a precarious position.

Things had improved a little by 1457, by which time York's protectorate had ended; the council to oversee Prince Edward's affairs was established in the early part of the year and Margaret made sure that she would direct it. London was too dangerous a base for them – the citizens there tending to be sympathetic to York – so she and Edward led a peripatetic lifestyle, generally in the Midlands or Cheshire where his own lands were and where they enjoyed greater support. During the ups and downs of the next few years she occasionally succeeded in wresting custody (there really is no more appropriate term) of the king away from her opponents and into her close circle, which meant that she could keep a firmer grip on power. Henry arrived at his wife's temporary base of Kenilworth in August 1457, when Edward was approaching his fourth birthday and presumably beginning to understand a little more of what was going on around him. What he might have thought of his father is impossible to guess.

Unfortunately we have no information about Edward's day-to-day life at this point, but we may assume that his early education was similar to that of other boys of his rank – learning letters, manners and some religion, playing and making a start on games that would lead to more formal martial training in later years. Unlike many others, though, his upbringing was imbued with a constant air of uncertainty and fear for the future, which might have communicated itself to him.

As Edward survived his infancy and moved into boyhood, his rights could be more properly promoted and his status proclaimed. This was made plain at the Battle of Blore Heath in September 1459, an engagement that is sometimes overlooked among the bigger battles of the Wars of the Roses. In short, the duke of York and the earls of Salisbury and Warwick had all been accused of treason in their absence at a council in Margaret's stronghold of Coventry in June 1459;[5] Salisbury then marched from Middleham in Yorkshire towards Ludlow to join up with the others, but he was ambushed by Lancastrian forces at Blore Heath in Staffordshire. He was outnumbered but managed to defeat his enemies and resume his journey to Ludlow, where he met up with the others, as we saw in the previous chapter. The battle was therefore not crucial in a military context, but its significance lies in one specific factor: the Lancastrian army did not wear the king's livery, but that of his son Edward, prince of Wales.

With York and his compatriots cornered, Edward accompanied both his parents to Ludlow, where the sudden overseas flight of all the major Yorkist lords left his party in the ascendant. They were able to ride back in some triumph to Coventry where, at a parliament in November 1459, Richard of York and his allies were attainted. At this same parliament the magnates recognized Edward as the heir to the throne, and he remained by Margaret's side as she became the undisputed ruler of England during York's absence in Ireland through the winter and spring of 1459–60.[6] Edward's status as the king-in-waiting seemed secure for the present but the period of stability was not to last long.

Following Richard of York's declaration of his Clarence/Mortimer claim to the throne in the autumn of 1460 and the subsequent Act of Accord, the 7-year-old Edward was disinherited, his future destroyed at a stroke. He lost not only his claim to the throne, but also his titles of prince of Wales, earl of Chester and duke of Cornwall, which were given to York; he was left with nothing. We do not know how the news was broken to him, or how much of the situation he understood, but his mother's reaction to it must have given him an idea of the severity of the situation. Terrified for Edward's personal safety, she gathered him up and fled immediately for Wales, where they were taken in by Jasper Tudor, the earl of Pembroke. He, as Henry VI's half-brother, was Edward's uncle; he was guaranteed to stay loyal to the Lancastrian cause because he had no future outside it. However, with York having great strength in the Welsh Marches, even this location was not considered safe, and mother and son soon fled to Scotland.

Scotland was at this point a realm enduring problems of its own. Its king was the 8-year-old James III, who had succeeded only a couple of months previously when his father, James II, was killed by an exploding cannon at the siege of Roxburgh. As a minor James could not govern in person; his mother, Mary of Guelders, was acting as his regent. The similarity in their situations – mothers acting on behalf of their sons in the absence of their husbands – gave Margaret and Mary something in common and the welcome in Scotland was friendly. Edward and James were of a similar age and as it happened they were distantly related; the late James II's mother had been a Beaufort, Joan, the sister of Margaret's long-standing ally and friend Edmund, duke of Somerset.

Negotiations took place between the two women, resulting in Margaret agreeing to cede the town of Berwick – long a bone of contention between the two realms – to Scotland in return for an army. To seal the deal, it was proposed that a marriage be arranged between Edward and Mary Stewart, King James's 6-year-old sister, although the wedding would not take place yet.

This is where the extent of Margaret's desperation becomes clear. She had no authority whatsoever to cede Berwick and she cannot possibly have imagined that this would be well received in England. However, the situation was such that she could only think in the short term; she had her army and it marched south wearing Edward's livery. However, this turned out to be another mistake, and one that would have serious and far-reaching consequences. As a Frenchwoman, it is possible that Margaret was not aware of the depth of hostility between England and Scotland – appearing in the north of England at the head of a ravening Scots army was counterproductive, to say the least, and could easily have been construed as treason. And on top of this Margaret had no ready cash with which to pay her new troops, so in lieu of wages she allowed them to take what they wanted while on the march and the Scots duly pillaged and ravaged their way south. Rumours of the horrors they inflicted flew ahead of them and became even more exaggerated in the telling.

Edward, of course, was with his mother on this march south, and the precarious balance of his position was tipped in his favour by an enormous stroke of luck: Richard, duke of York unwisely sallied out from Sandal castle and was killed at the Battle of Wakefield on 30 December 1460. However, Margaret once again did herself and Edward's cause no favours by mutilating the bodies of York, Salisbury and Rutland – a youth of just 17, let us not forget – after death, and then mocking York further with the paper crown. This smacked of nothing more than personal vindictiveness, which might have gone down well with her die-hard supporters such as the young duke of Somerset and earl of Northumberland, whose fathers had been killed by York at St Albans five years previously. However, it only served to antagonize others, and it certainly enraged Edward, earl of March and now duke of York.

At first Margaret and Edward's luck seemed to hold, despite the errors of judgement: after the Battle of Wakefield and its grisly aftermath they travelled south to find that Lancastrian forces had defeated Yorkists led by the earl of Warwick at St Albans (an encounter that came to be known as the Second Battle of St Albans, to differentiate it from the earlier engagement of 1455), and that King Henry had been released. Once again Edward was reunited with his father, though to a young boy already showing an interest in martial pursuits, the king must have cut a sorry figure when compared to the bellicose companions he had become used to in the army. Perhaps he wondered why and how Henry, revered in his position as the anointed king, could be so different from the battle-hardened men around him. Edward would, as the subsequent evidence shows, model himself more on the latter than the former.

Edward was still only 7, but in the absence of a viable kingly figure, he needed to be brought to the fore of the campaign, to show that the Lancastrians had a bright future. This had both positive and negative immediate consequences for him: he was knighted, a great honour, and then in turn knighted those who had distinguished themselves in battle … and then he pronounced the judgement on his defeated foes that led to their execution. It is possible that he even had to watch as the sentences were carried out, a mentally scarring experience for such a young child.

And it was at this point that Edward and Margaret's luck ran out. They could move no further towards London, which had declared for Edward of York, mainly because the citizens had been frightened – with good reason – by tales of the ravaging of Margaret's army on its way south from Scotland. Her tactics had worked against her. They were forced to flee back north while Edward of York entered London as its saviour and was proclaimed king.

Edward IV, as he now was, needed to go on the offensive: there could not be two kings in England. He followed Margaret and Edward – and Henry, who was being dragged around with them – north to Yorkshire. The two armies met at Towton, where the differences between the kingly candidates became horribly apparent: Edward, aged 19 and a virile giant of a man, led his own forces from the front, while the Lancastrian royal family were obliged to leave the fighting to others as they were too infirm, too female and too young to take part. They stayed 10 miles away in York – where the heads of the duke of York and the earls of Salisbury and Rutland still adorned Micklegate Bar – and were still there when they heard news of the catastrophic defeat on 29 March 1461 at the Battle of Towton.[7] Flight was once again the only option, and Scotland the only immediately viable destination: they sped northwards, 'full of sorrow and heaviness, no wonder'.[8]

Edward IV's first parliament was held in the autumn of 1461, and both Margaret and Edward were attainted, meaning that they were now the penniless outlaws that York had been just a year previously. Fortune's wheel was turning very fast indeed. King Edward, meanwhile, made it plain that he was not claiming to be king by right of conquest or by usurping Henry VI, but rather through his and his father's Mortimer/Clarence heritage:

> To the which Edmund [Mortimer], after the decease of the said King Richard, the right and title of the same crown and lordship, then by law, custom and conscience, descended and belonged; and of right belongs at this time unto our said Liege and Sovereign Lord King Edward the fourth […] Our said Sovereign and Liege Lord King Edward the fourth […] after the decease of the said right noble and famous Richard duke of York his father […] *took upon him to use his right and title* to the said realm of England.[9]

The wording of the declaration thus implied that Edward's was not a new claim to the crown; it had always been there and he was only now asserting his right to it. This, of course, had the knock-on effect of making young Edward of Lancaster's position worse. He was not the lawful heir overthrown, but merely the scion of a usurping dynasty that never had a right to the throne at all.

Edward, who turned 8 in the October of 1461 while all this was going on, had endured more – and more extreme – changes of fortune than many people might expect in a lifetime. And his hugely unstable upbringing continued apace: after a further year it was deemed that even Scotland was not safe, so he and Margaret sailed for Flanders. Henry VI returned to England; his supporters were defeated at Hedgeley Moor and Hexham in the spring of 1464 and he was captured and brought to London the following year, to be lodged in the Tower. This time there was no question of his being treated with royal dignity, as he had been in 1455: his feet were tied to his stirrups.[10] Indeed, his son Edward of Lancaster's existence was probably the only reason Henry was still alive; there would be no point in killing him if the only effect were to transfer the claims of the Lancastrians from a sad and pathetic invalid to an energetic and growing son.

Edward and Margaret arrived at the court of the duke of Burgundy 'poor and alone, destitute of goods and all desolate; [having] neither credence, nor money, nor goods, nor jewels to pledge'.[11] The duke, although unwilling to take up arms on their behalf, provided enough money to enable them to travel to join Margaret's father, René of Anjou, who was in Lorraine. From 1463 to 1470 – that is, from the ages of 9 to 16 – Edward lived at his grandfather's castle of Koeur, in north-eastern France, about 80 miles east of Reims, along with other exiled Lancastrians. The alliance with Scotland having come to nothing, there were various attempts at marriage negotiations on Edward's behalf, including one to Margaret, daughter of the French king Louis XI,[12] but with the situation in England still not clear the proposals fell through.

Once again we have very little information on Edward's day-to-day upbringing, but Margaret no doubt reminded him frequently of his lineage and his rights, and his education would have been geared towards the recovery of them: a mixture of academic and martial pursuits, but with the emphasis very much on the latter. We do have a couple of brief snapshots of Edward during these years and they seem to imply that (perhaps unsurprisingly, given the violence and uncertainty he had known throughout his life) he was growing up into a damaged young man. In 1467 a contemporary noted of him that 'this boy, though only thirteen years of age, already talks of nothing but cutting off heads or making war';[13] another wrote that 'as soon as he became grown up, [Edward] gave himself over entirely to martial exercises; and, seated on fierce and half-tamed steeds urged on by his spurs, he often delighted in attacking and assaulting the young companions attending him'.[14]

Edward might have stayed in north-eastern France, the prince of a court in exile, forever, but his position changed dramatically once more early in 1470. As it happened, this was none of his doing, nor that of his mother, but rather another arbitrary turn of Fortune's wheel. Edward IV had now been on the English throne for some nine years without challenge from the house of Lancaster, but he had managed to alienate his greatest supporter, his cousin Richard Neville, earl of Warwick. The reasons for this are complex and we will not go into them in any great detail here, except to note that one of the primary causes was King Edward's unorthodox marriage.

Edward had married in May 1464, in total secrecy, Elizabeth Woodville. She was unsuitable in the extreme: the daughter of Richard Woodville, a member of the minor gentry; the widow of Sir John Grey, who had been killed fighting for the Lancastrians at St Albans in 1461; the mother of two young sons; and five years older than Edward.[15] Like his distant relative the Black Prince, Edward had chosen to marry for affection rather than politics, but he, unlike the earlier Edward, was not in the position of being able to get away with it. His royal dynasty was very new, and his own position could still be classed as unstable – with a deposed but crowned and anointed king in his custody and a deposed king's son over the Channel – so it was incumbent upon him to find a bride who would bring diplomatic advantage. Indeed, Edward knew very well that such a match was not the right thing to do, which is why 'this marriage was kept full secretly long and many a day, that no man knew it'.[16] During four months of concealment Edward had allowed Warwick to go ahead with marriage negotiations with France, only revealing the truth in August when it became absolutely unavoidable. This, naturally, made Warwick look a fool, and it also damaged his standing as the king's most trusted advisor: how trusted could he be if he was not let into such an important secret? And to add to Warwick's travails, the new queen came complete with a huge family – not only her two sons, but also five brothers and seven unmarried sisters – who all needed to be provided for. The Woodvilles were married off to every heir and heiress available (the most egregious of these matches being the wedding in 1465 of the 19-year-old John Woodville to the dowager Duchess of Norfolk, then in her late sixties, which put all her estates and riches into his hands), and the male members of the family, particularly Elizabeth's father and her eldest brother Anthony Woodville, gained increasing influence over the king, to Warwick's detriment. Neither Warwick nor the king's mother, Cecily, dowager duchess of York, was present at the new queen's coronation when she was eventually brought to court, and the breach seemed irreconcilable.

The earl of Warwick first turned his attentions away from Edward and towards his next surviving brother, George, by now duke of Clarence; Warwick arranged for Clarence to be married to the elder of his two daughters, Isabelle Neville.[17] Clarence was at this time Edward IV's male heir: Edward and his queen had three daughters but no sons. This potentially put Warwick in a position of great influence, especially given that Clarence was much more easily manipulated than his brother. An uprising in Clarence's name, with the publicized intention of ridding the king's circle of the Woodvilles, took place in 1469; it resulted in the execution, at Warwick's order, of the queen's father and her brother John. However, enthusiasm for Clarence was generally weak and the alliance proved unsatisfactory for the earl, so eventually he took the momentous step of changing sides completely; he sailed to France and threw himself at the feet (literally; she kept him on his knees for quarter of an hour) of Margaret of Anjou.

Margaret's history with Warwick clearly made it difficult for them to be reconciled. To put it in its simplest terms, he had been responsible for deposing her husband and disinheriting her son, while she had been responsible for executing his father and putting his head on a spike. However, this was the best hope she had had in years of being able to make another push for the throne she saw as rightfully Edward's, so she pragmatically came to the conclusion that the enemy of her enemy, if not her friend, could at least be a useful ally. An agreement was reached whereby Edward would marry Warwick's younger daughter, Anne; in return, Warwick would fight for them and attempt to return the Lancastrian dynasty to power. If this succeeded, his own influence would be increased: to be the father-in-law of Edward of Lancaster would gain him more than to be the cousin of Edward of York.

The betrothal of Edward and Anne took place just a few days after the meeting, and Warwick sailed back to England leaving his daughter in Margaret's charge. Margaret, meanwhile, was still unwilling to risk the safety of her one and only precious son: Edward would not travel to England with Warwick, but would only embark *after* Warwick had made good his promises. It is unclear to what extent Edward might have agreed with this decision: he was now 16 and if he really had been talking 'of nothing but cutting off heads' for years, he might not have appreciated being coddled by his mother in such a way. But at this stage it is clear that she remained the one in charge.

Edward was thus still a pawn, and one who was in danger of being pulled several ways. A chronicler believed that, by marrying his daughters to Clarence and Edward, Warwick was seeking to play them off against each other:

> That the marriage of the prince should ever be a blot in the duke's eye, or the marriage of the duke a mote in the eye of the prince [...] each of them looking to be exalted, when the earl on him smiled, and each of them again thinking to be overthrown, when the earl of him lowered.[18]

Warwick now had a son-in-law of York and a son-in-law of Lancaster, hedging his bets; this was probably the best position he could hope for given that he had no sons and no royal blood to make a claim in his own name. As he left Margaret, however, it was certainly Lancaster that stood higher with him, and he even seemed to think that Clarence would go along with his plan. Warwick swore that he 'should never leave the war, until such time as King Henry the sixth, or the prince his son, were restored to the full possession and diadem of the realm', adding the not inconsequential proviso that

> The queen and the prince should dispute and appoint the duke [Clarence] and the earl [Warwick] to be governors and conservators of the public wealth till such time as the prince were come to man's estate to take upon him so high a charge and so great a burden.[19]

Edward and Margaret waited. And good news soon came from England: Warwick and Clarence had Edward IV on the run and in October 1470 the king fled to Holland. His pregnant queen, Elizabeth Woodville, sought sanctuary at Westminster Abbey with her three young daughters. Edward IV had no son to complicate matters; his brother and nominal heir George, duke of Clarence was in the Lancastrian camp and his only other surviving brother, the 17-year-old Richard, duke of Gloucester, was with him in exile. Warwick was, against all the odds, successful, so Edward and his mother could make plans to travel.

Fortune's wheel had lurched once more and Edward of Lancaster, without raising a hand, was again heir to the throne: more, indeed, for he would in name at least be his father's regent. Quite how he would have managed this with both his mother and his father-in-law trying to control him remained to be seen, but he was nevertheless in the best position he had been in for a decade. He now had to make good on his side of the agreement: in December 1470 the 17-year-old Edward was married to the 14-year-old Anne Neville, whose own feelings on the match are not recorded.

Over in England, a bemused King Henry was brought out of the Tower, where he had remained since his capture in 1465; he was paraded through the streets, the sorry spectacle only serving to confirm that he was merely a figurehead and that others would rule for and through him. But if real power was invested in the king's son, how was that any different to previous episodes in royal history? Such an arrangement could be seen as a return to something approaching normality. Part of the attraction of having Edward IV as king, for many nobles, citizens and traders, was the fact that he could bring stability as he was a much healthier and more determined man than Henry VI and thus a better king. But if Edward of Lancaster could provide the same, this cut away some of Edward IV's advantage, and the residual sympathy that Henry had always attracted began to resurface; to the general populace, he was the real king. After all, he had been on the throne for nearly five decades, and the Lancastrian dynasty in possession of it for seven; there could be few people alive who remembered otherwise.

Finally, in the spring of 1471, Edward and Margaret and their army sailed for England. But, unknown to them, Edward IV was not finished. He had begun regrouping almost as soon as he reached Holland and had himself embarked for England shortly before they did. He landed at Ravenspur on the Humber on 14 March, ten days before Edward and Margaret embarked and before any news of it could reach them. They were delayed by contrary winds, and it was not until 14 April that they landed at Weymouth. And it was on that very day – Easter Sunday, as it happened – that a great battle was fought at Barnet, north of London, between two pairs of brothers, the resurgent Edward IV and Richard of Gloucester facing off against the earl of Warwick and his brother John Neville, the marquis of Montagu. The result was decisive: both Nevilles were killed and the hapless Henry VI, captured once more, was returned to the Tower.[20]

News reached Edward and Margaret. There was at first some thought that they might turn round and sail away again, Margaret's first concern as ever being for Edward's safety. One chronicler depicts a conversation to that effect between her and the duke of Somerset, in which 'she allowed his counsel well, if so that she only might be in danger, and not her son'; 'fearing that when they fought most earnestly for their country, her son might be destroyed or cast away', she 'thought best either to put off and defer the battle to another time, or else to send her son into France'.[21] Of Edward's own opinion we hear nothing, but for a bellicose young man who had lived his whole life in expectation of this moment, the thought of turning tail must have been galling. Whoever it was that made the final decision, they would stay and fight it out.

Edward and Margaret's best chance was to head for Wales, where they could join forces with Jasper Tudor, still their ally; to this end they marched from Weymouth via Exeter and Bristol, but they had only reached Tewkesbury by 3 May when news reached them that the rampant Edward IV, fresh from his victory at Barnet and keen to wipe out the Lancastrian threat forever, had also marched, and he was encamped just 10 miles away at Cheltenham.

The choices were stark: engage in a pitched battle, or flee. Possibly Margaret's instincts were for the latter, and probably Edward's were for the former. His hour had come: he was 17, a knight, a prince, the son of a king and – in his own mind at least – the rightful heir to the throne. He had a force of around 6,000 men, including the earl of Devon, the duke of Somerset and Somerset's younger brother, the earl of Dorset. This, incidentally, was yet another duke of Somerset: Edmund, the 4th duke, the second son of Margaret's former ally Edmund, the 2nd duke. His elder brother Henry, who had inherited the title in 1455, had been captured and executed by John Neville, Lord Montagu, the earl of Warwick's brother, at the Battle of Hexham in 1464.

The men around Margaret had the final say; they would fight. And so, for almost the first time in his life Margaret had to let her beloved son out of her sight. She could not take the field so she bade him farewell and retired to a nearby religious house – an act she would regret bitterly for the rest of her life.

Edward was keen. He 'rode about the field, encouraging the soldiers, promising to them (if they did show themselves valiant against their enemies) great rewards and high promotions, innumerable gain of the spoil, and booty of their adversaries, and above all other fame and renown through the whole realm'.[22] As was customary, his army was divided into three divisions or 'battles'; that on the right would be commanded by Somerset, and the left by Devon, while Edward placed himself in command of the centre, just as his distant relative and namesake the Black Prince had done in different circumstances at a similar age. But Edward was not his great-great-great-uncle: the years of bullying his young companions at Koeur were not sufficient training for facing an enemy of the calibre of Edward IV.

The Battle of Tewkesbury, fought on 4 May 1471, was a disaster for the Lancastrian cause.[23] George, duke of Clarence, who had nominally been on Edward's side while the earl of Warwick was alive, had defected back to his brother several weeks previously; with Warwick dead, his interests would be better served by throwing himself on the mercy of his brother rather than relying on his wife's brother-in-law, who would see him as a threat. This deprived Edward of troops he might have expected, as did the death of Warwick himself. Meanwhile the Yorkist forces, led by Edward IV himself and his brother, the 18-year-old Richard, duke of Gloucester, were fresh from their triumph at Barnet and had the momentum with them. Edward's two closest advisors in the central part of the army both died on the field; accounts vary of what happened to Edward himself, but it is likely that he was fleeing for the tenuous safety of the town when he was killed – stories that he was captured and brought before Edward IV, proclaiming his defiance, and only then executed, are almost certainly a later invention. The most contemporary source is one written by a Yorkist adherent and eyewitness; it says that 'Edward, called prince' was 'put to discomfiture and flight' and 'was taken, fleeing towards the town, and slain in the field'.[24] His last moments were thus filled with the violence that had overshadowed his entire life.

The victorious Edward IV now sought to wipe out the last vestiges of the Lancastrian cause once and for all. Several of their lords had taken sanctuary in Tewkesbury Abbey, but he had them brought out and executed, including the duke of Somerset, whose one remaining younger brother, Dorset, had already died on the field. The wretched Henry VI, the sole surviving heir of Lancaster, was murdered as soon as King Edward returned to London.

Queen Margaret was captured a few days after the battle, 'almost dead for sorrow',[25] as well she might be after the crushing of all her hopes and dreams. King Edward could not get rid of her so easily – even in the context of the times the murder of a woman, a dowager queen, would have been beyond the pale – but he took his revenge for the death and humiliation of his father and younger brother by having her paraded through London in a cart as part of his victory procession. She was kept prisoner for several years, but following the death of her husband and especially that of her son, she was a broken woman. She was deemed no longer to be a threat and was returned into the custody of her cousin Louis XI in 1476, going on to live quietly until her death from natural causes in 1482. 'She passed her days in France more like death than life,' remarked one chronicler, 'languishing and mourning in continual sorrow, not so much for herself and her husband [...] but for the loss of Prince Edward her son.'[26]

Edward of Lancaster was buried in Tewkesbury Abbey. There was to be no grand tomb; a small plaque is all that marks his place of rest, itself not erected until much later. Even such an interment, however, might be seen as a concession: despite the mutilation of the bodies of his own father and brother by Margaret of Anjou, Edward IV declined to do the same to her son. He 'granted the corpses of the said Edward, and others so slain in the field, or elsewhere, to be buried there in church [...] without any quartering, or defouling their bodies'.[27]

And thus Edward of Lancaster's story ends. His was a tragic, wasted life, overshadowed by the conflict into which he was drawn from the moment of his birth. He would no doubt have made a stronger king than his father, but given his violent and unstable upbringing, the questions of how that 'strength' would have manifested itself, of how he would have ruled at a time of deep discord and revenge, are interesting ones. Would he have brought peace, or caused further war?

\*\*\*

The English royal line was now dangerously close to being extinguished. The legitimate Lancastrians were all dead. The bastard Beaufort line had also been all but wiped out;[28] the only survivors among them were Margaret Beaufort, daughter of John, 1st duke of Somerset, and her 14-year-old son by Edmund Tudor, Henry. Nobody thought them of any account; besides, the Lancastrian claim to the throne was based on the succession being in the male line only – as we have noted previously, the York claim was stronger if female inheritance were counted – so any claim of Margaret Beaufort, or of Henry Tudor through his mother, would be contradictory and self-defeating.

The Yorkists were almost as thin on the ground: Edward IV had two surviving brothers, neither of whom had children at this point, and three young daughters. But in one of its darkest moments the Yorkist dynasty had been blessed by a ray of light. While she was in sanctuary at Westminster Abbey during the king's exile, Edward's wife Elizabeth Woodville – uncertain from day to day whether she might be a queen or an outcast, a wife or a widow – had given birth to a son.

# Chapter 10

# Edward V, Edward of Middleham and Edward of Warwick

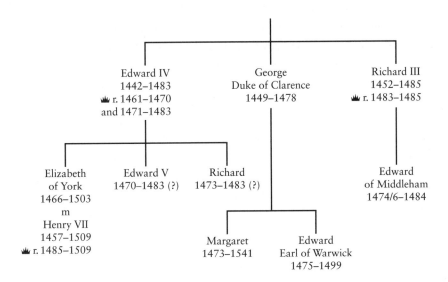

By the summer of 1471, that should have been that. Edward IV was once more secure on his throne; there were no rivals on the horizon; and he had a son and heir, the child who had been born in sanctuary in November 1470. The baby was named Edward after his father, and his future seemed assured. Life was good to the king; he ruled peacefully and unthreatened for another decade, his queen providing him with two more sons – Richard in August 1473 and George in 1477 – to ensure the succession. Sadly, George would die at the age of 2, but Edward was still left with a surviving family of two sons and six daughters, enough for any monarch. He also had two younger brothers who by the mid-1470s had a son each, so it was almost inconceivable that the house of York could be supplanted. However, the Middle Ages had one last upheaval in store for the crown and little Edward was to be at the centre of it.[1]

Edward was, as befitted his position, loaded with honours early. He was created prince of Wales and earl of Chester when he was just 7 months old; at the same time parliament took an oath to him as heir to the throne. A council was formed to oversee his affairs but, in a sign of things to come, it was headed by four individuals who did not get on particularly well: Edward's mother Queen Elizabeth; her eldest brother Anthony Woodville, by now earl Rivers; and the king's two brothers George, duke of Clarence and Richard, duke of Gloucester. In the first instance they were to rule over Edward's household and his estates until he reached the age of 14; it is not clear whether the intention was then to make a different arrangement or simply to declare the prince of full age, and we shall probably never know. One factor that was to be of crucial importance later on was that, although oversight of Edward's affairs was to be carried out by committee, his personal guardianship was entrusted to just one person, and that person was his maternal uncle, Anthony, earl Rivers. Rivers would be responsible for the prince's upbringing and education, and could exercise royal authority in his name. This was an unusual arrangement: normally such authority would have been vested in a man who was of royal blood himself, rather than a maternal relative. But the influence of the large Woodville family on the king was as strong as ever.

Edward and his infant brother Richard were made Knights of the Garter in May 1475, and Edward received further recognition of his status when he was named 'keeper of the realm' while Edward IV went abroad to France in June 1475 – this title was clearly honorific in nature, as he was just 4 at the time, but it showed where power was headed and it echoed the status held by the long-dead but still revered Black Prince.

In 1476, when he was approaching his sixth birthday, Edward and his household removed to Ludlow. This, of course, had been the scene of his grandfather's flight back in 1459, but it was also a pivotal stronghold in the Welsh Marches, one that had been in the family a long time and that was positioned to put a source of royal authority in the border region. In administrative terms such a relocation was a good idea, as Edward IV could not be everywhere at once; he was based mainly in London and the south, but with his son and heir in the west and his brother Richard of Gloucester in the north, he could maintain his authority through trusted lieutenants. However, this arrangement did have the knock-on effect that it removed little Edward completely from court, from his parents and from the king's family: he would be under the guardianship of Anthony Woodville for the formative years of his youth.

Edward was probably not much touched by the fall of his uncle George, duke of Clarence in 1478 – of which we will hear more later in this chapter – and he continued with his education regardless of wider family upheavals. Unusually, we do have some details of his day-to-day schedule, from the ordinances that were drawn up to regulate his household when it was formed. After rising he would hear Matins in his own chamber, followed by breakfast and Mass with the household. Lessons followed – 'such virtuous learning as his age shall now suffice to receive' – with other meals, 'disports and exercises' and periods of recreation all timetabled.[2] And while Edward was busy learning his lessons and practising his sword-drills, negotiations for his marriage were begun. Edward IV was not about to make the same mistake with his son that he had made himself; he would look for a foreign bride who would bring international political advantage. Various matches were proposed, including alliances with Spain, Milan and Burgundy, but the most serious candidate appears to have been Anne, heiress to the duchy of Brittany; a marriage treaty was drawn up in 1481 when the parties were aged 10 and 4.[3]

The peace of Edward's life in the Marches was shattered in April 1483 when his father died, suddenly and unexpectedly, just short of his forty-first birthday.[4] There was no question over who should succeed him, but problems were going to arise due to the new king's age. If Edward IV had lived to be 50 – not an unreasonable expectation – his heir would have been in his early twenties; if he had even managed to make his mid-forties then he could have left the throne to a king of 17 rather than a king of 12, a crucial difference. But his life of dissipation had taken its toll and England would reap the consequences: there would be another royal minority.

Edward was at Ludlow when the news reached him, and he was immediately hailed as Edward V. The fact that he is generally known as 'Edward V', and that he is included in the roll of English monarchs, demonstrates how the process of succession to the throne had developed over the centuries. During the Anglo-Norman and early Plantagenet periods, as we noted earlier, it was the coronation that was all-important, and an heir was not a king until the crown was put upon his head and until he was anointed. If 'being the eldest son of the previous incumbent' or 'being the designated and recognized heir' had been all that was necessary to accede, then England would have had a King Robert in 1087 and/or a Queen Matilda in 1135. But it did not. The first English monarch to be recognized as such before his coronation was Edward I, who was on crusade when his father died and who did not return to England until over a year later. It is a matter for debate as to whether he would still have been known as 'Edward I' if he had died in the intervening period, but the precedent of recognition and acclamation had been set, and certainly nobody else attempted to seize the opportunity of an absent heir to have himself crowned, as Henry I and Stephen had done in 1100 and 1135 respectively. By the late fifteenth century the double status of 'eldest son' and 'recognized heir' was enough to see young Edward called Edward V even though he had not been – and never would be – crowned.

Nobody in April 1483 could know that this would be the case, however, and arrangements for Edward's coronation were already in place when he heard of his father's death. He therefore set off from Ludlow to London, accompanied by his uncle earl Rivers and his half-brother Richard Grey, who was the younger of Elizabeth Woodville's two sons by her first marriage. Grey and his brother Thomas – who was in London with Elizabeth – were significantly older than Edward V, around 28 and 26 at this point; they were dangerous as, like the Tudor half-brothers of Henry VI, they had no prospects outside their uterine relationship to the king, so they might be expected to risk all for the chance of further gain.

It was at this juncture that the simmering resentment and conflict between the Woodvilles and the remaining royal Yorkist, Richard of Gloucester, became apparent. There was concern – not just from Gloucester but others as well – at how much influence the Woodvilles and Greys, parvenus of no royal blood, would wield in the new regime; and now here they were accompanying the new king as his principal advisors. Richard took the initiative straight away. He had been in the north when he heard the devastating news of his brother's death and he was also now on his way to London. He met up with his nephew's party at Stony Stratford in Buckinghamshire and immediately arrested both Rivers and Grey, claiming that they were plotting to seize power by force.[5] He had them taken to his own heartlands in Yorkshire, and announced he would escort Edward to London himself. 'And so' (says a deeply partisan later Tudor writer), 'the new king was separated from his loyal servants and was received like an innocent lamb into the hands of wolves.'[6]

Was Richard's suspicion justified? His action was precipitate, to be sure, but to a certain extent the answer to that question must be 'yes', as events in London demonstrate. Queen Elizabeth and her eldest son, Thomas Grey, marquis of Dorset, had been on the spot when the king died, so they had had more time to plan their next moves while the news was still galloping north and west. One way in which they did this was to seek to influence the royal council. A king's wishes were not legally binding after his death, but, knowing that Edward IV had on his deathbed added a codicil to his will designating his brother Richard as young Edward's protector, there were those who felt that this should be enacted; or, at the very least, that they should await Richard's arrival in London before discussing the matter further. However, Elizabeth and her faction dismissed this, with Dorset noting that 'we are so important, that even without the king's uncle we can make and enforce these decisions'.[7]

Meanwhile, in Stony Stratford, Richard had to face Edward in person to tell him why he had dismissed his closest advisors. He went through his reasons: such men had encouraged Edward IV in a life of overindulgence, resulting in his early death; they might influence the son in the same way; they were conspiring against Richard and plotting his death; they wished to overturn the wishes of the late king, who had wanted Richard to act for young Edward. He was met with a robust response:

> The youth, possessing the likeness of his father's noble spirit besides talent and remarkable learning, replied to this saying that he merely had those ministers whom his father had given him; and relying on his father's prudence, he believed that good and faithful ones had been given him. He had seen nothing evil in them and wished to keep them unless they otherwise proved to be evil. As for the government of the realm, he had complete confidence in the peers of the realm and the queen.[8]

There are two possible interpretations of this: either that Edward saw that Richard was lying, believed that Richard was acting in his own interest and wanted to warn Richard off; or that Richard was in fact correct, and that Edward was already so far under the thumb of the Woodville faction that extricating him would be very difficult. In either case, it appears that Richard had underestimated his nephew, and this might have very serious ramifications. Even if he now succeeded in entering into a regency for Edward, it would only last four or five short years – or not even that, if the original intention had been to declare Edward of full age when he reached 14 – and then the king would be his own man; he could re-invite anyone he liked to advise him, and he might want or encourage retribution. And in the meantime, even if they were formally excluded from power, the Woodville faction – Edward's mother, half-brothers and uncles – could expect to exert great influence over him informally. He knew them better than he knew Richard, who had been in the north for much of Edward's life while Edward had been based at Ludlow. And the Woodvilles would know how best to benefit from such influence.

When news reached the capital that Edward was approaching accompanied by Richard rather than by his Woodville relatives, Elizabeth Woodville and her eldest son Thomas took more direct action. There was no attempt at negotiation; they went straight in for the attack and tried to prepare for armed conflict. However, they did not get the response that they wanted:

> When they had exhorted certain nobles who had come to the city, and others, to take up arms, they perceived that men's minds were not only irresolute, but altogether hostile to themselves. Some even said openly that it was more just and profitable that the youthful sovereign should be with his paternal uncle than with his maternal uncles and uterine brothers.[9]

The power grab by the extended Woodville clan during the best part of the last two decades had been noted and they were not exactly popular. Seeing that this tactic would not work, Elizabeth fled into sanctuary at Westminster – where young Edward had been born twelve years earlier – with Dorset, her daughters and her youngest son, Richard, who was of course now heir presumptive to the throne. Richard, aged 9, had led a life separate from that of his brother Edward, but he was no less a pawn in the dynastic game. He was by this time a widower: he had been married at the age of 5 to the 4-year-old Anne Mowbray, sole heiress of the late duke of Norfolk, becoming duke of Norfolk, earl Warenne and earl of Nottingham to add to his existing title, duke of York, before he was even out of the royal nursery. Anne had died two years later, leaving Richard free to be used on the marriage market once more. At this point his value in the game of thrones was incalculable, as long as he could be kept apart from his brother Edward, and under Woodville control.

Edward and his uncle reached London on 4 May 1483. This was the date originally scheduled for the coronation, but planning it for just three weeks after Edward IV's death had always been ambitious, given the time taken for the news to reach the young king and for him to travel. It would need to be rescheduled. In the meantime, Richard of Gloucester was duly named protector during Edward's minority – an unremarkable appointment in the general scheme of things, for paternal royal uncles had done this before (John of Gaunt for Richard II; John, duke of Bedford for Henry VI); and if there was to be a protector at all he needed to be an adult man of the royal line, leaving Richard as the only possible candidate.

The coronation was now set for 22 June, and Edward was lodged in the Tower to await it. We should note at this point that this was an entirely normal course of events: there were royal apartments in the Tower, and it was where kings generally resided before their coronations as the procession to Westminster Abbey started from there. However, Edward must have been worried, or at least perplexed, by the fact that his mother and siblings were cowering in sanctuary rather than coming to meet and welcome him.

Events then moved very swiftly, perhaps too swiftly for a bemused, bereaved and pressured young boy to understand what was happening. In short, Richard of Gloucester appears to have taken leave of his senses. Perhaps he realized that he had made a mistake in arresting Rivers and Grey, and in underestimating Edward; perhaps he panicked and cast about him for a way to bolster his position; perhaps he had been planning it all along. On 10 June he wrote to his adherents in the north asking for reinforcements, and three days later he arrested a number of the late Edward IV's leading allies, going so far as to execute one of them immediately, without charge or trial.

On 16 June the move was made that would turn out to be crucial. The elderly archbishop of Canterbury, Cardinal Bourchier, was sent to persuade Elizabeth Woodville to release her youngest son Richard from sanctuary so that he could join his brother in the Tower. According to a (later, Tudor) chronicler he made several arguments in favour of the proposition: 'Her keeping of the king's brother in that place highly sounded, not only to the grudge of the people [...] but also to the grief and displeasure of the king's royal majesty, to whose grace it were a singular comfort to have his natural brother in company.'[10] Even the more neutral Mancini mentions the pressure brought to bear on the queen: 'He [Cardinal Bourchier] said that, since this boy was held against his will in sanctuary, he should be liberated, because the sanctuary had been founded by their ancestors as a place of refuge, not of detention, and this boy wanted to be with his brother.'[11] Whether or not the archbishop spoke in good faith (and there is no reason to suppose he did not) and whether it was the guilt trip or the implicit threat of force that did the trick, Elizabeth complied: Richard left Westminster Abbey and was taken to join Edward at the royal apartments in the Tower.

This, of course, was a tactical error of huge proportions – not to mention the catalyst for personal tragedy – though we may understand and sympathize that Elizabeth was hardly in a position to think straight. It is also unlikely that young Richard himself fully understood what was going on; perhaps he was keen to leave the boredom and confinement of holy sanctuary to stay with his brother and have the opportunity to run about in the fresh air. This is necessarily speculation, but during the early part of the summer both boys were seen playing and practising their archery in the Tower grounds, unaware that their fate was sealed. The only reason Henry VI had been kept alive in the Tower all those years was that his son and heir was at large and apart from him; harming Henry would just pass the royal claim on to someone who was less easily controlled. By the same token, the best way to protect Edward was to keep his brother apart from him and under strict supervision. But now they were together and, ominously, another royal child was rounded up: 'Gloucester gave orders that the son of the duke of Clarence, his other brother, then a boy of ten [*sic*] years old, should come to the city; and commanded that the lad should be kept in confinement in the household of his wife, the child's maternal aunt.'[12]

Once Edward and Richard were together, on 16 June, the coronation was postponed again, this time until November. After that the momentum was definite; business carried out under the name of Edward V began to tail off. And then, on 22 June, came the bombshell that was to seal Edward's fate: he was not the king at all.

That, at least, was the information put about by Richard of Gloucester, in a two-pronged attack on Edward's position. The first rumour was that Edward IV had been illegitimate; he was not the son of the duke of York at all. Such gossip had already been spread about him in the 1470s, when the earl of Warwick and the duke of Clarence had been trying to discredit him – but such gossip had also been heard about virtually every royal prince who had been born abroad. Promulgating it now was probably not much use, firstly as it was old news, and secondly as it put Richard in the difficult position of publicly insulting his (still very much alive) mother, by claiming that she had committed adultery.[13] But conveniently, at exactly this time it was additionally 'discovered' that Edward IV had never been legally married to Elizabeth Woodville and that therefore all their children were bastards who had no claim to the throne.

The reasons for this were, as it happened, frighteningly plausible. It was a matter of common knowledge that Edward IV had been a serial womanizer – he had the mistresses and the acknowledged illegitimate children to prove it – and it was also a matter of public record that he had married Elizabeth Woodville in secret, not revealing the fact until several months later. The reason for the marriage, given its complete lack of political advantage, was therefore assumed to be personal: Elizabeth would not have sexual relations with him unless they were married and she had got her way. However, it was now claimed (by the bishop of Bath and Wells, among others), that Edward had in fact entered into a similar arrangement with another woman *before* he had married Elizabeth – something that was all too easily believed, given his reputation – and therefore his marriage to Elizabeth was bigamous and their children were illegitimate. And illegitimate children had no right to the throne.

The timing of this revelation was, of course, stupendously convenient. And although coincidence can never quite be discounted, it does seem as though the discovery was a political expedient for Richard of Gloucester. And once the 'secret' was out in the open, events moved very quickly indeed. On 22 June a public sermon was preached to spread the news and to remind the public that bastards could not inherit. It was reiterated that the attainder passed on the late duke of Clarence extended to his heirs as well (otherwise his son and daughter would take precedence over Richard in the hereditary queue, a point to which we will return later in this chapter). The crown was therefore offered to Richard, and on 26 June he sat down in the king's seat at Westminster – the same one that his father had touched but never taken back in 1460 – and was proclaimed Richard III.

Young Edward could do nothing about any of this except to watch his whole world collapsing around him. The blows continued to fall:

any lingering hope he might have entertained that this was all a bad dream and that his uncle could be stopped were extinguished on 6 July when Richard and his wife Anne were crowned king and queen.[14] News may also have reached him at around this time that his uncle Anthony Woodville, earl Rivers, and his half-brother Richard Grey had both been executed in Yorkshire on 25 June. If he had not previously been afraid for his personal safety, he must have started to fear by now.

In late July an attempt was made to rescue Edward and Richard from the Tower, but it was unsuccessful. The only culprits named publicly were men of low standing, but it is reasonable to assume that someone of greater status may have been behind it. From that point on, sightings of the two boys grew less and less frequent: they stopped running around in the grounds and stayed inside; they appeared only behind barred windows; and then they appeared no more. By September, those who opposed Richard III had begun to coalesce around the unlikely figure of Henry Tudor, which suggests that Edward and Richard were dead, or at least that people thought them so.

\*\*\*

So, what happened? Over the centuries there has been plenty of speculation about the fate of the boys who became known as 'the princes in the Tower', but nothing has ever been substantiated. However, lest it be a disappointment to readers of this book to have come this far and not find any possible explanation, we will add to the conjecture. It is the opinion of this author that Edward and Richard were murdered; that this happened sometime in the late summer or autumn of 1483; that the murders were carried out on the orders of Richard III; and that Richard was motivated by fear – that this had not been his original plan, but that he had worked himself into a position where it ended up appearing the only possible option.

Richard of Gloucester had been his brother Edward's most loyal lieutenant. He had shared all the ups and downs of the reign – the triumphs in battle and the periods of exile – and never once let the king down. He would, perhaps, have extended the same loyalty to his brother's son if circumstances had been different. However, the situation was complicated by the Woodvilles: they had exerted a great deal of influence over Edward IV – malign influence, as far as Richard was concerned – and had the potential to exert even more over Edward V. The child had been in the care of Anthony Woodville, earl Rivers, since as long as he could remember, and who could say that Rivers was not drip-feeding him positive information about his own family and negative propaganda against Richard? The Woodville clan had for many years been increasing their riches and influence, but they did not completely control Edward IV; however, his sudden death gave them the opportunity to pull all of Edward V's strings and to rule England for their own benefit. Only one person stood in their way, and he was Richard of Gloucester. It was not only that he would seek to look out for Plantagenet interests; it was also that the lords and the general population would expect him to do so and would see this as natural – the only surviving brother of the late king and the only adult royal male. The scene was thus set for rivalry, but the stakes were so high that nothing less than the extermination of one party by the other would settle the matter. And this is where – again in the opinion of this author – the fear came in.

At the age of 7, Richard had stood with his mother and brother George at Ludlow, alone and facing the oncoming might of the royal army while his father, older brothers, uncle and cousin had got away. The potential existed for him to be attacked by armed men – executed, cut to pieces, whatever his child's imagination could come up with. And although he did survive, it is possible that the sheer, eye-watering terror of that day had never left him. Now he was a grown man who could fight his own battles, but he also had a son, Edward, who was around the same age that Richard had been on that fateful day. If the Woodvilles wanted rid of Richard, they would need to eliminate his heir as well. The thought of little Edward standing alone at Middleham while a murderous Woodville force approached might just have been too much for Richard, and might have caused him to panic, thus leading him down his eventual path. Fortunately, not many of us will ever be faced with the question, but if it came to a direct choice of murdering your nephew or allowing someone else to murder your son, what would you do?

Richard may not have originally intended to seize the throne. He might have thought that if he could only separate Edward V from his Woodville advisors, they could all get back on an even keel, and Edward would rule with the guidance of his paternal uncle. But Richard had completely underestimated both the character of his nephew and the influence to which he had already been subjected: to all intents and purposes, Edward was not a Plantagenet but a Woodville.

This being the case Richard had, by arresting Rivers and Grey, put himself in an impossible position: as soon as Edward was of age he would release them and retaliate, potentially costing Richard not only his own life but that of his son as well. This led to the next step: like his father before him, he could never consider himself safe while he was at the mercy of a king who would listen to his enemies, and, *ergo*, the only way he could be safe was to take the crown himself. This led to him taking drastic steps, ones that could not be retraced.[15]

The first of these was to postpone the coronation. Although Edward had been acclaimed as 'Edward V', he could still be considered only as a contender for the throne, and therefore one who might have a rival; once he was crowned and anointed it would be a different matter. Then Richard had to find a reason why Edward was not the legitimate king – and why Richard was. And finally, he had to have the crown put on his own head.

All this was achieved with almost extraordinary ease, and after his coronation on 6 July 1483 King Richard III could congratulate himself on his success. But he had one final problem: what to do with Edward and his brother? This is the point at which our guesswork necessarily becomes even more speculative, but we will plough on. Richard never produced the boys alive to counter rumours that they were dead – but equally he never produced them dead to counter rumours that they were still alive. This latter would have helped to quell any uprisings in their name (Henry VI's body, for example, had been displayed after he died for exactly that reason) but it would have confirmed beyond doubt that he was responsible for their deaths. The line between childhood and adulthood was not completely fixed in this era, particularly when it came to royalty, but it seems that it was drawn somewhere between the death of a 17-year-old in battle (such as those of Edmund of Rutland or Edward of Lancaster, which were uncomfortable but more or less palatable) and that of a 12-year-old in a darkened room.

Richard's major problem was that young Edward was guilty of no personal sin. The previous English kings who had been deposed – Edward II, Richard II and Henry VI – had all been accused of tyranny, misrule or (at the very least) incompetence so serious that it endangered the realm; thus their deposers suffered no ill consequences from demonstrating that they were dead. Indeed, it was to their advantage not to have pretenders springing up everywhere. The situation was very different for Richard III, and he was going to be damned either way: if he demonstrated that the boys were dead, then much propaganda would be made of him as child murderer; but if he did not, then he would be exposed to repeated uprisings in their name.

Richard had personal experience of the chaos into which a realm could descend when there were two living kings; he had been forced to flee overseas along with his brother King Edward when Henry VI was taken out of the Tower back in 1470. And Henry had only been lodged there because nobody wanted to kill him. The only viable solution to such a situation was a permanent one, and it was not going to happen by itself. If Edward V had been on his own it might just have been possible to get away with a proclamation of death by natural causes, but the sudden demise of both brothers – for there was no use getting rid of one without the other – would stretch credulity too far. Measures would need to be taken, although exactly how reluctant the king was to take them must forever be shrouded in mystery.

It is likely, then, that Edward and Richard died in the Tower in the late summer or autumn of 1483, at the respective ages of 12 or 13 and 10.[16] In all this talk of politics and crowns, it is easy to overlook the fact that at the centre of it all was a terrified pre-teen; a child. This must have been a time of unbearable stress and anguish for Edward. He had studied history, and he knew what happened to deposed kings. His father was dead; his uncle Rivers, the guardian he had known all his life, was dead; who was there to help him? He was imprisoned and afraid, and perhaps also bearing the additional burden of trying to keep up the spirits of his even younger brother, to keep the worst from him.

The very last contemporary account we have of Edward, that of his personal doctor (who told it to Dominic Mancini), indicates that Edward knew, or at least suspected, the fate intended for him:

> The physician Argentine, the last of his attendants whose services the king enjoyed, reported that the young king, like a victim prepared for sacrifice, sought remission for his sins by daily confession and penance, because he believed that death was facing him.[17]

It would appear that he was right.

\*\*\*

With Richard III now on the throne, England had a new royal heir: his only son Edward, known as Edward of Middleham after the place of his birth.

Very little is known about him: uniquely, for a prince of Wales, we do not even have his date of birth, which might have been in either 1474 or 1476.

As we noted above, it may be that many or most of Richard's actions were as much for his son as for himself, and once he was crowned he wasted no time in promoting Edward's claims. Naturally his wish was to be succeeded by his son, but he was well aware that wishes were not enough; promises made to a king to support his designated heir could be ignored, and indeed had been as long ago as 1135 – when Henry I's wish to pass the crown to his daughter Matilda was disregarded – and as recently as the previous year, as Richard himself could attest.

Edward was therefore created prince of Wales in August 1483, when he was aged somewhere between 7 and 9. The lords of England 'pledg[ed] their allegiance to Edward, King Richard III's only son, as their supreme lord, if anything should happen to his father',[18] and plans were drawn up for a formal investiture at York, where Richard's support was strongest. This took place on 8 September at York Minster, the ceremony and banquet lasting more than four hours.[19] Edward then returned to Middleham, rather than accompanying his parents back to London; perhaps Richard's plan was to secure the north by installing the prince's household there, much as Edward IV had done in the west by placing his son at Ludlow. The parliament of February 1484 confirmed Edward as heir apparent to the throne.[20]

However, Richard's plans were to come crashing down only two months later:

> Soon afterwards it was made plain how fruitless are the plans of men when they wish to arrange their own affairs without God. The following April [1484], on a day close to the anniversary of King Edward IV's death, this only son on whom rested all hope of the royal succession, expressed in so many oaths, died in Middleham Castle after a brief illness. Then you would have seen both the father and the mother, when they received the news in Nottingham where they were staying, go almost out of their minds for a time with sudden grief.[21]

The pointed mention of the anniversary of Edward IV's death – and the implicit reminder of his sons – together with the idea of Richard acting 'without God', make it clear that for one contemporary at least this course of events was divine justice. But Richard and Anne's grief was real, all the more so as the loss was probably unexpected. Edward's death at an early age has led to speculation about his general health and he is often referred to as 'sickly', but there is no specific or contemporary evidence of this (no comment was made, for example, about Edward's fitness to withstand the gruelling four-hour investiture ceremony). The idea seems to have developed in hindsight, thus forming a circular argument: he died young, therefore he must have been sickly; he was sickly, therefore he died young. But children who were otherwise healthy could sicken and die with frightening rapidity, and Edward may have been one of these.

The loss of his son was not just a devastating personal blow for Richard; it was also a political disaster. He had fought, and possibly murdered, to get to the throne, and now he had no successor of his own blood at all. No English king had died childless since his namesake Richard II – and that situation certainly had not ended well.

Richard did not know it but his own time was also running out. Opposition to him had now strengthened the very dubious claim to the throne of Henry Tudor, who invaded, defeated and killed the king at the Battle of Bosworth in August 1485, and had himself crowned as Henry VII.[22]

***

Henry VII's claim to the English throne was tenuous in the extreme, so he needed to bolster it by any means possible. One of his first steps was to marry Elizabeth of York, the eldest daughter of Edward IV and Elizabeth Woodville, thus giving himself (and the heirs he planned to produce) some Yorkist credibility. However, there was one final Yorkist male further up the hereditary queue.

Edward, earl of Warwick, was the son of George, duke of Clarence and his wife Isabelle Neville; his grandfathers were Richard, duke of York and Richard Neville, earl of Warwick, the 'Kingmaker'. He had been born for greatness, but his position was severely weakened by the erratic behaviour of his father. George of Clarence had been a danger to everybody. He was handsome, wrote one contemporary, and 'he possessed such mastery of popular eloquence that nothing upon which he set his heart seemed difficult for him to achieve';[23] but despite his superficially appealing personality he had no political acumen at all. He had been just 12 when his brother ascended the throne, and he was recognized as the heir until Edward had children of his own; he had been loaded with estates and titles. Crucially, however, these had come to him through his brother's efforts and his bloody triumphs on the battlefield; George had not won them himself. This may have been one factor in his slightly overinflated sense of importance – in short, he expected everything to be handed to him on a plate.

Dissatisfied with Edward, George had joined Warwick in his rebellion and had been happy to spread the rumours about Edward being illegitimate – which of course meant that he, George, was the true king. However, this idea failed to gain much traction and Warwick, as we saw earlier, turned his attentions to the house of Lancaster. Once George realized that he would play second fiddle to Margaret of Anjou's son Edward, he defected back to his brother – and was, somewhat inexplicably, forgiven and restored. But he still resented his position and eventually rebelled once too often: he was attainted and convicted of treason. He was executed in February 1478, privately and by means unknown, although the gossip soon had it that he was drowned in a barrel of wine. His body was taken to Tewkesbury, where he was buried alongside his wife, who had died from childbirth complications fourteen months previously.[24]

Clarence left two orphaned children: Margaret, aged 4, and Edward, who was just shy of his third birthday. Edward's wardship and custody of his estates were granted to Thomas Grey, Elizabeth Woodville's eldest son. Despite his father's attainder he was still valuable; Clarence's own estates were forfeit and so could not be inherited, but the lands he held in right of his wife were not, so Edward was still earl of Warwick and heir to valuable properties via his Neville heritage.

Attainders could, of course, be reversed, depending on the prevailing political situation. Richard III had recognized this when he took Edward into his household during his own campaign for the crown: 'He feared that if the entire progeny of King Edward [IV] became extinct, yet this child, who was also of royal blood, would still embarrass him.'[25] However, this was custody rather than imprisonment: Edward and his sister Margaret were taken north to Sheriff Hutton Castle in Yorkshire, where they were lodged as befitted their status and their relationship to both the king and the queen.

When Richard's son Edward of Middleham died, he was short of an heir. However, he could not name Edward of Warwick: his own claim to the throne was predicated on the children of both his older brothers being barred from it, so to name Warwick as his heir might prompt the question of why Warwick was not king already.[26] Instead he went for a different option; there was no formal announcement but it was generally thought that he chose his nephew John de la Pole, the earl of Lincoln (the eldest son of Richard's sister Elizabeth, duchess of Suffolk), who was already at Sheriff Hutton acting as the guardian of Edward and Margaret.[27]

On Richard III's death at Bosworth in August 1485, Edward's position became very dangerous. He was the only surviving grandson in the male line of Richard, duke of York; he was the only survivor in the male line of Edmund of Langley, son of Edward III; he was also descended from Lionel of Antwerp, Edmund of Langley's older brother. Given that his paternal grandmother, Cecily Neville, was herself descended from John of Gaunt, it could even be argued that Edward combined the lines of York and Lancaster.[28] Moreover, an Act of Parliament supposedly passed during the readeption of Henry VI had vested the succession in the duke of Clarence and his heirs, should Henry VI's own line fail to continue.[29]

Richard III was safely dead, so Henry VII was spared fears of a further rebellion in the name of his predecessor, and his position was reinforced by a factor sometimes overlooked: such had been the rate of attrition during the Wars of the Roses that all the other potential claimants to the throne were children. He collected them all and placed them in the household of his formidable mother: Edward and Margaret, the children of Clarence; the five surviving daughters of Edward IV; and the 7-year-old duke of Buckingham who, as a descendant of Thomas of Woodstock, fifth and youngest son of Edward III, carried his own distant claim.[30] Henry then made his own position both more stable and more difficult by marrying Elizabeth, the eldest of Edward IV's daughters: more stable because he could now claim, in right of his wife, the most senior line of descent from Edward IV; and more difficult because he had to re-legitimize her to do so, thus putting his wife's claims below those of Edward V or his brother Richard, should they still be alive. This also had potential consequences for Edward of Warwick: if bastardy could be reversed, why not an attainder?

Henry was efficient. Edward IV's other daughters were now his in-laws and could be married off or given to the Church to keep them under control, as could young Edward's sister Margaret, who was married in 1487 to Henry's cousin, a man well below her own rank. Margaret, incidentally, would live a long life but would eventually fall victim to the monstrous and paranoid Henry VIII, who overturned many centuries of custom by showing no scruples over executing noblewomen, even if they were his mother's first cousin. Margaret had lived sensibly, managing her estates, raising a family and keeping out of trouble, but her adherence to the Catholic faith in the 1530s brought her to prominence again and perhaps reminded Henry that she carried a blood claim to his throne. She was imprisoned in the Tower without being convicted of any crime, kept there for two and a half years, and finally dragged out to be beheaded in 1541. She was 67 years old and the execution was carried out by a reserve headsman, 'a wretched and blundering youth [...] who literally hacked her head and shoulders to pieces in the most pitiful manner'.[31]

Henry VII's position improved with the birth of his own son and heir, Arthur, in 1486, but he still feared a Yorkist insurgency and in the same year the now 11-year-old Edward of Warwick was taken from household custody to be imprisoned in the Tower. Unlike his cousins he was not kept in comfortable royal lodgings; his confinement appears to have been harsh, as a later commentator noted that he was 'kept out of all company of men, and sight of beasts, in so much as he could not discern a goose from a capon'.[32]

In 1487 there was a bizarre episode. A young boy, Lambert Simnel, had been trained to impersonate Edward; he was proclaimed 'Edward VI' and banners were raised in his name. It was a strange thing to do, given that Henry could stop the insurrection in its tracks via one simple expedient, which he did: he commanded that 'Edward the young earl of Warwick should be brought from the Tower through the streets of London to the cathedral church of St Paul. This young gentleman (as he was commanded) show[ed] himself openly to everybody [...] having communication openly with many noble men.'[33] Edward himself was not implicated in the ill-conceived plot, so he survived – for now.

Henry might have thought himself safe as the years wore on, but a more serious threat occurred in 1494. Nobody had ever proved categorically that the princes in the Tower were dead, and now a young man appeared on the scene claiming to be Richard, duke of York and Edward V's younger brother. So far, so implausible, but the pretender had the not inconsiderable backing of Margaret, the dowager duchess of Burgundy – who also happened to be the sister of Edward IV and Richard III, therefore making her this young man's aunt, if he was who he said he was.

The claims were a thorn in Henry's side for several years, but eventually he won out; the young man was captured and he confessed to being a Fleming named Perkin Warbeck, and not Richard of York after all.[34] He was initially lodged at court, but after attempting to flee he was put in the Tower, where Edward of Warwick was still confined, having by now spent more than half his life there. Warbeck tried to escape from his prison in 1499, a plan in which Edward was (almost certainly wrongly) implicated. Warbeck was condemned to death and Henry took the opportunity to rid himself of the last male-line Yorkist heir at the same time. The Tudor historian Polydore Vergil was no friend to the Yorkist dynasty, but even he had sympathy for Edward by this point:

> Why indeed the unhappy boy should have been committed
> to prison not for any fault of his own but only because of
> his family's offences, why he was retained so long in prison,
> and what, lastly, the worthy youth could have done in prison
> which could merit his death [...] could not be comprehended
> by many.[35]

Like many of his forebears who have featured in this book, Edward was no personal threat and had committed no crime, but his blood represented danger to a suspicious king. So – again like many others – he had to die. On 28 November 1499 he was led from his cell at three o'clock in the afternoon and taken to Tower Hill. He was 24 years old and had been in custody since he was 8 and in prison since he was 11; his entire life had been wasted, and he may not even have been aware of what was happening as he stumbled to the block and laid down his head.

The blade rose; the blade fell; and the last of a long line of unfortunate medieval heirs was no more.

# Endnotes

**Chapter 1: Robert Curthose and William Clito**

1. It is perhaps surprising that the eldest son of William the Conqueror should be so little known, although this is no doubt due to the fact that he never became king. Robert is the subject of two notable scholarly biographies: see David, C.W., *Robert Curthose, Duke of Normandy* (Cambridge, MA: Harvard University Press, 1920); and Aird, W.M., *Robert Curthose, Duke of Normandy, c. 1050–1134* (Woodbridge: Boydell, 2008). See also Thompson, K., 'Robert [called Robert Curthose], duke of Normandy, b. after 1050, d. 1134', ODNB.
2. The question of Matilda's height has in the past been a vexed one, with her reported stature being as small as 4ft 2in. However, an examination of remains recovered from her tomb showed her to have been 5ft tall, not much under average height for a woman at the time. She survived at least nine pregnancies and childbirths, so must have enjoyed reasonable health. See Dewhurst, J., 'A Historical Obstetric Enigma: How Tall was Matilda?', *Journal of Obstetrics & Gynecology*, 1.4 (1981), pp. 271–2.
3. OV, vol. II, p. 357.
4. OV, vol. III, p. 97.
5. The nickname 'Rufus' means 'red', but may refer more to a ruddy complexion than red hair; see AB, p. 71; Barlow, F., *William Rufus* (Berkeley: University of California Press, 1983), pp. 11–12.
6. On this incident, see Aird, *Robert Curthose*, p. 87.
7. OV, vol. III, p. 111.
8. Thompson, 'Robert [called Robert Curthose]'.
9. The practice of noble families 'donating' one of their children to the Church was common at this time, with the children themselves generally having no say in the matter. However, once they had taken vows they were expected to become high-ranking members of

the clergy rather than simple monks and nuns, and would thus be considered at an equal social level to the lay nobility.

10. OV, vol. IV, p. 115.
11. A mark was 13*s* 4*d*, or two thirds of a pound; a pound in money literally meant a pound in weight, so this represented 6,667 lbs of silver in the form of 1.6 million silver pennies – a huge sum by contemporary standards.
12. HH, p. 42.
13. Wace, p. 200.
14. RCaen, p. 46.
15. WM, *Chron.*, p. 421.
16. See Morris, M., *A Great and Terrible King: Edward I and the Forging of Britain* (London: Windmill, 2009), p. 104.
17. Tinchebrai was in south-west Normandy, about 30 miles south-west of Falaise and on the border with the county of Mortain; the count of Mortain was one of the magnates loyal to Robert.
18. OV, vol. VI, p. 87.
19. For more on the Battle of Tinchebrai, see Bradbury, J., 'Battles in England and Normandy, 1066–1154', in Strickland, M. (ed.), *Anglo-Norman Warfare* (Woodbridge: Boydell, 1992), pp. 182–93; Morillo, S., *Warfare under the Anglo-Norman Kings, 1066–1135* (Woodbridge: Boydell, 1994), pp. 169–70.
20. OV, vol. VI, p. 93.
21. Robert's daughter's own name is not recorded, as is often the case at this time; the individual names and personalities of women, even noble ones, were of less interest to chroniclers than their dynastic role.
22. WM, *Chron.*, pp. 423 and 443.
23. OV, vol. VI, p. 287.
24. WM, *Chron.*, p. 423.
25. Aird, *Robert Curthose*, pp. 251–2. The Pipe Rolls are the records of the medieval English exchequer, so called because they were kept rolled up like pipes.
26. OV, vol. VI, p. 237.
27. For more on the Battle of Brémule, see Morillo, *Warfare under the Anglo-Norman Kings*, pp. 171–3; Strickland, M., 'Henry I and the Battle of the Two Kings: Brémule, 1119', in Crouch, D. and Thompson, K. (eds), *Normandy and its Neighbours, 900–1250* (Turnhout: Brepols, 2011), pp. 77–116.

28. Hollister, C.W., 'William Clito, 1102–1128', ODNB.
29. HH, p. 61.
30. OV, vol. VI, p. 377.
31. Wace, p. 207.
32. HH, p. 61.
33. OV, vol. VI, p. 359.
34. As translated in Aird, *Robert Curthose*, p. 275; originally published in *The Gentleman's Magazine*, vol. 64, in 1794.
35. OV, vol. IV, p. 115.

**Chapter 2: William Adelin and Empress Matilda**

1. On William, see principally Mason, J.F.A., 'William [William Ætheling, William Adelinus] (1103–1120)', ODNB.
2. WM, *Chron.*, p. 454.
3. For further details on this battle, see above p. 13.
4. OV, vol. VI, p. 241.
5. OV, vol. VI, p. 297.
6. The tales are recounted by Orderic Vitalis (OV, vol. VI, p. 298), and William of Malmesbury (WM, *Chron.*, p. 456). Modern historians tend to the view that they are apocryphal: see Hollister, C.W., *Henry I* (New Haven, Yale University Press, 2003), p. 278; King, E., *King Stephen* (New Haven: Yale University Press, 2012), p. 18; and Hanley, C., *Matilda: Empress, Queen, Warrior* (London: Yale University Press, 2019), p. 44.
7. Wace, p. 206.
8. Wace, p. 206; WM, *Chron.*, p. 456.
9. HH, p. 56.
10. The reasons for this remain unclear, but his nickname of 'the Simple' and a note from a contemporary that Adela 'wisely set aside her first-born because he was deficient in intelligence and seemed second rate' hint that he may have been disabled in some way that was not properly understood at the time.
11. Thanks to her fight for the English throne, we know more about Matilda than we do about many of her female contemporaries. Among other works, see Chibnall, M., *The Empress Matilda: Queen Consort, Queen Mother and Lady of the English* (Oxford: Wiley-Blackwell, 1991); Castor, H., *She-Wolves: The Women Who Ruled England before Elizabeth* (London: Faber and Faber, 2010),

pp. 35–126; Hanley, *Matilda*. Matilda also features strongly in the many books written about King Stephen and about the period known as 'the Anarchy', including Bradbury, J., *Stephen and Matilda: The Civil War of 1139–53* (Stroud: Sutton, 1996).

12. The word 'queen' is not – or at least was not at the time – appropriate for the position Matilda was seeking, for it meant simply 'the wife of the king' and did not imply ruling authority. For discussions on this point see Beem, C., *The Lioness Roared: The Problems of Female Rule in English History* (New York: Palgrave MacMillan, 2008), pp. 30–4 and 49–52; Castor, *She-Wolves*, p. 66; and Hanley, *Matilda*, pp. 145–6.
13. HH, p. 64.
14. This was discussed in Chapter 1; see above p. 8.
15. RW, vol. I, p. 483.
16. This has often been interpreted as simple stupidity by Stephen and therefore luck for Matilda, but she may actually have acted with great strategic insight: see Hanley, *Matilda*, pp. 114–17.
17. On the contemporary usage of the word 'queen', see note 12 in this chapter.
18. Titles in the Empire can be confusing, but in brief, the emperor was not officially emperor until he had been crowned by the pope in Rome; before that, he was either king of the Germans or king of the Romans (or both). Matilda had been crowned queen in Mainz in 1110, at the age of 8, before she ever went to Italy; the honour was sacred and lifelong, even though the husband from whom she derived the title had died.
19. GS, p. 113.
20. For more on the Battle of Lincoln (sometimes known as the First Battle of Lincoln, to differentiate it from a later engagement in 1217), see among others Bradbury, *Stephen and Matilda*, pp. 94–109; Beeler, J., *Warfare in England 1066–1189* (Ithaca: Cornell University Press, 1966), pp. 110–19.
21. HH, p. 81.
22. GS, p. 119.
23. GS, p. 121.
24. GS, p. 123.
25. WM, *Hist.*, p. 66.
26. AB, p. 79.
27. GS, p. 143.

28. WM, *Hist.*, p. 77.
29. GS, p. 145.
30. JW, p. 250.
31. Translation of the Peterborough manuscript, a continuation of the *Anglo-Saxon Chronicle*, available at http://omacl.org/Anglo/part7.html.

**Chapter 3: Eustace, William and Mary of Blois**

1. Very little has been written on Eustace personally, though he does appear in some of the many works on King Stephen and the period of the 'Anarchy'. The most complete information is in King, E., 'Eustace, count of Boulogne (c. 1129–1153)', ODNB.
2. HH, p. 73. Louis VII was the second son of Louis VI, but his elder brother had been killed in a fall from a horse as a young man; he left no children and thus catapulted the teenage Louis into a role for which he was not entirely suited.
3. See above, p. 29.
4. WM, *Hist.*, p. 57
5. HH, p. 87.
6. GS, p. 221.
7. GS, p. 219.
8. GS, p. 223.
9. Innocent II had died in 1143, to be succeeded by Celestine II in 1143, Lucius II in 1144 and Eugenius III in 1145.
10. JS, pp. 85–6.
11. HH, p. 88.
12. HH, p. 88.
13. GS, p. 239.
14. GS, p. 239.
15. GS, p. 239.
16. HH, p. 92.
17. RT, p. 73.
18. HH, p. 92.
19. Translation of the Peterborough manuscript, a continuation of the *Anglo-Saxon Chronicle*, available at http://omacl.org/Anglo/part7.html.
20. Contemporary writers did not tend to dwell on the lives of women, or certainly not their personal lives, but Constance had endured many

ups and downs as Eustace's wife, her status varying wildly from queen-in-waiting to prisoner in the Tower. Her second marriage does not seem to have been particularly serene, either. Raymond of Toulouse was involved in the crisis that led to the murderous Albigensian Crusade; Constance bore him four children before the marriage was dissolved on the grounds of consanguinity; her youngest son would later be executed on the orders of her eldest.

21. As we noted in Chapter 1, 'donating' a child to the Church was common practice. Mary's uncle Henry of Blois, for example, had been placed in a monastery at just 2 or 3 years of age and had risen to become, successively, abbot of Glastonbury, bishop of Winchester and papal legate. The opportunities for women were fewer, as abbesses did not generally take on public roles as bishops did, but they lived in some luxury, wielded authority within their Orders, and were regarded with great respect.

22. See above, p. 27.

23. Henry already controlled England, Normandy, Maine, Anjou and Aquitaine, but he still seemed unsatisfied. Aquitaine had long held out a claim to the overlordship of the county of Toulouse, and it was this that Henry was seeking to gain, ostensibly on behalf of his wife.

24. This affluent foundation was a popular choice for royal females. Henry I's queen, Edith/Matilda, had been educated there in her youth (although she was not a nun), at a time when her aunt was the abbess.

25. RT, p. 92.

26. The count was Thierry of Alsace, who had held the title for over thirty years since the death of William Clito back in 1128.

27. 'Letter from Marie of Boulogne and Blois to Louis VII', *Epistolae: Medieval Women's Letters*, at https://epistolae.ctl.columbia.edu/letter/46.html.

28. Henry II had kept Mortain for the use of his own sons; it was true that the county had once belonged to Stephen, but only because Henry I had bestowed it on him, so this could be considered a precedent that the county was in the royal gift so the king could bestow it on minor members of his own family. The title of Mortain was vacant for some years before being bestowed upon Henry's youngest son John in 1189.

29. Philip was Matthew's older brother and the heir of Thierry, who had died in 1168. The life of a twelfth-century heiress was not an

easy one, and Ida suffered as others had done: after two very short marriages (both husbands dying within a year of their wedding), neither of which produced children, she was kidnapped and forced to marry for a third time by an ambitious noble who coveted the county of Boulogne. Ida bore him only one child, a daughter, so the unfortunate cycle was perpetuated.

**Chapter 4: Henry the Young King**

1. Until recently Henry the Young King was not a terribly well-known figure, being mentioned only in passing in studies of his father or brothers. An important recent biography has remedied this: see Strickland, M., *Henry the Young King, 1155–1183* (London: Yale University Press, 2016).
2. Henry's mother Eleanor of Aquitaine had once been the wife of Margaret's father King Louis, but after their divorce Louis had remarried, to Constance of Castile; Margaret was Constance's daughter so the young couple shared no blood relationship, however murky the spiritual ties might have been. Constance died in 1160 giving birth to a second daughter – who would in turn be betrothed to Henry II's second son Richard – but leaving Louis still without a male heir. He would marry again within weeks; to muddy the genealogical waters further, his new queen was Adela of Blois-Champagne, who was the sister of his elder daughters' husbands Henry of Champagne and Theobald of Blois: they therefore became Louis's brothers-in-law as well as his sons-in-law. His third queen finally gave him a son, Philip, in 1165.
3. RH, vol. I, p. 258.
4. Sending children away from home at an early age was common at this time for both sexes and at all levels of society. For the lower classes it might mean being engaged as a servant; for upper-class boys, education or knightly training; and for noble or royal girls, being brought up in the household of their future husband. See Orme, N., *Medieval Children* (London: Yale University Press, 2003), pp. 317–21 and 334–7.
5. The Scottish king was by now Malcolm IV, grandson of the David I who had been uncle to, and a great supporter of, Henry II's mother Empress Matilda. Wales was at this time not a unified entity, but was rather divided into separate principalities, each with its own lord.

6. Hallam, E., 'Henry the Young King, 1155–1183', ODNB.

7. As noted in the previous chapter, English kings of this period often arranged for their sons to do homage for French lands in their stead, to avoid having one king kneel to another. At this same ceremony Young Henry also performed homage to his brother-in-law, Louis's son and heir Philip (then aged 4), thus anticipating that the amicable relationship between the two dynasties would continue into the next generation.

8. RT, p. 111. The specific details of the coronation are not described at any great length by contemporaries, but for a reconstruction based on the known ordinances for other coronations, see Strickland, *Henry the Young King*, pp. 85–7.

9. Pope Alexander was so incensed by this disregard for Church custom that he formalized the arrangement so a similar situation could not arise in future: in 1171 he issued a papal bull, *Quanto majorem*, decreeing that the sole right to conduct coronations in England was henceforward to be invested only in archbishops of Canterbury. This in turn caused problems for later kings; see Church, S., *King John: England, Magna Carta and the Making of a Tyrant* (London: Macmillan, 2015), pp. 67–8; Hanley, C., *Louis: The French Prince Who Invaded England* (London: Yale University Press, 2016), pp. 120–1.

10. GH, vol. I, p. 6.

11. MP, vol. I, p. 353. Empress Matilda was dead by this time; it might have been interesting to find out whether her grandson would have dared to make the same remark about Henry II's parentage in her presence.

12. RH, vol. I, p. 326.

13. It was not an uncommon occurrence for a woman who held titles in her own right to pass them to an adult or almost-adult son as soon as he was old enough; Matilda of Boulogne, for example, had similarly relinquished control of her county to her son Eustace when he was knighted in 1147. See above, p. 38.

14. JF, ll. 21–2.

15. HWM, vol. I, pp. 99 and 101.

16. RT, p. 116; see Strickland, *Henry the Young King*, p. 112.

17. HWM, vol. I, p. 101.

18. HWM, vol. I, p. 107. There is conflicting testimony that Henry had in fact already been knighted by Henry II immediately prior to his coronation in 1170: see Strickland, *Henry the Young King*, pp. 82–4.

19. HWM, vol. I, p. 103.
20. RH, vol. I, pp. 366–7.
21. Young Henry was not old enough to remember the bitter civil war in England fought by his grandmother and father, or he might have been more aware of the dangers of forming such close ties with the house of Blois. Counts Henry and Theobald were King Stephen's nephews, and Matthew was at this time ruling Boulogne in right of his daughters, King Stephen's only legitimate grandchildren.
22. JF, ll. 17–20.
23. RH, vol. I, p. 367.
24. Philip had no children of his own, so his brother Matthew had been his heir to the rich county of Flanders; Matthew himself left only two young daughters. In search of an adult male heir Philip was forced to turn to his one remaining brother, Peter, who was a clergyman; it took some time to arrange for him to leave the Church and marry in order that the family line could be continued. As it transpired, Peter produced no children either, so Philip was eventually succeeded in 1191 by his sister Margaret, whose husband Baldwin, count of Hainaut, became count of Flanders in right of his wife.
25. RT, p. 119; RH, vol. I, pp. 370–1.
26. RH, vol. I, p. 374.
27. This was £15,000 in Angevin pounds, the currency used in Henry's continental lands. An Angevin pound was worth approximately one quarter of a pound sterling, so Young Henry's allowance equated to £3,750 in English currency; this was still a huge sum, many times the annual income of an earl, and it would allow him to live in a lavish fashion.
28. HWM, vol. I, p. 123.
29. At this time tournaments were not the elaborate jousts of later centuries. Rather, they took the form of realistic training for real war: two sides fought against each other in a melee, ranging over a wide area, and real weapons were used. On Young Henry's participation in tournaments, see Strickland, *Henry the Young King*, pp. 239–58; more generally, see Barber, R. and Barker, J., *Tournaments* (Woodbridge: Boydell, 2000).
30. 'He never indulged himself in any peace or quiet […] he mounted his swift horse at break of dawn, and passed the day in a state of restless activity […] when he arrived at home in the evenings, you

would scarcely ever see him sitting down [...] it was his habit to weary the whole court by standing continually' (GW, p. 49).

31. RH, vol. II, p. 14.
32. GC, vol. I, pp. 303–4.
33. HWM, vol. I, p. 323.
34. Geoffrey had been ruling Brittany directly since 1181, and had already managed to end up in armed conflict with his father. He had a reputation for being duplicitous: one chronicler calls him a 'son of iniquity' (RH, vol. II, p. 25), while another says that he was 'flowing over with speech, soft as oil [...] having the power to tear asunder things most united, able to corrupt two kingdoms with his tongue' (GW, p. 26).
35. Geoffrey of Anjou, the husband of Empress Matilda and the father of Henry II, had been known by the soubriquet 'Plantagenet' thanks to his habit of wearing a sprig of broom (*planta genista*) in his hat. Although Henry II did not use the name himself (the first member of the family to resurrect it would be Richard, duke of York, as we shall see), it is generally used to describe him and his descendants.
36. It is not clear which of the two was the driving force behind this decision. It seems more likely to have been Geoffrey, partly on the basis that Young Henry had hitherto shown little indication of cruelty, and partly on the basis that it would have been in Geoffrey's personal interest to exploit the war between his two older brothers as much as possible by fomenting further discord.
37. RH, vol. II, p. 26.
38. RH, vol. II, p. 26.
39. HWM, vol. I, p. 353.
40. RH, vol. II, p. 27.
41. RT, p. 146.
42. His son had cost him much, said King Henry, but 'would that he were still costing me!' (HWM, vol. I, p. 365).
43. GW, p. 13.

## Chapter 5: Arthur and Eleanor of Brittany

1. For a discussion of the significance of this name to the Bretons, see Warren, W. L., *King John* (London: Yale University Press, 1997), pp. 81–2. Arthur has not been the subject of a dedicated biography,

though he does appear in various works on the reign of King John; for fullest details see Jones, M., 'Arthur, duke of Brittany (1187–1203)', ODNB.

2. Arthur was 3 years old at the time. Nobody was particularly interested in noting which of Tancred's three daughters would be his bride, but as the eldest was only around 5, the point remains valid.

3. RW, vol. II, p. 95; see also RH, vol. II, p. 165.

4. HWM, vol. II, p. 71.

5. On this incident see Gillingham, J., *Richard I* (New Haven and London: Yale University Press, 2002), p. 298.

6. One chronicler noted that 'when the king was now in despair of surviving, he devised to his brother John the kingdom of England and all his other territories' (RH, vol. II, p. 453), though others do not mention it.

7. Since we last saw him at the deathbed of Young Henry in 1183, Marshal had risen high in Plantagenet service, working for Henry II and then Richard, and being rewarded with an earldom and the hand of a rich heiress.

8. HWM, vol. II, p. 93.

9. HWM, vol. II, p. 95.

10. HWM, vol. II, p.95.

11. Warren, *King John*, p. 48.

12. RW, vol. II, p. 180.

13. RH, vol. II, pp. 462–3; RW, vol. II, pp. 182–3.

14. RH, vol. II, p. 481.

15. Arthur and Eleanor were John's only young relations in the male line, but as well as his deceased brothers Henry, Richard and Geoffrey he also had three sisters; the second of them, Eleanor, had married King Alfonso VIII of Castile, and Blanche was one of their daughters. Eleanor of Aquitaine, despite her great age, had travelled over the Pyrenees to Castile to collect Blanche in person and bring her to France for the wedding. Blanche would go on to become a pivotal figure in the history of the French monarchy; for more on her life, see Grant, L., *Blanche of Castile, Queen of France* (London: Yale University Press, 2016).

16. Constance was 40, which even at the time was not considered particularly elderly. Bizarrely, contemporary sources disagree as to whether her death was due to childbirth or leprosy.

17. There is a vast literature on John's marriage to and subsequent relationship with Isabella of Angoulême, much of it either hysterical or hopelessly over-romanticized. For proper analytical accounts set in appropriate historical context, see Nicholas Vincent's chapter on Isabella in Church, S.D. (ed.), *King John: New Interpretations* (Woodbridge: Boydell, 2003), pp. 165–219 and Church, S. *King John: England, Magna Carta and the Making of a Tyrant* (London: Macmillan, 2015), pp. 82–92.

18. AB, p. 93.

19. All sources agree that one of the gates was unsecured, though whether this was through negligence or just because it was faulty and would not shut properly is unclear.

20. One account gives us the splendid detail that Geoffrey de Lusignan, brother of the jilted Hugh and one of the Poitevin leaders, was still eating his breakfast, a dish of pigeons (AB, p. 94).

21. AB, p. 95.

22. For a thorough discussion of this engagement and the sources for it, see McGlynn, S., *Blood Cries Afar: The Forgotten Invasion of England 1216* (Stroud: Spellmount, 2011), pp. 36–40.

23. RW, vol. II, p. 205.

24. RCog, pp. 139–41 and 145.

25. WB, pp. 173–4.

26. Margam, p. 27.

27. RW, vol. II, p. 248; AB, pp. 112–15.

28. For a detailed analysis of all the contemporary sources for Arthur's death, see Powicke, F.M., *The Loss of Normandy (1189–1204)* (Manchester: Manchester University Press, 1913), pp. 453–81.

29. RW, vol. II, p. 206.

30. It was proclaimed at the French court in 1213 and 1215 (as part of a justification of why King Philip's son Louis should invade England to take the crown) that John had been deposed for killing Arthur. This was not legally useful in the context – Philip might have been able to deprive John of lands that he held as Philip's vassal, but Philip had no power to deprive him of the throne of England – but the statements, and the lack of attendant surprise, do show that Arthur's murder was fairly common knowledge. See Bradbury, J., *Philip Augustus: King of France 1180–1223* (Harlow: Longman, 1998), p. 318, and Hanley, C., *Louis: The French Prince Who Invaded England* (London: Yale University Press, 2016), pp. 60–1 and 78–9.

31. All of these were highly fortified and forbidding places, and must have been frightening for a young woman in Eleanor's circumstances, but Corfe held an additional horror at the time: some other Poitevin prisoners kept there made a partial break-out, but they were surrounded and their food supplies cut off until they surrendered; twenty-two of them starved to death (Margam, p. 26).

32. Although not necessarily clothing fit for her rank; one order for cloth to make gowns for Eleanor stipulated that the fabric should be 'not of the king's finest'. See Jones, M., 'Eleanor of Brittany, 1182×4–1241', ODNB; and Warren, *King John*, p. 83.

33. It may be of interest to note that, in contrast to the sometimes tortured situation in England, the French crown passed in an unbroken line from father to eldest surviving son for 329 years from 987 to 1316.

34. This sad state of affairs incidentally deprived England of its first King Alfonso; Edward and Eleanor's third son, who was heir to the throne between his elder brothers' deaths and his own, was given a name from the queen's homeland. Edward and Eleanor's daughters are the subject of a recent book: Wilson-Lee, K., *Daughters of Chivalry: The Forgotten Children of Edward I* (London: Pan Macmillan, 2019).

## Chapter 6: Edward the Black Prince

1. Edward is probably the best known of the heirs featured in this book, and the one who has been the subject of most attention from historians. See, among others: Barber, R., *Edward, Prince of Wales and Aquitaine: A Biography of the Black Prince* (Woodbridge: Boydell, 1978); Green, D., *Edward the Black Prince: Power in Medieval Europe* (Harlow: Pearson, 2007); Jones, M., *The Black Prince* (London: Head of Zeus, 2017). A collection of primary sources and letters relating to Edward may be found in Barber, R. (ed.), *Life and Campaigns of the Black Prince* (Woodbridge: Boydell, 1986).

2. Barber, *Edward, Prince of Wales*, pp. 29–30.

3. Edward II was also known as 'Edward of Caernarvon'; part of the justification for the creation of the title was that he had been born in Wales. The Black Prince, on the other hand, was known by the title for the rest of his life without ever actually setting foot in the

principality. From this time onwards 'prince of Wales' became the recognized position of the eldest son of the monarch, without necessarily implying any direct rule.

4. Louis X's wife was pregnant at the time of his death in 1316, so the succession had been put on hold until the birth. The child was a boy, John 'the Posthumous', and he was immediately declared king, but he died just five days later (thus becoming both the youngest and one of the shortest-reigning kings in history), and the crown passed to Louis's next brother Philip V. Louis had been the king of Navarre as well as the king of France; Navarre had no laws against female succession so his daughter Jeanne became queen of Navarre in her own right even though she would never rule France.

5. JB, p. 171.

6. JB, p. 172.

7. CH, p. 88.

8. Barber, ed., *Life and Campaigns*, p. 18.

9. JB, pp. 167–8.

10. GB, p. 44.

11. GB, pp. 44–5.

12. Froissart, p. 92.

13. Ostrich feathers still feature on the arms of princes of Wales, though the number has now changed from one to three. There are numerous works available on the Battle of Crécy; see for example Ayton, A. and Preston, P., *The Battle of Crécy, 1346* (Woodbridge: Boydell Press, 2002); Livingston, M. and Devries, K. (eds), *The Battle of Crécy: A Casebook* (Liverpool: Liverpool University Press, 2015). See also Barber, *Edward, Prince of Wales*, pp. 65–72; Green, *Edward the Black Prince*, pp. 34–47; Jones, *The Black Prince*, pp. 98–108.

14. The queen was Joan of Burgundy, a capable woman whom Philip had married before he had any expectation of becoming king; she had acted as his regent on several occasions. The future queen was Bonne of Luxembourg, daughter of the blind King John of Bohemia who had perished at Crécy; she was married to the French heir, John, and was the mother of ten children all aged under 12.

15. It is sometimes said that medieval parents, producing so many offspring and losing them in such great numbers, could not possibly love their children in the way that modern parents do. This is contradicted by the expressions of grief that may be found in multiple

sources, including a letter King Edward wrote to the king of Castile to inform him of this event. In it he writes of being 'desolated by the sting of this bitter grief' at the death of 'our dearest daughter', whom 'we have loved with our life'. A full transcript of the letter may be found in Horrox, R., *The Black Death* (Manchester: Manchester University Press, 1994), p. 250.

16. King John of England had lost many of his French lands, including Normandy, to Philip Augustus in the early thirteenth century. The northern half of Aquitaine, comprising Poitou and the Limousin, had been conquered by Philip's son Louis VIII during the somewhat ineffective reign of John's son Henry III, but England still held the south-western part including the coast of Gascony and the city of Bordeaux.

17. JB, pp. 222–3. See also the accounts in GB, pp. 61–70; Froissart, pp. 120–6.

18. JB, p. 223.

19. Barber, ed., *Life and Campaigns*, pp. 50–2.

20. Charles was the first French heir to be known as the dauphin, following the acquisition of the dauphiné of Vienne by the French crown in 1350. Some modern writers also refer to previous heirs by this title, but this is erroneous.

21. The length of the campaign was also a factor here; Edward's army, composed of the same personnel, had been fighting together for over a year while the French army was disparate and recently mustered. Several of the French noblemen had quarrelled with each other over the best way to approach the battle. For more information on the Battle of Poitiers, see Green, D., *The Battle of Poitiers, 1356* (Stroud: The History Press, 2008); Witzel, M. and Livingstone, M., *The Black Prince and the Capture of a King: Poitiers 1356* (London: Casemate, 2018); also Barber, *Edward, Prince of Wales*, pp. 139–45; Jones, *The Black Prince*, pp. 205–21.

22. GB, p. 79.

23. GB, pp. 81–2 and Froissart, p. 144, respectively.

24. The unfortunate David II – who had inherited the Scots throne and a whole lot of trouble at the age of 5 upon the death of his father Robert I the Bruce – had now been in English custody for eleven years since his capture at the Battle of Neville's Cross, and he was brought out for the procession in order to emphasize King Edward's

position of power and dominance over both neighbouring realms. David would finally be released in October 1357 after a ransom agreement was reached, the sum of 100,000 marks to be paid off in instalments over ten years.

25. This was a boy named Roger, later Sir Roger Clarendon, who was at this point around 8 years old; he would go on to be executed in 1402 by the new and suspicious king, Henry IV, as a possible rival to the throne. See below p. 98.

26. Joan was the only surviving child and heiress of Edmund, earl of Kent, the younger of Edward I's two sons by his second wife. She was also, as it happened, a second cousin of Queen Philippa – both being descended from Philip III of France – so she was related to her new husband twice over.

27. This, at least, is the accepted narrative. An alternative theory is that Joan and Holland fell for each other *after* her marriage to Salisbury, and that they concocted the story of the earlier wedding in order to annul her present union so they could be together. This would at least make the age gap between them slightly more palatable to modern sensibilities, as they would have consummated their relationship at the respective ages of 17 and 31, rather than 12 and 26; see Jones, *The Black Prince*, pp. 130–4. Holland, of course, stood to gain from the marriage as he would become earl of Kent in right of his wife.

28. Barber, ed., *Life and Campaigns*, p. 83; CH, p. 105.

29. See Barber, *Edward, Prince of Wales*, p. 174. For a detailed investigation of Edward's household and accounts see Green, *Edward the Black Prince*, pp. 107–40.

30. Barber, R., 'Edward of Woodstock, prince of Wales and Aquitaine, 1330–1376', ODNB.

31. John II, as we saw earlier, had been captured at Poitiers in 1356 and taken to England. There he had remained for four years until the Treaty of Brétigny (the same by which Aquitaine had been made a sovereign state) finalized his ransom at an enormous 3 million crowns. Once agreement was reached he was released – along with his now 18-year-old youngest son, Philip, who had remained with him throughout – so that he could return to France and raise the ransom; he left his second son Louis, duke of Anjou, in English-held Calais as a guarantee. However, in violation of his word, Louis later escaped; King John, in a striking act of chivalry equal to anything

the Black Prince might have done, voluntarily surrendered himself back into English hands in the name of 'faith and honour'. He died in London in 1364, still in captivity.

32. On the Battle of Nájera, see CH, pp. 124–30; Barber, *Edward, Prince of Wales*, pp. 199–201; Jones, *The Black Prince*, pp. 309–14.
33. Froissart, pp. 177–8.
34. Chandos Herald notes briefly that both the garrison and the citizens 'were all killed or taken by the prince' (CH, pp. 137–8) but gives no further details.
35. TW, vol. I, p. 36.

**Chapter 7: Edmund Mortimer**

1. See the character assessment in Tuck, A., 'Edmund of Langley, 1341–1402', ODNB, where the author writes of 'the impression of feebleness of character and idleness of disposition which modern historians have identified in Edmund'.
2. Isabella was the younger sister of Constance, John of Gaunt's second wife; both were daughters of the murdered Peter I 'the Cruel' of Castile who had been supported by the Black Prince to his own detriment. John of Gaunt thus carried a claim to the throne of Castile in right of his wife, which he would pursue sporadically throughout his life.
3. Philippa of Clarence's husband was Edmund Mortimer, 3rd earl of March, the great-grandson of the Roger Mortimer who had been the lover of Queen Isabella and ruled England with her before being executed by the young Edward III (see above p. 77); the family had since rehabilitated itself and its lands and titles had been restored. It is unfortunate for us that virtually every male member of the Mortimer family, for several generations, was called either Roger or Edmund, but we will attempt to differentiate them as we go along.
4. AU, p. 21. Charles VI had succeeded his father Charles V 'the Wise', whom we met in Chapter 6, in 1380.
5. Froissart, p. 431.
6. Froissart, p. 423.
7. Edmund's genealogy is given in excruciating detail by the chronicler Adam of Usk, who name-checks, among others, Empress Matilda, William the Conqueror, Alfred the Great, the royal houses of Scotland and Wales, and the kings of France, Spain and (somehow) ancient Troy. See AU, pp. 36–9.

8. AU, pp. 52–4.

9. See above p. 76.

10. Edward III's succession arrangements in this regard were important to his claim to the crown of France, which was via his mother; he could hardly deny or ignore the male-line-only rules of Salic Law in France and then introduce them in his own kingdom.

11. AU, p. 55; my emphasis.

12. Edmund had one younger brother (somewhat inevitably called Roger), of whom little is known; he was not much more than an infant at this time, and he died in his teens in 1413 or shortly afterwards. Of course, Henry IV was not to know this in 1399, so it was important for him to keep both boys in his custody. Edmund and Roger also had two sisters, Anne and Eleanor; they posed less of a threat to Henry and were therefore allowed to remain with their mother rather than being taken into the king's keeping. Anne would go on to marry Richard of Conisbrough, the second son of Edmund of Langley, duke of York (and thus her grandmother's first cousin); we shall hear more of her later.

13. See, among others, Saul, N., *Richard II* (New Haven: Yale University Press, 1997), pp. 424–5; Tuck, A., 'Richard II, 1367–1400', ODNB. Richard's widow, the 10-year-old Isabella, was shipped back to France 'clad in mourning weeds, and showing a countenance of lowering and evil aspect to King Henry'; AU, p. 99.

14. Given-Wilson, C., 'Clarendon, Sir Roger, *c*. 1350–1402', ODNB. See also Given-Wilson, C. and A. Curteis, *The Royal Bastards of Medieval England* (London: Routledge and Kegan Paul, 1984), pp. 143–6.

15. Griffiths, R.A., 'Mortimer, Edmund (V), 1391–1425', ODNB.

16. Taken from the Parliament Roll of 1415, and as translated in Pugh, T.B., *Henry V and the Southampton Plot of 1415* (Stroud: Sutton, 1998), p. 182. For more on the plot see the rest of Pugh's volume, and also the 'July' and 'August' chapters in Mortimer, I., *1415: Henry V's Year of Glory* (London: Vintage, 2010).

17. GHQ, p. 19; AU, p. 177 (my emphasis).

18. Henry had revived his family's generations-old claim to the crown of France and was keen to go to war. By now this claim was tenuous in the extreme, four Valois kings in a row having succeeded since the end of the direct Capetian line, but after some unexpected victories against

the rather feeble Charles VI 'the Mad', Henry ended up being named heir to the French throne. However, he would never live to take it, the elderly and infirm Charles outliving him by six weeks.

19. GHQ, p. 59. The figure of 5,000 is probably an exaggeration, but not by too much: rolls listing the sick from this campaign survive, and even though they are incomplete they give some 1,700 names (GHQ, p. 59 n. 5).

20. Catherine was the youngest of Charles's daughters; her eldest sister Isabella had, many years previously, been the second queen of Richard II.

21. As quoted in Griffiths, 'Mortimer, Edmund'.

22. Pugh, *Southampton Plot*, p. 64.

23. His pivotal importance was later parodied by Sellar and Yeatman, who gave 'Are you Edmund Mortimer? If not, have you got him?' as the key questions to be answered by any kingly candidate during the Wars of the Roses. Sellar, W.C. and Yeatman, R.J., *1066 and All That: A Memorable History of England* (Stroud: Sutton, 1997; originally published in 1930), p. 54.

### Chapter 8: Richard, duke of York

1. Richard has been the subject of two modern biographies: Johnson, P.A., *Duke Richard of York, 1411–1460* (Oxford: Clarendon Press, 1988); and Lewis, M., *Richard Duke of York: King by Right* (Stroud: Amberley, 2016). He also features in dedicated chapters in a number of books on the Wars of the Roses, including Gillingham, J., *The Wars of the Roses: Peace and Conflict in Fifteenth-Century England* (London: Phoenix Press, 1981), pp. 65–75; and generally in other works including Lander, J.R., *The Wars of the Roses* (Stroud: Sutton, 1990).

2. Pugh, T.B., *Henry V and the Southampton Plot of 1415* (Stroud: Sutton, 1988), p. 24.

3. Gillingham, *Wars of the Roses*, p. 68; Lewis, *Richard Duke of York*, p. 60.

4. Harriss, G.L., 'Beaufort, John, duke of Somerset, 1404–1444', ODNB.

5. Like most princesses of this era, Catherine had been allowed no choice about her marriage to Henry V (despite what Shakespeare's play might have you believe); she had been 18 when she married, 19 when she saw her husband for the last time, and 20 when she was

widowed. Stuck in a foreign court surrounded by various factions trying to take control of her infant son, it would not be surprising if she had felt the need for companionship. In fact she would go on to marry again, but not to Edmund Beaufort: we will hear of her second marriage later in this chapter.

6. As we noted earlier (see Chapter 7, note 18), Charles VI of France had named Henry V as his heir, but had then outlived him. Upon Charles's death the English claimed that Henry VI was therefore the rightful king of France, although the disinherited erstwhile dauphin – the sister of Catherine of Valois and thus young Henry's uncle – was immediately proclaimed by his supporters as Charles VII. Charles held the lands around Reims, where all French coronations took place, so Henry VI's guardians had to content themselves with crowning him in Paris.

7. The text of the commission is reproduced in full in Johnson, *Duke Richard of York*, pp. 226–7.

8. 'It was for his good rule of the duchy [of Normandy] and for his genuine attempts to deal with the problems created by a declining military occupation that York would be remembered in France.' Watts, J., 'Richard of York, 1411–1460', ODNB.

9. Edward's height is confirmed by analysis of his skeleton; see Gillingham, *Wars of the Roses*, p. 134. A chronicler said of Lionel of Antwerp that 'in all the world was then no prince like him in stature'; he notes that Lionel stood head and shoulders above anyone else in a room (Hardyng, p. 334). For further analysis of the question of Edward's parentage, see Lewis, *Richard Duke of York*, pp. 88–90.

10. A recent biography sheds more light on Henry VI's life and personality: Johnson, L., *Shadow King: The Life and Death of Henry VI* (London: Head of Zeus, 2019).

11. Humphrey, duke of Gloucester and Henry V's last surviving brother, was still alive but he had retired from public life following the arrest and subsequent conviction of his wife on charges of witchcraft. He would die in 1447 without ever regaining his previous influence at court.

12. One of the reasons for Charles's reluctance was that the childlike and borderline mentally unstable Henry VI was his nephew, so his daughters were Henry's first cousins – and all of them were grandchildren of the mad king Charles VI. The science of genetics

was obviously not understood at this time, but everyone knew enough to realize that any children of such a match would stand a much greater chance of inheriting ill health. Margaret of Anjou, as the niece of Charles's wife, shared no such blood connection and was thus a safer bet.

13. Queen Catherine's rumoured affair with Edmund Beaufort has led to speculation that he might have been the real father of Edmund Tudor, the eldest of Catherine's second family; see Richmond, C., 'Beaufort, Edmund, duke of Somerset, c. 1406–1455)', ODNB. Given that Edmund Tudor married Margaret, the niece of Edmund Beaufort, this raises the intriguing possibility that their son Henry Tudor (later Henry VII) might have had parents who were first cousins to each other, and that the house of Tudor was actually the house of Beaufort.

14. Hardyng, p. 399.

15. CWR, p. 208.

16. This defeat led to the loss of Bordeaux and the rest of Gascony; its eventual consequence was that the English lost all of their lands in France except Calais, which would hold out until 1558. The Battle of Castillon is now generally considered to mark the end of the Hundred Years' War.

17. For a fuller discussion of the possible causes of Henry's illness and its effects on him, see Ross, J., *Henry VI: A Good, Simple and Innocent Man* (London: Allen Lane, 2016), pp. 65–9.

18. CWR, p. 212.

19. *Benet's Chronicle*, as quoted in Watts, 'Richard of York'.

20. CWR, p. 212; Paston, vol. I, p. 296 n.2.

21. Paston, vol. I, p. 265.

22. Paston, vol. I, pp. 263–4.

23. Paston, vol. I, p. 315.

24. It may seem odd that a father and son were both earls at the same time, but each held his title in right of his wife; the Nevilles' aggressive marriage strategy meant that they were by now related to many of the realm's highest families.

25. This Henry Percy was the son of the Henry 'Hotspur' Percy who had been killed fighting against Henry IV at Shrewsbury in 1403, but he had served Henry V well and had been allowed to inherit his grandfather's earldom. Coincidentally his mother, Hotspur's

widow, was Elizabeth Mortimer, the daughter of Philippa of Clarence; this made Percy the duke of York's first cousin once removed. He was also, as it happens, related to York by marriage as their wives, Cecily Neville and Eleanor Neville, were sisters. So intermarried were the noble houses of England that there were very few antagonists in the Wars of the Roses who did not share some ties of kinship.

26. Paston, vol. I, p. 315.
27. The full text of the letter may be found in Paston, vol. I, pp. 325–6.
28. Gregory, p. 198. For more on the battle see, among others, Boardman, A., *The First Battle of St Albans 1455* (Stroud: Tempus, 2006); Burley, P., Elliott, M. and Watson, H., *The Battles of St Albans* (Barnsley: Pen and Sword, 2007); Gillingham, *Wars of the Roses*, pp. 85–91.
29. Grafton, *Hist.*, vol. I, p. 659.
30. Richard and Cecily had twelve or thirteen children, of whom only four sons and three daughters survived infancy. The sons were in two distinct pairings: the births of Edward and Edmund in 1442 and 1443 had been followed by two daughters and two infant losses, with George and Richard not making their appearance until 1449 and 1452 respectively.
31. Gregory, p. 208.
32. Grafton, *Hist.*, vol. I, pp. 666–8.
33. There is a wealth of literature available on the Battle of Towton. See for example, Sadler, J., *Towton: The Battle of Palm Sunday Field* (Barnsley: Pen and Sword, 2014); Goodwin, G., *Fatal Colours: Towton, 1461* (London: Weidenfeld & Nicolson, 2011); Boardman, A.W., *Towton: The Bloodiest Battle* (Stroud: The History Press, 2009); Gillingham, *Wars of the Roses*, pp. 132–5.
34. CWR, p. 224.

**Chapter 9: Edward of Lancaster**

1. Grafton, *Hist.*, vol. I, p. 651.
2. The quote is from Piero da Monte, a papal emissary to Henry VI's court who knew the king personally; the emphasis is mine. For further discussion on Henry's chastity and/or sexuality, including on da Monte's opinions, see Lewis, K., *Kingship and Masculinity in Late Medieval England* (Oxford: Routledge, 2013), pp. 198–202.

3. For a fuller discussion of the circumstances surrounding Edward's birth, see Ross, J., *Henry VI: A Good, Simple and Innocent Man* (London: Allen Lane, 2016), pp. 22–5.

4. Grafton, *Hist.*, vol. I, p. 655.

5. See above, p. 119.

6. This assumption of power by Margaret was accepted because she was claiming to act on behalf of her husband and son; as we saw in Chapter 2 when discussing Empress Matilda and Queen Matilda of Boulogne, female power was tolerated as long as the woman in question was exercising it for a male relative and not attempting to do so in her own right.

7. See Chapter 8, note 33 for further references on the Battle of Towton.

8. Gregory, p. 217.

9. Edward's Act of Parliament, as translated in Lander, J.R., *The Wars of the Roses* (Stroud: Sutton, 1990), p. 98; my emphasis.

10. Ross, *Henry VI*, p. 92.

11. Georges Chastellain, the duke of Burgundy's official historiographer, as quoted in Lander, *Wars of the Roses*, p. 108.

12. Charles VII had died in July 1461, to be succeeded by his eldest son Louis XI. Louis was to prove a formidable force in European politics, as evidenced by his various nicknames: 'the prudent', 'the cunning' and 'the universal spider'.

13. A letter home from the Milanese ambassador to France, as quoted in Lander, *Wars of the Roses*, p. 110.

14. Sir John Fortescue, as quoted in Griffiths, R.A., 'Edward of Westminster, prince of Wales', ODNB.

15. The match was so outrageous that it has been called 'not so much politically inappropriate as politically inconceivable'. Castor, *She-Wolves*, p. 386.

16. Gregory, p. 226.

17. Richard Neville and his wife Anne Beauchamp had no sons, so the Warwick title would go to their eldest daughter Isabelle, and the lands would be divided between Isabelle and her younger sister Anne Neville. This would (in theory at least) happen on the death of their mother, not their father, as it was Anne Beauchamp who was countess of Warwick in her own right.

18. Grafton, *Hist.*, vol. II, p. 22.

19. Grafton, *Hist.*, vol. II, p. 22.

20. For more on the Battle of Barnet, see Cass, F., *The Battle of Barnet* (London: British Library Historical Print Editions, 2011); Clark, D., *Barnet, 1471: Death of the Kingmaker* (Barnsley: Pen and Sword, 2006); Hammond, P.W., *The Battles of Barnet and Tewkesbury* (London: St Martin's Press, 1990).
21. Grafton, *Cont.*, p. 459.
22. Grafton, *Hist.*, vol. II, p. 42.
23. For further details of the engagement, see Hammond, *Battles of Barnet and Tewkesbury*; Goodchild, S., *Tewkesbury: Eclipse of the House of Lancaster 1471* (Barnsley: Pen and Sword, 2005); Gillingham, J., *The Wars of the Roses: Peace and Conflict in Fifteenth-Century England* (London: Phoenix Press, 1981), pp. 202–7.
24. *Arrivall*, p. 30.
25. Grafton, *Hist.*, vol. II, p. 42.
26. Grafton, *Hist.*, vol. II, p. 43.
27. *Arrivall*, p. 31.
28. The Beauforts had paid a heavy price for their involvement in the dynastic wars of the fifteenth century. To recap: John, the 1st duke of Somerset, had died of illness or suicide. His brother Edmund had been killed at St Albans in 1455; Edmund's eldest son Henry had been executed after the Battle of Hexham in 1464; Henry's younger brothers Edmund and John were executed and killed (respectively) at Tewkesbury in 1471. The wider nobility had also suffered in a manner not seen since the Norman Conquest: Gillingham notes that between 1455 and 1471 twenty-six peers had been killed and a further thirteen executed, while six of Edward III's descendants in the male line had met violent ends (Gillingham, *Wars of the Roses*, p. 217).

### Chapter 10: Edward V, Edward of Middleham and Edward of Warwick

1. Given the brevity of his life and reign and the dearth of available evidence, Edward has unsurprisingly not been the subject of much scholarly biographical attention: most of the information we have on him must be found in the many works on Edward IV and Richard III, or on the Wars of the Roses more generally. Two exceptions are Horrox, R., 'Edward V', ODNB; and Hicks, M., *The Prince in the Tower: The Short Life and Mysterious Disappearance of Edward V* (Stroud: Tempus, 2007).

2. Hicks, *Prince in the Tower*, pp. 76–7.
3. As it transpired, this marriage would never take place. Anne inherited the duchy of Brittany in 1488 upon the death of her father; she was first married to Maximilian I, the Holy Roman Emperor, and then (uniquely) she was queen consort of France twice. Her marriage to Charles VIII of France produced seven children, none of whom survived infancy, so the crown passed to his second cousin Louis XII; he, keen to keep hold of Brittany, divorced his wife and married Anne instead.
4. The cause of Edward IV's death has variously been ascribed to appendicitis, a stroke or pneumonia brought on by a bout of fishing (Horspool, D., *Richard III: A Ruler and His Reputation* (London: Bloomsbury, 2015), p. 138). Whatever the precise cause, the illness was such that the king died within days, but not so suddenly that he did not have time to make a will and arrangements for the succession.
5. CC, pp. 155–7.
6. CWR, p. 279. All medieval chroniclers wrote with their own opinions and loyalties at the backs of their minds (as do modern historians, if we are honest with ourselves), but the accounts of the events of 1483 are particularly caught up in a web of tangled allegiances and hindsight. We will attempt to disentangle them as we go along.
7. Mancini, p. 75. Dominic Mancini was an impartial observer to these events, an Italian who was visiting England during 1482–3 and who wrote an explanatory account for the archbishop of Vienne (in France), which has survived. He acknowledges in his writing those occasions when he has spoken to an observer or informant on a particular matter, and those when he has no specific information and so is drawing his own conclusions. As Mancini was writing very soon after the events he describes (he finished his account in December 1483), and as he had no vested interest in the success of any of the factions, his text is valuable and it will be our main source in this chapter. Interestingly, Mancini's own name for his work, the relatively neutral *De Occupatione Regni Anglie per Riccardum Tercium* (*The Occupation of the Throne of England by Richard III*), was changed by a later editor to *The Usurpation of Richard III*, a distinctly more negative connotation.
8. Mancini, p. 77.
9. Mancini, p. 79.

10. Grafton, *Hist.*, vol. II, p. 166.
11. Mancini, p. 89.
12. Mancini, p. 89. In fact Edward, Clarence's son, was just 8, having been born in 1475.
13. On Edward IV's supposed illegitimacy, see above, p. 110; and Pollard, A.J., *Edward IV: The Summer King* (London: Allen Lane, 2016), pp. 10–12.
14. Richard's wife was Anne Neville, the daughter of Richard, earl of Warwick and the widow of Edward of Lancaster. Her sister Isabelle had been married to Richard's brother George, meaning that the vast Neville/Warwick/Salisbury inheritances were parcelled out between them.
15. Richard was made into a pantomime villain by William Shakespeare, but perhaps the Shakespearean lines that represent him best are from another play: 'I am in blood / Stepp'd in so far that, should I wade no more, / Returning were as tedious as go o'er' (*Macbeth*, Act III, Scene 4).
16. Edward's biographer sums up the dating thus: the last recorded sighting of the brothers alive was in July 1483; by November they were 'politically dead' (that is, the political landscape functioned with no reference to them); by the end of 1483 they were presumed dead; and in January 1484 the first accusation of murder was made, at the French royal court (Hicks, *Prince in the Tower*, pp. 180–1).
17. Mancini, p. 93.
18. CWR, p. 298.
19. Horspool, *Richard III*, pp. 192–3.
20. Pollard, A.J., 'Edward of Middleham, prince of Wales, 1474×6–1484', ODNB.
21. CC, p. 171; CWR, p. 298.
22. This book is about heirs, not kings, so we will not go into detail about Henry's usurpation of Richard here. There is a vast amount of literature available on both Richard III and Henry VII, as well as on the Battle of Bosworth itself. More recent works, following the discovery of Richard's remains in 2012, have been able to shed detailed and horrific light on Richard's last moments: see in particular Appleby, J. et al., 'Perimortem Trauma in King Richard III: A Skeletal Analysis', *The Lancet*, 385 (2014), pp. 253–9.
23. Mancini, p. 63.

24. This is a very brief summary, and Clarence's life, actions and motives were more complex than we have space for here. For further information see, among other works, Hicks, M., *False Fleeting Perjur'd Clarence: George, Duke of Clarence, 1449–78* (Stroud: Alan Sutton, 1980).
25. Mancini, p. 89.
26. This echoed the situation we examined back in Chapter 1, where Henry I, left with no legitimate son, was unwilling to name the son of his older brother, William Clito, as his heir for the same reason. See above p. 14.
27. John de la Pole was at this point in his early twenties and was, as the eldest grandson of Richard, duke of York, the logical choice as Richard III's heir. The family would later suffer for their blood links to the crown: John and one of his brothers would be killed in battle, another would be executed, and the last would die in prison under Henry VIII.
28. Cecily Neville's mother had been Joan Beaufort, the daughter of John of Gaunt by his mistress (and later third wife) Katherine Swynford. This meant that Edward's descent from John of Gaunt came only through a female of the legitimated Beaufort line; but then again, so did Henry VII's.
29. Pierce, H., *Margaret Pole, Countess of Salisbury 1473–1541* (Cardiff: University of Wales Press, 2003), ch. 1 (n.p.).
30. Edward Stafford, the 7-year-old duke of Buckingham, survived this episode, but his Plantagenet blood eventually proved fatal; he was executed in 1521 on the orders of Henry VIII.
31. Pierce, H. 'Pole, Margaret, *suo jure* countess of Salisbury', ODNB.
32. Edward Hall, as quoted in Pierce, *Margaret Pole*, ch. 1 (n.p.). Some later historians have taken this as evidence that Edward had a mental incapacity all his life, but there is no evidence that he was anything other than normally intelligent before he disappeared into the Tower, at which point all education ceased, his development was apparently ignored, and he may even have been kept in solitary confinement.
33. Grafton, *Hist.*, vol. II, p. 166.
34. For more on Perkin Warbeck, see Wroe, A., *Perkin: A Story of Deception* (London: Jonathan Cape, 2003).
35. Polydore Vergil, as quoted in Pierce, *Margaret Pole*, ch. 1 (n.p.).

# Selected Further Reading

## Biographies

The Yale English Monarchs series includes detailed academic biographies of all the crowned kings mentioned in this book; see http://yalebooks.yale.edu/series/the-english-monarchs-series. For a briefer introduction to all those who occupied the throne, see the recent Penguin Monarchs collection: https://www.penguin.co.uk/series/PMO/penguin-monarchs/. Entries for all individuals featured in this book, crowned or not, may be found in the *Oxford Dictionary of National Biography*, at www.oxforddnb.com.

Other book-length biographies – of both the principal subjects of the present volume and others mentioned – include:

**Aird, William M.**, *Robert Curthose, Duke of Normandy, c. 1050–1134* (Woodbridge: Boydell, 2008)

**Asbridge, Thomas**, *The Greatest Knight: The Remarkable Life of William Marshal, the Power Behind Five English Thrones* (London: Simon and Schuster, 2015)

**Barber, Richard**, *Edward, Prince of Wales and Aquitaine: A Biography of the Black Prince* (Woodbridge: Boydell, 1996; orig. 1978)

**Barber, Richard**, *Henry Plantagenet* (Woodbridge: Boydell, 2001; orig. 1964)

**Bradbury, Jim**, *Philip Augustus: King of France 1180–1223* (London: Longman, 1998)

**Castor, Helen**, *She-Wolves: The Women Who Ruled England before Elizabeth* (London: Faber and Faber, 2010)

**Chibnall, Marjorie**, *The Empress Matilda: Queen Consort, Queen Mother and Lady of the English* (Oxford: Wiley-Blackwell, 1991)

*Lost Heirs of the Medieval Crown*

**Church, Stephen**, *King John: England, Magna Carta and the Making of a Tyrant* (London: Macmillan, 2015)

**David, Charles Wendell**, *Robert Curthose, Duke of Normandy* (Cambridge, MA: Harvard University Press, 1920)

**Given-Wilson, Chris and Alice Curteis**, *The Royal Bastards of Medieval England* (London: Routledge and Kegan Paul, 1984)

**Green, David,** *Edward the Black Prince: Power in Medieval Europe* (Harlow: Longman, 2007)

**Green, Judith A.,** *Henry I: King of England and Duke of Normandy* (Cambridge: Cambridge University Press, 2006)

**Hanley, Catherine**, *Louis: The French Prince Who Invaded England* (London: Yale University Press, 2016)

**Hanley, Catherine**, *Matilda: Empress, Queen, Warrior* (London: Yale University Press, 2019)

**Hicks, Michael**, *False Fleeting Perjur'd Clarence: George, Duke of Clarence, 1449–78* (Stroud: Alan Sutton, 1980)

**Hicks, Michael** *The Prince in the Tower: The Short Life and Mysterious Disappearance of Edward V* (Stroud: Tempus, 2007)

**Horspool, David**, *Richard III: A Ruler and His Reputation* (London: Bloomsbury, 2015)

**Johnson, Lauren**, *Shadow King: The Life and Death of Henry VI* (London: Head of Zeus, 2019)

**Johnson, P.A.,** *Duke Richard of York 1411–1460* (Oxford: Clarendon, 1988)

**Jones, Michael**, *The Black Prince* (London: Head of Zeus, 2017)

**LoPrete, Kimberley**, *Adela of Blois: Countess and Lord (c. 1067–1137)* (Dublin: Four Courts Press, 2007)

**Maurer, Helen**, *Margaret of Anjou: Queenship and Power in Late Medieval England* (Woodbridge: Boydell, 2003)

**Norton, Elizabeth**, *England's Queens: The Biography* (Stroud: Amberley, 2012)

**Pierce, Hazel**, *Margaret Pole, Countess of Salisbury 1473–1541* (Cardiff: University of Wales Press, 2003)

**Strickland, Matthew**, *Henry the Young King* (London: Yale University Press, 2016)

**Turner, Ralph V.**, *Eleanor of Aquitaine: Queen of France, Queen of England* (New Haven: Yale University Press, 2009)

# General works

**Barlow, Frank**, *The Feudal Kingdom of England 1042–1216*, 5th rev. ed. (Harlow: Longman, 1999; orig. 1955)

**Bartlett, Robert**, *England under the Norman and Angevin Kings, 1075–1225* (Oxford: Oxford University Press, 2000)

**Bates, David and Curry**, **Anne** (eds), *England and Normandy in the Middle Ages* (London: Hambledon, 1994)

**Beeler, John**, *Warfare in England, 1066–1189* (Ithaca: Cornell University Press, 1966)

**Beem, Charles**, *The Lioness Roared: The Problems of Female Rule in English History* (New York: Palgrave MacMillan, 2008)

**Bradbury, Jim**, *Stephen and Matilda: The Civil War of 1139–53* (Stroud: Sutton, 1996)

**Bradbury, Jim**, *The Routledge Companion to Medieval Warfare* (London: Routledge, 2004)

**Brown, R. Allen**, *The Normans and the Norman Conquest*, 2nd ed. (Woodbridge: Boydell, 1985; orig. 1969)

**Carpenter, David**, *The Struggle for Mastery: The Penguin History of Britain 1066–1284* (London: Penguin, 2004)

**Chibnall, Marjorie**, *Anglo-Norman England, 1066–1166* (Oxford: Blackwell 1986)

**Clanchy, M.T.**, *England and its Rulers, 1066–1272* (London: Wiley-Blackwell, 1983)

**Duggan, Anne** (ed.), *Queens and Queenship in Medieval Europe* (Woodbridge: Boydell, 1997)

**Dyer, Christopher**, *Everyday Life in Medieval England* (London: Hambledon and London, 2000; orig. 1994)

**Dyer, Christopher**, *Making a Living in the Middle Ages: The People of Britain 850–1520* (New Haven and London: Yale University Press, 2009; orig. 2002)

**Erler, Mary and Kowaleski, Maryanne**, (eds), *Women and Power in the Middle Ages* (Athens, GA: University of Georgia Press, 1988)

**Gillingham, John**, *The Wars of the Roses: Peace and Conflict in Fifteenth-Century England* (London: Phoenix Press, 1981)

**Gillingham, John**, *The Angevin Empire*, 2nd ed. (London: Bloomsbury, 2001)

**Gillingham, John**, *Conquests, Catastrophe and Recovery: Britain and Ireland 1066–1484* (London: Vintage, 2014)

**Hicks, Michael**, *Who's Who in Late Medieval England* (London: Shepheard-Walwyn, 1991)

**Hicks, Michael**, *The Wars of the Roses* (London: Yale University Press, 2010)

**Jones, Dan**, *The Plantagenets: The Kings Who Made England* (London: William Collins, 2013)

**Jones, Dan**, *The Hollow Crown: The Wars of the Roses and the Rise of the Tudors* (London: Faber and Faber, 2015)

**Keen, Maurice**, *England in the Later Middle Ages* (London: Methuen, 1973)

**Lander, J.R.**, *The Wars of the Roses* (Stroud: Sutton, 1992)

**Lewis, Katherine J.**, *Kingship and Masculinity in Late Medieval England* (Oxford: Routledge, 2013)

**Leyser, Henrietta**, *Medieval Women: A Social History of Women in England 450–1500* (London: Weidenfeld & Nicolson, 1995)

**McGlynn, Sean**, *By Sword and Fire: Cruelty and Atrocity in Medieval Warfare* (London: Weidenfeld & Nicolson, 2008)

**Morillo, Stephen**, *Warfare under the Anglo-Norman Kings 1066–1135* (Woodbridge: Boydell, 1994)

**Morris, Marc**, *The Norman Conquest* (London: Hutchinson, 2012)

**Orme, Nicholas**, *From Childhood to Chivalry: The Education of the English Kings and Aristocracy 1066–1530* (London: Methuen, 1984)

**Orme, Nicholas**, *Medieval Children* (New Haven and London: Yale University Press, 2001)

**Pollard, A.J.**, *Richard III and the Princes in the Tower* (Stroud: Sutton Publishing, 1991)

**Pugh, T.B.**, *Henry V and the Southampton Plot* (Gloucester: Alan Sutton, 1988)

**Saul, Nigel**, *A Companion to Medieval England 1066–1485*, 3rd ed. (Stroud: Tempus, 2005; orig. 1983)

**Tyerman, Christopher**, *Who's Who in Early Medieval England* (London: Shepheard-Walwyn, 1996)

**Wagner, John A.**, *Encyclopaedia of the Wars of the Roses* (Santa Barbara, CA: ABC-CLIO, 2001)

**Warren, W.L.**, *The Governance of Anglo-Norman and Angevin England, 1086–1272* (Stanford: Stanford University Press, 1987)

# About the Author

J.F. Andrews is the pseudonym of an academic historian who has written extensively on war and politics in the Middle Ages.

# Index

All individuals are listed by first name. An entry in **bold** indicates that the person is the subject of a chapter.

George Neville, archbishop of
    York, 121
George Plantagenet, duke of
    Clarence, 120, 134–6, 138, 142,
    143, 148, 149, 151, 155–6, 157
George, son of Edward IV, 141
Gerberoy, 3
Gisors, 15
Gloucester, 18, 28, 29, 32
Gravelines, 53
Guy of Thouars, duke of Brittany,
    65, 74

Hamelin of Anjou, illegitimate
    son of Geoffrey of Anjou, 45
Harfleur, siege of (1415), 103
Hedgeley Moor, Battle of
    (1464), 132
Helias de St-Saëns, son-in-law
    of Robert Curthose, 11, 13
Henry I, count of Champagne, 40,
    52–3, 55
Henry I, king of England, 2, 4, 5,
    8–9, 10–12, 13–16, 18, 19–27,
    34, 38, 67, 144, 154
Henry II, king of Castile, 89
Henry II, king of England, 26, 33,
    34–5, 38–40, 42, 44–6, 47–61,
    62, 65, 121
Henry III, king of England, 8, 75,
    84, 96
Henry IV, king of England, 94,
    96–100, 101, 104, 105,
    107–8
Henry V, Holy Roman Emperor,
    15, 19, 24–5
Henry V, king of England, 100–4,
    105, 107, 110

Henry VI, king of England,
    103–5, 107–23, 124–40, 144,
    148, 152, 153, 157
Henry VII, king of England, 140,
    150, 155, 157–9
Henry VIII, king of England, 158
Henry Beaufort, 3rd duke of
    Somerset, 119, 130, 137
Henry Beaufort, cardinal, 109, 111
Henry Scrope, 3rd Baron Scrope,
    101–2
Henry of Blois, bishop of
    Winchester, 23, 27, 28, 29,
    31, 37
Henry of Grosmont, 1st duke of
    Lancaster, 84, 87, 91, 96
Henry Percy, 2nd earl of
    Northumberland, 117–18
Henry Percy, 3rd earl of
    Northumberland, 119, 130
Henry Percy, 'Hotspur', son of the
    1st earl of Northumberland, 98
Henry Plantagenet, son of
    Richard, 3rd duke of York, 110
**Henry the Young King**, 47–61
Hexham, Battle of (1464),
    132, 137
Hubert de Burgh, 1st earl of
    Kent, 71
Hugh Bigod, 1st earl of Norfolk,
    44–5
Hugh IX de Lusignan, count of
    La Marche, 69
Humphrey of Gloucester, son of
    Thomas of Woodstock, 94
Humphrey of Lancaster, duke
    of Gloucester, 102, 104, 108,
    109, 111